JULIE MOORE & RICHARD STORTON

Oxford Academic Vocabulary **Practice**

LOWER INTERMEDIATE | **B1**

OXFORD

UNIVERSITY PRESS

OXFORD
UNIVERSITY PRESS

Great Clarendon Street, Oxford, OX2 6DP, United Kingdom

Oxford University Press is a department of the University of Oxford.
It furthers the University's objective of excellence in research, scholarship,
and education by publishing worldwide. Oxford is a registered trade
mark of Oxford University Press in the UK and in certain other countries

© Oxford University Press 2017

The moral rights of the author have been asserted

First published in 2017

2021 2020 2019 2018 2017

10 9 8 7 6 5 4 3 2 1

ISBN: 978 0 19 400088 8

Printed in China

This book is printed on paper from certified and well-managed sources

ACKNOWLEDGEMENTS

*The authors and publisher are grateful to those who have given permission to
reproduce the following extracts and adaptations of copyright material*: p.25
Definition from *A Dictionary of Education (Second Edition)*, edited by Susan
Wallace (Oxford University Press, 2015). By permission of Oxford
University Press. p.27 Extracts from *Oxford IB Diploma Programme: Theory
of Knowledge Course Companion* by Eileen Dombrowski, Lena Rotenberg
and Mimi Bick (Oxford University Press, 2013). Reproduced by
permission of Oxford University Press. p.38 Definition from *A Dictionary
of Construction, Surveying and Civil Engineering* by Christopher Gorse,
David Johnston, and Martin Pritchard (Oxford University Press, 2013).
By permission of Oxford University Press. p.66 Extract from *Making
Sense: A Student's Guide to Research and Writing: Psychology (Second Edition)* by
Margot Northey and Brian Timney © Oxford University Press Canada,
2015. Reproduced by permission of Oxford University Press. p.73
Definition from *A Dictionary of the Internet (Third Edition)* by Darrel Ince
(Oxford University Press, 2013). By permission of Oxford University
Press. p.74 Adapted extracts from *The Oxford Dictionary of Sports Science
& Medicine (Third Edition)* by Michael Kent (Oxford University Press,
2007). By permission of Oxford University Press. p.75 Adapted extracts
from *A Dictionary of Human Resource Management (Second Revised Edition)*
by Edmund Heery and Mike Noon (Oxford University Press, 2008). By
permission of Oxford University Press. p.91 Adapted and abridged
definition from *A Dictionary of Marketing (Fourth Edition)* by Charles Doyle
(Oxford University Press, 2016). By permission of Oxford University
Press. p.97 Definitions from and adapted extracts from *A Dictionary of
Environment and Conservation (Second Edition)* by Chris Park and Michael
Allaby (Oxford University Press, 2013). By permission of Oxford
University Press. p.98 Adapted definition from *A Dictionary of Sociology
(Fourth Edition)*, edited by John Scott (Oxford University Press, 2015).
By permission of Oxford University Press. p.103 Adapted definition
from *A Dictionary of Law (Eighth Edition)*, edited by Jonathan Law (Oxford
University Press, 2015). By permission of Oxford University Press.
p.105 Adapted definition from *The Concise Oxford Dictionary of Politics
(Third Edition)* by Iain McLean and Alistair McMillan (2009) © Oxford
University Press, 1996, 2003. By permission of Oxford University Press.
p.54 Extracts from *IB Biology: Course Companion* by Andrew Allot (Oxford
University Press, 2012). Reproduced by permission of Oxford University
Press. p.58 Extracts from *AQA GCSE Science: Science B: Science in Context*
by James Hayward, Jo Locke, Nicky Thomas, Louise Burt and Andrea
Johnson. (Oxford University Press, 2014). Reproduced by permission of
Oxford University Press. pp.52, 62–63 Extracts from *AQA Certificate in
Geography (iGCSE), Level 1/2* by Stephen Durman and Simon Ross (Oxford
University Press, 2014). Reproduced by permission of Oxford
University Press. p.51 Extracts from *AQA GCSE Statistics* by Shaun Procter-Green and
Paul Winters, (Nelson Thornes, 2009), reproduced by permission of the
publishers, Oxford University Press. p.56 Data for graph taken from *Life
expectancy at birth: Number of years*, OECD (2016), OECD Factbook 2015–
2016: Economic, Environmental and Social Statistics, OECD Publishing,
Paris, DOI: http://dx.doi.org/10.1787/factbook-2015-en, (accessed on
11 August 2016). Reproduced by permission.

Sources: p.82 *Water: A Very Short Introduction (Very Short Introductions)* by
John Finney (Oxford University Press, 2015). p.39 *Biology for You: Fifth
Edition for All GCSE Examinations* by Gareth Williams (Oxford University
Press, 2016). p.40 *Physics for You: Fifth Edition for All GCSE Examinations*
by Keith Johnson (Oxford University Press, 2016). pp.100–101 *AQA
GCSE Science Student Book* by Graham Bone, Simon Broadley, Philippa
Gardom Hulme, Sue Hocking, Mark Matthews and Jim Newall (Oxford
University Press, 2011).

*The publishers would like to thank the following for their kind permission to
reproduce photographs*: 123RF pp.6 (building construction/Christian
Delbert), 33 (lecture hall/kasto), 33 (presentation/racorn), 66 (woman
using laptop/Sutichak Yachiangkham), 68 (tablet/ymgerman), 71 (man
with grandchildren/goodluz), 84 (Vietnam boat tour/Thi Hong Hanh
Mac), 92 (Chicago Mercantile Exchange/Visions of America LLC),
94 (USB connection/Joanne Weston), 101 (doctors sterilising/Tyler
Olson); Alamy Stock Photo pp.24 (male portrait/Sergio Azenha),
24 (woman using laptop/Glow Asia RF), 26 (scientist/Hero Images Inc.),
26 (female technician/Tetra Images), 33 (teacher and student/Blend
Images), 62 (abandoned facility/Jack Laurenson), 86 (York flooding/
Steve Allen Travel Photography), 89 (Apple logo/Mira), 90 (aerial view
of London/Gibson Blanc), 102 (barrister/Mike Abrahams); Getty Images
pp.19 (teen using laptop/Anne Ackermann), 24 (female portrait/Nick
Dolding), 26 (researcher, Ecuador/Pete Oxford), 33 (student in lecture/
Skynesher), 41 (MRSA colonies/By R Parulan Jr.), 46 (adolescents/
Peopleimages) 53 (ecologist/Hero Images), 58 (bacteria/PASIEKA),
61 (Hydrothermal Vents/Ralph White), 77 (Chinese class/Ingram
Publishing), 78 (Carl Safina and albatrosses/Mint Images – Frans
Lanting), 95 (binary code/Science Picture Co); Oxford University Press
p.21 (bicycle/Photodisc); Shutterstock pp.12 (dead fish/kessudap),
14 (bird feeding/Sari ONeal), 17 (shoe shopping/Dmitry Kalinovsky),
21 (wooden table/horiyan), 22 (female student/Click Images), 22 (Asian
woman/leungchopan), 22 (male portrait/A and N photography),
31 (elephant/red-feniks), 33 (classroom/Monkey Business Images),
42 (city crowd/TonyV3112), 49 (cyclist/maxpro), 54 (girl with inhaler/
wavebreakmedia), 72 (Ronan O'Gara/Paolo Bona), 81 (man in
supermarket/Ditty_about_summer), 82 (girl studying/wavebreakmedia),
96 (dam/Alexandru Chiriac), 105 (voting/Ververidis Vasilis).

Cover photographs: Shutterstock; (motherboard/Olga Miltsova), (optical
fibres/ktsdesign), (student/wavebreakmedia), (coral/antos777).
Back cover photograph: Oxford University Press building/David Fisher
Illustrations by: ODI pp.21 (migratory cycle), 35 (print icon), 57 (stove)
*The publisher would like to thank the following people for their advice and
assistance in developing the material for this series*: Elif Barbaros (Erciyes
University), Kenneth Anderson (Edinburgh University), Alison
Macaulay, Fatos Eskicirak (Bahçeşehir University), Ros Gallacher
(University of Strathclyde), Ilkay Gökçe (Ege University SFL, Izmir),
Anne Kelly (University of Strathclyde), Mümin Şen (Yıldırım Beyazıt
University), Libor Stepanek (Masaryk University, Brno) and Irmak Çiçek
Yücel (Bosphorus University, Istanbul).

Contents

Section 4   Analysis and evaluation

Section 5   Functions in academic writing

Section 6   Disciplines

Introduction

Who is this book for?

Oxford Academic Vocabulary Practice is designed for anyone who is studying, or plans to study, at college or university level in English. It aims to help you build your knowledge of academic vocabulary and, through practice, give you the confidence to use this language in your own writing. The book can be used either for self-study or in class. The language reference, answer key and glossary at the back of the book make it ideal for independent study.

What vocabulary is included?

The book mostly focuses on vocabulary which will be useful to students of any academic subject. The last section (Units 38–45) deals with language which is particularly relevant to different disciplines (business, law, medicine, etc.), but it doesn't include highly specialized subject vocabulary.

The book contains vocabulary that students at university level might need to use in their own writing; thus the focus is on *productive* vocabulary rather than *receptive* vocabulary (which you might need to understand when reading).

The research for the book was also heavily informed by the *Oxford Corpus of Academic English*. This was used to check the frequency and usage of words, and also provided many of the examples in the activities.

The *Academic Word List*

The book includes many words from the *Academic Word List* (AWL). This is a list of words that are typically used in academic writing. These words are highlighted in the Words to learn lists and the glossary using the AWL symbol (AWL). This book focuses on the AWL items that are most frequent and which are most useful for academic writing (productive vocabulary). Many other words from the AWL word families are included in the glossary at the back of the book.

The book also covers many words that are not on the AWL. These are very frequent words in all contexts, and at this level it is important to master this vocabulary too. A good control of this vocabulary will give you the confidence to express your ideas in a variety of academic contexts and situations.

Use a good dictionary for learners of English alongside this book. Try the *Oxford Learner's Dictionary of Academic English*. Keep an organized vocabulary record so you can review new vocabulary regularly and easily.

How is the book organized?

The book is divided into 45 main units and five review units. These are organized into broad sections focusing on core vocabulary skills, academic life, describing basic concepts and relationships, and expressing evaluation. There is also a section that explores key concepts and skills in understanding how to learn and use common functions in academic writing. The units are designed to be independent, so you can either work through the units in order or choose units that are most interesting to you.

At the back of the book you will find:

- A language reference section containing useful information relating to the vocabulary in the main units.
- A glossary giving definitions of all the keywords in the book, based on the *Oxford Learner's Dictionary of Academic English*. It also contains information about pronunciation and word families.
- An answer key for all the exercises.

For teachers

Many of the reading texts could form the basis for discussion and further comprehension activities in class. Some units end with a writing task which is also suitable for a classroom context.

Abbreviations used in the book

adj	adjective	phr	phrase
adv	adverb	prep	preposition
AWL	*Academic Word List*	sb	somebody
conj	conjunction	sth	something
det	determiner	v	verb
n	noun	WF	word family

How to use a unit

Words to learn

About 12–15 keywords or phrases to learn. These words/phrases are the focus of the whole unit. The Words to learn list shows you:
- the part of speech
- whether the word/phrase is on the *Academic Word List*.

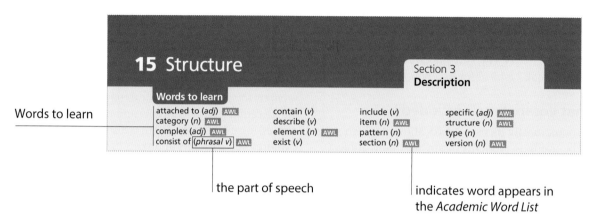

Words to learn →

15 Structure

Section 3
Description

Words to learn

attached to *(adj)* AWL	contain *(v)*	include *(v)*	specific *(adj)* AWL
category *(n)* AWL	describe *(v)*	item *(n)* AWL	structure *(n)* AWL
complex *(adj)* AWL	element *(n)* AWL	pattern *(n)*	type *(n)*
consist of *(phrasal v)* AWL	exist *(v)*	section *(n)* AWL	version *(n)* AWL

the part of speech

indicates word appears in the *Academic Word List*

Input texts

A short text or a series of short texts present the vocabulary in a typical academic context.

Physical structures

A In very basic terms, a building is defined as a **structure** which is used to provide shelter to humans. However, a building has an important cultural and social role, which can often change during the building process. Architects and construction teams look at buildings in **specific** stages. The building 'envelope' is the skeleton of the building which **contains** columns, beams, floors and the roof, without any internal fittings. These are the first parts of a building which are **attached to** outer walls. In modern methods of construction, many **sections** of a building are prefabricated. This means that **elements** of the structure are made in a factory, and then assembled on-site. With more **complex** designs, different **items** such as glasswork or heating and lighting systems need to be carefully fitted into the build.

Both builders and architects use computer-generated **versions** of the design to ensure that the final building matches their plans.

highlighted words

Source: Adapted from Gorse, C. *et al.* (2012). 'building.' 'building system.' *A Dictionary of Construction, Surveying and Civil Engineering.* Oxford: Oxford University Press. p.237.

Highlighted words show the first use of a Word to learn. When you have read the text, use the glossary at the back of the book to help you if you are still unsure about meaning. The glossary includes:
- a definition of the word as it is used in this book
- the unit number
- whether the word is in the *Academic Word List*
- how to pronounce the word
- information about word families (see Unit 4 for more information on this).

Note that many words have other meanings, so the glossary is not a replacement for a good dictionary.

Academic Word List

definition

achieve AWL /ə'tʃiːv/ *v* to succeed in reaching a particular goal or result, especially by effort or skill **U7** WF achievable *adj,* achievement *n*
activity /æk'tɪvəti/ *n* (pl. -ies) a thing that a person or group does or has done, usually in order to achieve a particular aim **U28** WF active *adj,* actively *adv*
actually /'æktʃuəli/ *adv* used to emphasize a fact or the truth about a situation **U33** WF actual *adj*
address /ə'dres/ *v* to think about a problem or a situation and decide how you are going to deal with it **U26**

unit number   pronunciation   word family information

Practice of keywords

The exercises help you to use the vocabulary and develop your understanding of the words to learn.

> **3 Replace the highlighted words in the sentences with one of the keywords or phrases from text A.**
>
> ▶ EXAMPLE: There are two ways of playing <u>versions of</u> the game, one long and one short.
> 1 There are particular _____ differences between the two species.
> 2 I found this part _____ of the story very boring – not much happened.
> 3 People with serious allergies should avoid eating foods that include _____ additives.
> 4 Research into the form _____ of DNA molecules has helped our understanding of genetics.
> 5 Maintaining good customer relations is an important aspect _____ of business success.

Answers to all the exercises are in the answer key at the back of the book.

Unit 14

1 a, b, d

2 1 communicate
   2 access
   3 slides
   4 administration
   5 registered, log on
   6 connection (you can also say *internet access*, but *access* is an uncountable noun so it isn't used with *an*)
   7 links

3 1 Y
   2 Y

2 The website gives information about more than 200 **academic** institutions in the US. ____
3 To become a lawyer, you need a university **degree**. ____
4 He **teaches** courses in the history of science and the history of technology. ____
5 The history **department** is on the third floor. ____

Usage note noun + noun
We often use noun + noun combinations to talk about academic study and academic departments:
  a(n) law/science/university/undergraduate student
  the history/geography/engineering department (or the department of history/geography/engineering)
  a(n) science/law/undergraduate/university degree
But, we use the adjective *medical*: *a medical student/degree* (NOT ~~a medicine student/degree~~)

6 Match the sentence halves.

1 She's studying for an engineering
2 There are some differences between the **higher**
3 Political science is an **academic**
4 The university welcomes **international**
5 We have changed the way we **teach**

a **discipline** that focuses on politics.
b **degree** at Tokyo University.
c **students** from all over the world.
d **education** systems in the two countries.
e science **subjects** at high school level.

7 Write a short profile (two or three sentences) describing your own academic studies or what you plan to study. Try to use some of the words from the unit.

Academic study | Unit 8 **23**

Units often end with a writing task so you can use the new words in relevant contexts.

Usage notes

The usage notes give information about grammar, the different meanings of related words, dictionary skills, and much more.

1 Learning vocabulary

Using a dictionary

AWL: The *Academic Word List* is a list of words that are typically used in academic writing. These are useful words to learn if you plan to study at university level in English.

Pronunciation: This shows you how a word is pronounced. If you are using a digital dictionary (e.g. a dictionary app or an online dictionary), you may be able to click on a symbol (◀») to hear the word.

> **evi·dence** AWL /ˈevɪdəns/ *noun* **1** [U, C] the facts, signs or objects that make you believe that sth is true; **~ of sth** *There is clear evidence of culture in chimpanzees.* **~ for sth** *These studies have been widely cited as evidence for the existence of intelligence in pigeons.* **2** [U] the information that is used in court to try to prove sth: *Due to a lack of evidence, the case against her was dropped.*
> IDM **(be) in evidence** present and clearly seen: *There is little brand loyalty from customers in evidence in the market today.*

Part of speech: It is important to find the correct form of the word (*noun*, *verb*, *adjective* or *adverb*) when you are looking in the dictionary. Remember that sometimes two parts of speech are spelled the same. For example, *study* can be a noun or a verb.
▶ For more about parts of speech, see Unit 4.

Phrases and idioms: Fixed phrases and idioms are usually shown at the end of an entry. Always check whether a word is part of a fixed phrase by looking at the end of the entry. The phrase may have a different meaning from the word used on its own.
▶ For more about phrases, see Units 5 and 6.

Patterns: Information about the common patterns that follow a word are often shown before the examples. This includes information about prepositions that typically follow a noun (*evidence of, evidence for*) and structures that follow a verb (*find that …*).
▶ For more about patterns and structures, see Unit 6.

Irregular forms: Irregular verb and noun forms are usually shown at the start of an entry.
▶ For more about common irregular nouns and verbs, see pp.108 and 110.

> **find** /faɪnd/ *verb* (**found, found** /faʊnd/) **1** [T] to discover or learn that sth is true after you have tried it, tested it or experienced it:
> **~ (that)…** *Khanna and Palepu (1999c) found that the performance of groups increased after economic reforms were implemented.* **2** [T] **~ sth/sb** to discover sth/sb by searching, studying or thinking carefully: *West (1948) found no convincing evidence for telepathy.* ◊ *Our aim was to find support for our initial hypothesis.*

Grammar labels: These labels tell you about how a word is used grammatically.
- At nouns, the label [C] tells you the noun is *countable* and [U] tells you it is *uncountable*.
▶ For more about nouns, see Unit 2.
- At verbs, the label [T] tells you that a verb is *transitive* and [I] tells you it is *intransitive*.
▶ For more about verbs, see Unit 3.
If there are two labels, the most common use is usually shown first. For example, *evidence* [U, C] is usually uncountable and only sometimes countable.

Collocations: Example sentences often show words that are frequently used together – collocations. For example, *find + evidence, find + support*.
▶ For more about collocation, see Unit 5.

1 Read the information about the dictionary entries and answer the questions.

1 What does 'AWL' refer to? _____
2 Is *evidence* mostly used as a countable or an uncountable noun? _____
3 Which prepositions are frequently used after *evidence*? _____ / _____
4 If something is *in evidence*, what does it mean? _____
5 What is the past tense form of *find*? _____
6 Which two nouns are frequently used after *find*? _____ / _____

2 a The glossary on pp.127–141 at the back of this book contains some of the information you find in a dictionary. Tick the information it includes.

a part of speech _____
b AWL labels _____
c pronunciation _____
d irregular forms _____
e grammar labels _____
f definitions _____
g phrases _____
h examples _____

b Check these words in the glossary on pp.127–141. What information can you find?

1 study   2 progress   3 term   4 create

Recording vocabulary

VOCAB

evidence

noun, U

There is clear evidence of major changes.

clear/strong/good evidence

find (verb)

past: found

The research found that the condition
is more common in boys than girls.
They found significant differences.
(find + differences)

Usage note recording vocabulary

Recording useful words in a notebook or digitally will help you to improve your vocabulary.
• Write down whatever information will help you remember the word: a definition, a translation, notes, etc.
• Write down example sentences. This will help you remember how the word is used.
• Make a note of any important features, for example if a noun is uncountable or a verb is irregular.
• Record new words, and also **new uses** or **new phrases** with words you already know.
• Add to your notes when you meet the word again. For example, add a new example or a new collocation.

3 Look up these words in a dictionary. Write a vocabulary note for each word. Choose one meaning that you think may be useful in academic writing. Write down information that will help you remember the word and how it is used.

• create   • security   • numerous   • occur   • discipline

Usage note choosing a dictionary

Try to use an English **learner's dictionary**, as this will contain the information you need to learn vocabulary. There are several good learner's dictionaries available for free online. Try www.oxfordlearnersdictionaries.com.

2 Nouns and adjectives

Words to learn

aware (*adj*) AWL	information (*n*)	media (*n*) AWL	particular (*adj*)
developed (*adj*)	life (*n*)	necessary (*adj*)	use (*n*)
developing (*adj*)	low (*adj*)	news (*n*)	work (*n*)

Understanding nouns

A Technology plays a vital role in our everyday **lives**. We rely on computer technology for **work** and for study. We use the internet as a source of **information** and, increasingly, it is also the way we access the mass **media**. We read **news** online, we watch videos and even TV on our laptops or other devices.

Young people who have grown up since the **use** of digital technology became common are known as 'digital natives'. For this generation, computers, the internet, social media and mobile apps are just a normal part of everyday **life**.

Usage note types of nouns

We use nouns to refer to people, things (*laptops*, *computers*) and ideas (*work*, *life*). Nouns can be:
• **countable**, labelled [C] in a dictionary. These words can be used in a plural form: *computer – computers*
• **uncountable**, labelled [U] in a dictionary. These words cannot be used in a plural form: *information*
Some nouns can be both. They are **uncountable** when they are describing a general idea, but **countable** when they refer to a specific example:
• *Technology* (U, in general) *plays a vital role in our everyday lives.*
• *Engineers are developing new **technologies*** (C, specific machines, devices, etc.) *all the time.*
For more about countable and uncountable nouns, see the language reference section on pp.108 –114.

1 **Find the words in text A. Are they used as countable nouns (C) or uncountable nouns (U)? Check the words in a dictionary.**

1 technology __	3 work __	5 information __	7 use __
2 role __	4 study __	6 device __	8 generation __

Usage note irregular nouns

Remember that some nouns have an irregular plural form: *life – lives   person – people*
Media is an irregular plural noun. The singular form is *medium*.
*the mass **media*** (plural: TV, radio, newspapers, etc.)   *social **media*** (plural: Facebook, Twitter, Instagram, etc.)
• *His work has reached a mass audience only through **the medium** of television.*
Some nouns, like *news*, are always plural. But note that *news* is used with a singular verb: *The **news** is positive.*
For a list of common irregular nouns, see the language reference section on pp.108 –114.

2 **Choose the correct option to complete the sentences.**

1 For more *information* / *informations* about this theory, see chapter 12.
2 Recent *work* / *works* suggests a link between diet and the risk of some diseases.
3 People are most concerned about decisions that affect their own *lifes* / *lives*.
4 The mass *medias* / *media* such as television and newspapers influence our ideas about the world.
5 Medical researchers are hoping to find new *use* / *uses* for existing drugs.

3 **Complete the sentences using the present simple form of the verb in CAPITALS. Think carefully about the agreement between the highlighted noun and the verb.**

▶ EXAMPLE: Nowadays **news** about an event <u>is</u> available online within minutes. BE
1 The **lives** of most people _____ in a number of ways as they grow older. CHANGE
2 The **use** of digital technology _____ the registration process much quicker. MAKE
3 Detailed **information** about the products _____ online shoppers to make their choices. HELP
4 Much more **work** on these issues _____ necessary to find positive solutions. BE

Understanding adjectives

B Developing countries claim that their standard of living is much **lower** than in more **developed** countries. They argue that increased use of fossil fuel is **necessary** for economic growth.

C We live in a shrinking world. We are becoming increasingly **aware** that when we pollute a **particular** location, we are polluting the world.

Glossary
fossil fuel (*n*): substances such as coal and oil that are burned to produce power or heat
shrink (*v*): to become smaller in size

4 **Read texts B and C. Mark the statements true (T) or false (F) according to the texts.**

1 People in developing countries usually have less money than those in developed countries. __
2 Developing countries want to use less fossil fuel. __
3 People do not realize that pollution in one place can have a wider effect. __

5 **Complete the sentences using adjectives from the box. Think about meaning and sentence position.**

| aware   low   necessary   particular |

1 Advertising is usually aimed at _____ groups of people, for example teenagers.
2 Within cities, transport costs are quite _____ compared to rural areas.
3 Doctors should be _____ of the most common problems in pregnancy.
4 As the technology develops, it may become _____ to give staff further training.

3 Verbs and adverbs

Words to learn

abroad (*adv*)	easily (*adv*)	in general (*phrase*)	survive (*v*) AWL
continue (*v*)	generally (*adv*)	largely (*adv*)	
damage (*v*)	globally (*adv*) AWL	overseas (*adv*) AWL	
deal with (*phrasal v*)	happen (*v*)	spread (*v*)	

Understanding verbs

A A river can naturally **deal with** a certain amount of pollution. The water dilutes the pollutants to safe levels. However, beyond a certain point this natural process cannot **continue**. When this **happens**, the water is not safe to drink. The pollutants **damage** the habitat and fish cannot **survive**. As the pollution **spreads**, the whole river can be affected.

Glossary
dilute (*v*): to make a liquid weaker by adding water
pollutant (*n*): a substance that causes pollution

Usage note types of verbs

Transitive verbs, labelled [T] in a dictionary, are followed by an object:
• *The river can **deal with** <u>pollution</u>.*
Intransitive verbs, labelled [I] in a dictionary, are not followed by an object:
• *When this **happens**, fish cannot **survive**.*
Some verbs can be both **transitive** and **intransitive**:
• *This natural process cannot **continue**. [I]*
• *He **continued** <u>his work</u>. [T]*

For more about transitive and intransitive verbs, see the language reference section on pp.108–114.

1 a Match the sentence halves. Think about meaning and grammar.

1 The same thing **happened**
2 Rapid economic growth can also **damage**
3 It is difficult to **deal with**
4 The government uses the media to **spread**
5 We hope to **continue**
6 About 72% of patients **survive**

a such a huge global problem.
b our research into this issue.
c the environment.
d for more than five years after treatment.
e in a number of different cities.
f important public health messages.

b Are the highlighted verbs in 1a being used in a transitive (T) or intransitive (I) form?

1 __   2 __   3 __   4 __   5 __   6 __

2 Complete the sentences using the past simple form of the verb in CAPITALS. Check the verb forms on page 110 if necessary.

► EXAMPLE: Each of the families <u>dealt with</u> the situation in different ways. DEAL WITH

1 News of the accident _____ quickly via social media. SPREAD

2 Nearly half of all the workers _____ their jobs. LOSE

3 In the study, 63% of people _____ the wrong option. CHOOSE

4 The research _____ no difference between the groups. FIND

5 In total, the project _____ more than seven billion dollars. COST

Usage note irregular verbs

Remember that some verbs have irregular past forms:
• *No one **dealt with** the problem.*
• *Eventually the pollution **spread** to the whole river.*
• *The water **became** unsafe to drink.*
• *Many fish species were **lost**.*

You can find irregular verb forms in a dictionary and in the language reference section on pp.108–114.

Understanding adverbs

B According to UNESCO, in 2012 at least four million students went **abroad** to study.

- That number represents almost 2% of university students **globally**.
- The most mobile student population comes from Central Asia, and the proportion of students from this region studying **overseas** is increasing rapidly.
- The US and UK are still the most popular destinations, **largely** due to the attraction of studying in English.
- Regional hubs are becoming more popular, as students prefer to stay closer to home. Dubai, for example, is doing very well at attracting students from the region. Studying in a nearby country reduces travel costs and students **generally** adapt to the culture more **easily**.

Source: UNESCO. (2016). UNESCO Institute for Statistics.

Glossary
hub (*n*): a central or important place for an activity

3 Read the paraphrases of ideas in text B. Mark them correct (C) or incorrect (I).

1 International students make up nearly 2% of the student population worldwide. __
2 The largest proportion of students go to Central Asia to study. __
3 The number of Central Asian students studying abroad is growing fast. __
4 It is becoming more popular for students to stay in their own country to study. __

Usage note irregular adverbs

Most English adverbs end in *-ly*:   *globally   rapidly   largely   generally   easily*
There are some irregular adverbs:
  *four million students go **abroad**   students studying **overseas***
  *Dubai is doing very **well*** (NOT ~~very good~~)   *this number is growing **fast*** (NOT ~~fastly~~)

Note: ***overseas*** can be used as an adverb or an adjective: *study/move **overseas*** (adv), *an **overseas** student/market* (adj). But ***abroad*** is always an adverb, used after a verb: *study/work/travel **abroad***

---

4 Choose the correct adjective or adverb form to complete the sentences.

1 People are going *abroad / international* in search of higher incomes.
2 Many firms have encountered problems in *abroad / overseas* markets.
3 Use simple explanations that customers can *easy / easily* understand.
4 This approach works *good / well* for relatively simple devices.
5 Wages are rising *fast / rapid* in certain areas.
6 *In general / In generally*, coastal areas have higher rainfall.

Usage note adverbs and adverb phrases

As well as adverbs, there are some common adverb phrases used in academic writing:
in general   in particular   at first   on average to some extent
Generally and ***in general*** have a similar meaning and are used in a similar way:
- *There is, **in general**, no risk to people's health.*
- *The process **generally** takes four to six weeks.*
For more about common phrases, see Unit 5.

5 Complete the text using verbs and adverbs from the Words to learn list.

In 2014, there was an outbreak of the Ebola virus in West Africa. The first case was reported in Guinea, but the disease [1]_____ quickly. As people travelled [2]_____ , they took the virus to neighbouring countries. Health care services struggled to [3]_____ so many sick people, and there were fears that the virus could spread [4]_____ . Thankfully, through 2015 the number of cases fell, and by the end of the year the outbreak was [5]_____ over.

4 Word formation

Words to learn

academic (*adj*) AWL	critical thinking (*n*)	provide (*v*)	useful (*adj*)
attract (*v*)	differ (*v*)	reliable (*adj*) AWL	
behave (*v*)	measure (*v*)	repeat (*v*)	
compete (*v*)	misunderstand (*v*)	unfortunately (*adv*)	

Word families

A To test whether birds **behave** differently throughout the day, we **measured** the amount of water they drank in the morning, at midday and in the late afternoon.

B To find out whether birds' behaviour **differs** depending on the time of day, the researchers took measurements at three different times.

C Researchers investigated behavioural differences in birds throughout the day by recording their drinking patterns.

1 Read text A and the students' paraphrases B and C and complete the table using the keywords from the texts.

Noun	Verb	Adjective	Adverb
1 _____	behave	2 _____	-
3 _____	4 _____	5 _____	differently
6 _____	measure	-	-

Usage note word families

Many English words can have more than one form: as a **noun** (*difference*), as a **verb** (*differ*), as an **adjective** (*different*) or as an **adverb** (*differently*). Together, these are called a **word family**.

Knowing different words in a word family can help you to find the best way to express an idea. It can also help you to **paraphrase** ideas from texts. Remember to record words from the same word family together. For more about word families, see the glossary on pp.127–141.

D Internet providers have to **compete** with each other to **attract** users. They can do this by offering either a better service or lower prices.

E Companies that **provide** internet services are in competition with each other. Each attempts to make their services seem more attractive to users.

F The provision of internet services is a highly competitive market.

Usage note -er/-or and -sion/-tion endings

Sometimes there are two different noun forms in the same word family. The ending can help you understand the meaning:

-er/-or: a person or thing that does something: *provider competitor*

-sion/-tion: an action or process: *provision competition*

2 Read paraphrases D, E and F and complete the table using the highlighted keywords. Use the glossary on pp.127–141 to help you.

Noun	Verb	Adjective
provider [1] _____	2 _____	-
competition [3] _____	4 _____	5 _____
attraction	6 _____	7 _____

3 a Complete the sentences using the correct form of the word in CAPITALS.

▶ EXAMPLE: People's attitudes to work _differ_ around the world. DIFFERENT
1 Psychology is the study of the human mind and our _____ . BEHAVE
2 Market research includes finding out about _____ and their products. COMPETE
3 The city launched a marketing campaign to _____ more visitors. ATTRACTIVE
4 The software calculates accurate _____ of the building. MEASURE
5 Many websites _____ free information about weather, transport, sport, etc. PROVIDER

b Identify the form (noun, verb, adjective or adverb) of each of the answers in 3a.

1 ____   2 ____   3 ____   4 ____   5 ____

Prefixes and suffixes

G Unfortunately, some of the participants **misunderstood** the instructions. So we **reworded** the instructions and **repeated** the test with a new group of people.

Usage note prefixes

Prefixes at the beginning of some words tell you about the meaning:
un- = not: _unfortunately unattractive unaware_
Other negative prefixes include: **in-** (_incorrect_), **non-** (_non-profit_)
mis- = badly or wrongly: _misunderstand misbehave_
re- = again: _reword repeat recycle reuse_
For more prefixes, see the language reference section on pp.108 –114.

4 Choose the best word to complete the sentences.

1 The measurements were _repeated / reworded_ every three days.
2 _Fortunately / Unfortunately_, there is a simple way of solving the problem.
3 If a patient has _understood / misunderstood_ something, then the nurse should explain it again.
4 Some students didn't apply for funding because they were _aware / unaware_ it was available.
5 Solar heating is an _attractive / unattractive_ option in some regions because it is cheap and easy to install.
6 Customers are encouraged to _use / reuse_ plastic bags instead of getting new ones on each visit.

H **Critical thinking** is asking questions about what you read. Is the information **useful**? Is it from a **reliable** source?

An **academic** resource has authority when its writers are experts in the subject and the information is reliable.

Usage note suffixes

Suffixes at the end of words can tell you about the form of the word:
• Adjective endings: **-al** (_critical_) **-ful** (_useful_) **-able** (_reliable_) **-ic** (_academic_) **-ive** (_attractive, competitive_)
• Noun endings: **-tion** (_question_) **-ity** (_authority_) **-ment** (_measurement_) **-ence** (_difference_) **-ability** (_reliability_)
For more about suffixes, see the language reference section on pp.108 –114.

5 Identify the form, noun (N) or adjective (A), of the highlighted words in the sentences. Use the endings to help you.

1 Teachers should encourage **critical** thinking and problem-solving skills. __
2 The site provides some **useful** advice. __
3 Some experts have questioned the **reliability** of the data. __
4 Over 40% of the university's **academic** staff are from other countries. __
5 Below is an **illustration** of the basic structure of a flower. __
6 Solar power is a clean, **renewable** source of energy. __

5 Collocation

Words to learn

come into contact with (phr) AWL	information technology (n)	make sense (to do sth)	questionnaire (n)
complete (v)	in order that (phr)	on a ... basis (phr)	skill (n)
guidelines (n)	in return for (phr)	on behalf of (phr) AWL	together with (phr)
	in terms of (phr)	option (n) AWL	

Collocation

A At the start of the course, I felt my **information technology skills** were weak. Consequently, I allowed more time to create my webfolio. By following the **guidelines**, I successfully created an organized and well-researched webfolio. Using this, I was able to give a successful presentation. The feedback from my presentation was generally positive.

B I designed my own **questionnaire** for the study. To keep it as simple as possible, I gave only three **options** for each question: 'yes', 'no' and 'sometimes'. This approach worked well because participants were able to **complete** the questionnaire quite quickly, giving us more time for the interview stage.

Source: student reports

Glossary
webfolio (n): information collected from the internet by someone on a particular topic; a *portfolio* is a collection of someone's work

---

1 Read student reports A and B and answer the questions.

1 How did student A use the information from their webfolio?_____

2 Why was the questionnaire successful?_____

2 a Complete the sets of collocations using words from the box.

> feedback ~~guidelines~~ option positive skills questionnaire work

▶ EXAMPLE: follow / provide / develop + *guidelines*

1 information technology / language / communication + _____

2 design / complete / use + a/an _____

3 give / provide / choose + a/an _____

4 positive / negative / regular + _____

5 _____ + well / hard / together

6 generally / very / extremely + _____

Usage note collocation

Particular words are typically used together in academic writing; these are called **collocations**.
• verb + noun: *follow + guidelines   give + a presentation   complete + a questionnaire*
• adjective + noun: *positive + feedback*
• adverb + adjective: *generally + positive*
You can find collocations in the dictionary. They are shown in the example sentences or sometimes in a collocations box. Remember to record useful collocations. Learning which words are used together will make your writing more natural.
For more on collocation, see the language reference section on pp.108 –114.

b Complete the sentences using an appropriate collocation from 2a.

1 Customers are asked to _____ one of three **options**: good, OK or poor.

2 All research projects must _____ the university's ethical **guidelines**.

3 The manager provides _____ **feedback** to the trainees at the end of every week.

4 All patients _____ a **questionnaire** when they arrive about their health and lifestyle.

5 Good _____ **skills** are essential for staff dealing directly with customers.

Fixed phrases

C Some websites sell products **on behalf of** many small producers. The website advertises the products **in return for** a small fee. It also provides the technical skills to manage the online sales process **in terms of** taking orders and online payments. These specialist services, **together with** the more effective advertising of a larger site, benefit the seller.

Usage note prepositional phrases

There are many common phrases used in academic writing that include a keyword plus one or more prepositions: *at first for example in common in return for in terms of on behalf of together with*
Recording and learning these fixed phrases can improve the style of your writing.

3 Choose the correct phrase to complete the sentences.

1 Participants were given a café voucher *in return for / on behalf of* taking part in the study.
2 The document includes the names of all the workers, *in terms of / together with* their ages.
3 One woman stood up to speak *in return for / on behalf of* the whole group.
4 Students are put into mixed groups *in terms of / together with* academic ability.

D In the retail sector, staff **come into contact with** customers **on a regular basis**. Thus, it **makes sense** to train staff well **in order that** they deliver a good level of customer service.

Glossary
retail sector (*n*): the area of business that involves selling goods to the public, usually in shops

4 Complete the sentences using one word in each gap.

1 The figures are updated _____ a daily basis.
2 The guidelines must be followed by all other staff who _____ into contact with patients.
3 It _____ sense to try and prevent illness where possible.
4 Germany is the largest country in Europe _____ terms of population.
5 Problems need to be identified quickly _____ order that they can be dealt with.
6 The manager signed the contract _____ behalf of the company.

Usage note phrases in academic writing

A phrase can be any group of words that are typically used together with a fixed meaning: *come into contact with sb make sense (to do sth) keep sth simple*
Recording and learning phrases commonly used in academic writing can improve your own writing.
In some phrases, one word or part can change: *on a regular/daily/temporary basis*
You can find many fixed phrases in the dictionary. They are often shown in **bold** followed by an example sentence, or sometimes in the idioms section, where they have a full definition.

5 Find collocations to go with the words. Use a dictionary or find examples in other units in this book. Write an example sentence for each collocation.

▶ EXAMPLE: <u>take</u> (*verb*) + notes *During seminars students should listen carefully and take notes.*
1 _____ (*verb*) + questions
2 a developing + _____ (*noun*)
3 the _____ (*adjective*) + media
4 _____ (*verb*) + a role in sth

6 Patterns and structures

Vocabulary skills

Words to learn

advise (v)
approach (n) [AWL]
aspect (n) [AWL]
be concerned with (phr)

capable (adj) [AWL]
concentrate (v) [AWL]
enable (v) [AWL]
ensure (v) [AWL]

focus (v) [AWL]
impact (n) [AWL]
need (n)
participate (v) [AWL]

purpose (n)

Preposition patterns

A Each chapter **focuses** on a different **aspect** of international law.

B The **purpose** of this book is to present an integrated **approach** to the design and manufacturing of products.

C Chapter 5 **is concerned with** the **impact** of digital technology on the music industry.

Glossary
integrated (adj): with many parts working successfully together

1 **Read the information from three academic books, A, B and C. Complete the paraphrases using the best preposition (on, of, to, etc.) in each gap.**

1 In the first book, the author focuses _____ different aspects _____ international law in each chapter.

2 The purpose _____ the second book is to describe a particular approach _____ product design.

3 The third book includes a chapter concerned _____ the impact _____ digital technology _____ the music industry.

Usage note word + preposition patterns

Some words are typically followed by a particular preposition:
- noun + preposition: *aspect of   purpose of   approach to*
- verb + preposition: *focus on   compete with   communicate with*
- adjective + preposition: *different from   aware of*

You can find information about the prepositions typically used with a word in the dictionary:

aspect [AWL] /ˈæspekt/ *noun* **1** [C] a particular feature of a situation, an idea or a process; a way in which something may be consistent; **~ of sth**: *Age is shown to have an important influence on many aspects of health.*

When you record new vocabulary, remember to note down any prepositions that are used with a word.

---

2 **Complete the sentences using the words given. Add any prepositions or other words that are needed.**

▶ EXAMPLE: purpose | research
The first chapter explains <u>the purpose of the research</u>.

1 new | approach | language learning
Lewis developed _____.

2 concerned | human rights issues
Organizations like Amnesty International are _____.

3 impact | floods | local people
The pictures show _____.

4 aspect | contemporary culture
The exhibition explores several _____.

5 focus | role | technology | education
This article _____.

6 aware | health risks | smoking
Nowadays most people are _____.

Verb patterns and structures

D We always **advise** students to take notes during lectures. Most lecturers put their slides online, so there's no **need** to write down every detail. Students should **concentrate** on noting down interesting points. Sometimes it's a good idea to write down questions that you want to ask later.

E We offer some of our courses via distance learning. Distance learning students should **ensure** that their computer has a webcam and a microphone. The microphone should be **capable** of picking up good quality sound. This will **enable** them to **participate** fully in online seminars.

Usage note following verb patterns

Some words (verbs, nouns and adjectives) are typically followed by a verb in a particular form:
+ **to do sth**: *advise sb to do   no need to do   enable sb to do   decision to do*
• We **advise** students **to take** notes.
+ **preposition + -ing sth**: *concentrate on doing   be capable of doing   focus on doing*
• Students should **concentrate on noting** down interesting points.

---

3 **Read texts D and E. Complete the answers in the Q&A using the correct form of the verb in brackets.**

1 Q: Do I need to take notes in lectures?
  A: Yes, we **advise** students _____ (take) notes, either on paper or using a laptop or tablet. There's no **need** _____ (write) down everything, but you should especially **concentrate** on _____ (note) down things you find interesting.

2 Q: What computer equipment do I need to take part in your distance learning courses?
  A: To **enable** you _____ (participate) fully in online seminars, you need a webcam and microphone. The microphone should be **capable** of _____ (pick up) good quality sound so we can hear you clearly.

4 **Choose the best option to complete the sentences.**

1 She's **capable** *of achieving / to achieve* a good result in her exam.
2 Research so far has **focused** *on found / on finding* the cause of the problem.
3 He explained his **decision** *for leaving / to leave* the company in an interview.
4 The guidelines **advise** *not to drive patients / patients not to drive* after taking the medication.

5 **Match the sentence halves. Think about meaning and grammar patterns.**

1 Regular checks **ensure**
2 Recent studies show
3 The farmers **concentrated**
4 Two hundred and fifty people **participated**

a on improving the quality of the fruit.
b in the first stage of the research.
c that the quality stays the same.
d that average rainfall has increased.

Usage note verb + *that*

Some verbs are typically followed by *that* + a clause: *ensure that …   show that …   argue that …*
• Students should **ensure that** <u>their computer has a webcam and a microphone</u>.
This pattern is often shown in the dictionary.

7 Academic language

Words to learn

achieve (v) AWL	cycle (n) AWL	odd (adj) AWL	strategy (n) AWL
attempt (v)	employ (v)	receive (v)	table (n)
correct (adj)	enjoy (v)	right (n)	

Formal and informal vocabulary

A Motivating teenage students can be challenging. There are, however, a wide range of **strategies** that can be **employed** to help them **achieve** academic goals.

B Sometimes it's hard to motivate teenagers. There are lots of ways you can use to help them get to their goals.

C When a student using the app **attempts** to answer a question, they **receive** positive feedback even if their answer is not completely **correct**.

D If you try to answer a question, you get positive feedback even if your answer isn't quite right.

Glossary
motivate (v): to make someone want to do something

1 Read the extracts from two academic texts, A and C. Match the words to words with a similar meaning in the spoken paraphrases, B and D.

▶ EXAMPLE: strategies – ways

1 employ – _____
2 achieve – _____
3 attempt – _____

4 receive – _____
5 correct – _____

Usage note formal and informal vocabulary

Academic writers typically use more formal words than we use in informal speech. Vocabulary in academic writing needs to be precise in meaning. For example, the verb **get** has many possible meanings, so academic writers use verbs like **achieve** and **receive**, which have a more precise meaning:

   achieve a goal/a result/success   **receive** feedback/attention/information

2 Replace the highlighted words in the sentences with a more formal word with a similar meaning.

▶ EXAMPLE: Both approaches get _achieve_ the same result.
1 All participants get _____ written information about the study.
2 Psychologists try _____ to explain human behaviour.
3 Only 44% identified the right _____ answer.
4 Each company uses different ways _____ to attract new customers.
5 The group used _____ various methods to solve the problem.

Usage note academic writing

As well as vocabulary, there are some other differences between general conversation and academic writing.
• Contractions (_isn't, don't_) are not normally used in academic writing.
• Personal pronouns (_I, you_) are less common in academic writing.
• Sentences are longer and contain more detailed information. In conversation, your listener can ask questions, but in writing, you need to give your reader all the information they need.
Find examples of these differences in texts A–D.

General and academic meanings

E The **table** shows the number of seats won by each political party.

F Many migratory animals travel in annual **cycles** over extremely long distances.

G European Union citizens **enjoy** the same voting **rights** in all member states.

H Researchers found that people were less likely to choose **odd** numbers (3, 5, 7, etc.).

Glossary
migratory (*adj*): (of animals) moving from one part of the world to another according to the season

3 Choose the two most appropriate pictures to illustrate texts E and F.

UK Elections 2015

Party	Seats	change
Conservatives	64	74
Labour	6	6
SNP	19	18
Lib Dem	13	13
DUP	8	0
Plaid Cymru	3	0
SDLP	3	0
UKIP	1	1

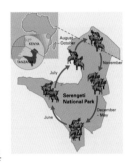

1   2   3   4

1 Text E: Picture_____   2   Text F: Picture_____

Usage note general and academic meanings

Sometimes the meaning of a word in academic writing is different from the most common, everyday meaning. When you check a word in the dictionary, remember to look at all the senses until you find the one that fits best.

table /'teɪbl/ *noun* **1** a piece of furniture that consists of a flat top supported by legs: *a kitchen table* [...] **2** a list of facts or numbers arranged in a special order, usually in rows and columns: *Table 2 shows how prices and earnings have increased over the past 20 years.*

4 Match the highlighted words from texts G and H to the correct definition, a or b. Think about the meaning of the words in the texts.

1 enjoy ___   a to have fun doing something
              b to have something good that is an advantage to you
2 right ___   a a thing that you are allowed to do according to the law
              b the right side or direction (opposite = left)
3 odd ___   a strange; unusual
              b (used about a number) that cannot be divided by two (opposite = even)

5 a Complete the sentences using words from the box.

cycle   enjoy   odd   right   table

1 Large businesses _____ certain advantages over smaller firms.
2 The number keypad is on the _____ of the keyboard.
3 The life _____ of a species is the way organisms are born, grow, reproduce and die.
4 This may seem like a slightly _____ question to ask.
5 The third column of the _____ shows the figures for this year.

b Are the keywords in 5a used with the same meaning (S) as in texts E–H or with a different meaning (D)?

1 ___   2 ___   3 ___   4 ___   5 ___

8 Academic study

Words to learn

academic (*adj*) AWL
course (*n*)
degree (*n*)
department (*n*)

discipline (*n*)
faculty (*n*)
higher education (*n*)
institution (*n*) AWL

international student (*n*)
student (*n*)
study (*v*)
subject (*n*)

teach (*v*)
undergraduate (*n*)
university (*n*)

Studying at university

Rebecca

Yasuko

Dipak

A I'm a **student** at the **University** of Oxford. I'm **studying** medicine and I plan to become a doctor.

B I'm a law student at Melbourne University. I'm doing a **course** in international law.

C I'm from Mumbai in India, but at the moment I'm at university in London. I'm an **undergraduate** in the first year of a three-year engineering course. There are lots of other **international students** on my course.

1 **Complete the sentences about the three students using words from the box.**

course   international student   student   studying   undergraduate   university

1 Rebecca is a _____ in Oxford. She's in her second year at the moment.
2 She's doing a _____ in medicine and hopes to become a doctor when she finishes.
3 Yasuko is _____ law, in particular international law.
4 She's at _____ in Melbourne, Australia.
5 Dipak is an _____ / _____ doing a course in engineering in London.

Usage note talking about your studies

Notice the different ways you can talk about your studies:
• *I'm studying (medicine/law).*
• *I'm a student at (Bristol University).*
• *I'm a (law) student.*

• *I'm at university in (Istanbul).*
• *I'm doing a course in (international law).*
• *I'm an undergraduate.*

2 **Choose the correct word to complete the sentences.**

1 There are around 8,900 international students *at* / *of* Oxford University.
2 In 2014, around 11,700 students altogether were *doing* / *making* undergraduate courses at the university.
3 In 2015, 952 undergraduates were *student* / *studying* medicine.
4 Around 960 students were doing courses *of* / *in* history.
5 There were around 664 law *students* / *studying*.

Higher education

D **Higher education** includes courses at universities and other **institutions**, such as art colleges. A higher education course leads to a **degree**, such as a BA (Bachelor of Arts) or a BSc (Bachelor of Science). A degree course usually lasts for three or four years.

E Most universities are divided into **faculties**, such as the Faculty of Science or the Faculty of Law. Each faculty is divided into **departments**. An **academic** department **teaches** courses in a particular **subject** or **discipline**, such as the Department of Engineering or the Department of History.

3 **Read texts D and E about higher education. Mark the statements true (T) or false (F).**

1 Higher education includes high schools, colleges and other institutions. __
2 At the end of a university course, students get a degree. __
3 A university faculty is larger than a department. __
4 A *discipline* is another word for a subject that you study. __
5 A university department usually teaches many different subjects. __

4 **Complete the web page using words from the box.**

Department	
Faculty	**¹_____ of Clifton**
University	²_____ of Sciences | Engineering ³_____
courses	Our ⁴_____
	• BSc in Civil Engineering
	• BSc in Mechanical Engineering
	• BSc in Electronic Engineering

5 **Write the part of speech (noun, verb or adjective) of the highlighted word in each sentence.**

▶ EXAMPLE: She's a professor in the **Faculty** of Medicine at the University of London. *noun*

1 We spoke to students from different **disciplines**, including history, economics and engineering. ____
2 The website gives information about more than 200 **academic** institutions in the US. ____
3 To become a lawyer, you need a university **degree**. ____
4 He **teaches** courses in the history of science and the history of technology. ____
5 The history **department** is on the third floor. ____

> **Usage note** noun + noun
>
> We often use noun + noun combinations to talk about academic study and academic departments:
> *a(n) law/science/university/undergraduate student*
> *the history/geography/engineering department (or the department of history/geography/engineering)*
> *a(n) science/law/undergraduate/university degree*
> But, we use the adjective *medical*: *a medical student/degree* (NOT *a medicine student/degree*)

6 **Match the sentence halves.**

1 She's studying for an engineering
2 There are some differences between the **higher**
3 Political science is an **academic**
4 The university welcomes **international**
5 We have changed the way we **teach**

a **discipline** that focuses on politics.
b **degree** at Tokyo University.
c **students** from all over the world.
d **education** systems in the two countries.
e science **subjects** at high school level.

7 **Write a short profile (two or three sentences) describing your own academic studies or what you plan to study. Try to use some of the words from the unit.**

9 Arts and social sciences

Words to learn

ancient (*adj*)	field (*n*)	perspective (*n*) **AWL**	religious (*adj*)
art (*n*)	history (*n*)	philosophy (*n*) **AWL**	sociology (*n*)
artist (*n*)	literature (*n*)	professor (*n*)	topic (*n*) **AWL**
education (*n*)	modern (*adj*)	programme (*n*)	

Arts subjects

Dr Emily Nelson
Department of English

Dr Marco Cavallo
Department of History of Art

Dr Susan Lee
Department of Philosophy

A My main research interest is 19th-century British and American **literature**. I teach on the undergraduate English Literature **programme**, including courses in Poetry, American Literature (1830–1945), and Creative Writing.

B Marco Cavallo is a lecturer in the History of Art. He studied **Ancient** and **Modern** History at Oxford University and gained his PhD in Medieval Art History. His research focuses on Italian **artists** of the 12th century. He teaches on courses including Introduction to Medieval Art, and **Religious** Art.

C Dr Lee is a **Professor** of Philosophy. She teaches on courses including Philosophy of Science, and Medical Ethics. She is author of the textbook *Introduction to the Philosophy of Science* (2009).

1 Read the academic staff profiles, A–C. Choose the correct option to complete the sentences.

1 Dr Nelson *teaches / studies* English literature to undergraduates.
2 Dr Cavallo teaches *Ancient and Modern History / History of Art*.
3 Dr Lee teaches in the *philosophy department / Department of Medicine*.
4 She wrote a book about *the philosophy of science / medical ethics*.

2 Match the student comments, 1–4, to the courses they are studying, a–d.

1 We're learning about the work of 15th-century artists, like Leonardo da Vinci and Michelangelo.
2 We discuss questions like the link between scientific theories and the actual data that scientists collect.
3 On this course, we're studying Greek culture and civilization from the period around 480 BC.
4 At the moment, we're reading a novel called *The Bluest Eye* by the US writer Toni Morrison.

    a Ancient History
    b History of Art
    c Philosophy of Science
    d American Literature

Academic perspectives

> **D** An interdisciplinary course of study looks at more than one academic discipline to create a **perspective** on **topics** common to both. Thus, one might use ideas from the **fields** of **education** and **sociology** to examine the topic of cultural deprivation, for example.
>
> Glossary
> **deprivation** (*n*): the fact of not having the things that people in a society normally have
>
> Source: In Wallace, S. (ed.). (2015). *A Dictionary of Education*. (2nd ed.). Oxford: Oxford University Press.

3 Read text D from *A Dictionary of Education*. What is it a definition of?

a cultural deprivation   b the field of education   c interdisciplinary study

---

Usage note academic word families

We use nouns to talk about different academic disciplines: *education, sociology, history, economic*
We use adjective + noun to talk about topics connected to a discipline: *a **philosophical** problem*
We use different nouns to talk about the people who study or work in a particular field: *sociologist, historian*
All these words are part of a word family (e.g. *history – historical – historian*).

---

4 Complete the table using the correct form of the words. Use the word families in the glossary on pp.127–141 to help you.

Academic subject (noun)	Perspective adjective	Person (noun)
history	historical	1 _____
philosophy	2 _____	philosopher
3 _____	educational	educator
sociology	4 _____ , social	sociologist
economics	economic	5 _____
6 _____	legal	lawyer
politics	7 _____	political scientist, politician

5 Read a paragraph from a student essay about cultural deprivation. Complete the paragraph using words from the box.

> field   perspective   social   sociologists   topic

> 'Cultural deprivation' is a theory which says that children from some [1]_____ backgrounds do not learn the intellectual and linguistic skills they need to be successful in life. They come from homes where there are few books or other activities to help them develop. So from an educational [2]_____ , this means that when they start school, they lack the skills they need to progress. This leads to low academic achievement, few qualifications and poor job prospects. The idea of 'cultural deprivation', then, is clearly a [3]_____ that is of interest to those working in the [4]_____ of education, as well as to [5]_____ .

6 Choose the correct word to complete the sentences.

1 Aristotle was a Greek *philosopher* / *philosophy* who was born in 384 BC.
2 The book shows, from a *history* / *historical* perspective, how much the legal system has changed.
3 He is best known for his work in the field of international *economic* / *economics*.
4 In recent years, there have been major changes to the *politics* / *political* system.
5 Many well-known *literature* / *literary* works have been adapted to film.

Words to learn

applied science (*n*)   experiment (*v*)   observe (*v*)   scientific (*adj*)
biologist (*n*)   laboratory (*n*)   physical (*adj*) AWL   scientist (*n*)
chemist (*n*)   methodology (*n*) AWL physicist (*n*)   team (*n*) AWL
engineering (*n*)   objective (*n*) AWL   science (*n*)

Scientists

A The kinds of things that draw **scientists** into this area of knowledge are as various as the individuals. As **biologist** Peter Medawar said about his colleagues, "There is no such thing as a **Scientific** Mind. Scientists are people of very dissimilar temperaments doing different things in very different ways."

The picture of 'the scientist' becomes even less clear in contemporary science because scientists generally work in **teams** – teams of **physicists**, **chemists**, environmental scientists, and increasingly, interdisciplinary teams. They spend their time **experimenting** in **laboratories**, **observing** in the field, or working in offices connected to very powerful computers.

Source: Adapted from Dombrowski, Rotenberg & Bick. (2013). *Theory of Knowledge.* Oxford: Oxford University Press. p.328.

Glossary
temperament (*n*): a person's nature and the way they behave
interdisciplinary (*adj*): involving different areas of study
in the field (*phr*): doing practical work or study, not in a library or a laboratory

1 Read text A about scientists. Mark the statements true (T) or false (F) according to the text.

1 People become scientists for many different reasons. __
2 Peter Medawar says that his colleagues have a similar type of personality. __
3 Different types of scientists usually work separately. __
4 Scientific work can happen in many different types of places. __

2 Which of the pictures, A–C, shows a scientist working:

1 in the field? __   2 in a laboratory? __   3 at a computer in an office? __

3 Complete the sentences using the best word from the box.

experimented   laboratory   observe   physicists   scientific   team

1 A moving object will carry with it the energy of its motion – what _____ call 'kinetic energy'.
2 Michael Faraday _____ with electricity early in the 19th century.
3 Nowadays, our understanding of how the human body works is based on _____ research.
4 We used hidden cameras to _____ the animals' natural behaviour.
5 Work in the _____ has helped us to understand exactly how water freezes to make ice.
6 The study was carried out by a _____ of researchers from the University of Southampton.

Basic and applied sciences

> **B** The terms basic science and **applied science** refer to the **objectives** of the work more than the **methodology** and activities; roughly whether it's to determine some property of the **physical** world or to design something for a specific purpose.
>
> **Engineering**, applied science and design are always about something new. If it weren't new, we would just buy an existing product. And the activities are truly engaging – figuring out what the real problem is, drawing on things you already understand, identifying what you don't understand, working out the new bits, trying out an experimental version, working through the stress and excitement of getting the final version finished by the deadline and seeing the happy faces of clients. Who wouldn't love working like that?
>
> Source: Jim Cavers. In Dombrowski, Rotenberg & Bick. (2013). *Theory of Knowledge.* Oxford: Oxford University Press. p.331.

4 Read text B, part of an interview with engineer Jim Cavers. What is the main difference between basic science and applied science?

5 Choose the correct words to complete the definitions.

1 *A methodology / An objective* is something you are trying to achieve: your goal.
2 *Engineering / Methodology* is the use of scientific knowledge to design and build something.
3 *Objective / Applied science* is the use of scientific knowledge in a practical way.
4 Your *objective / methodology* is the way you carry out a particular activity, especially a piece of research.

6 a Complete the sentences using the correct form of the keyword provided. Use the glossary on pp.127–141 to help you.

1 science – scientists – scientific
   a Advances in _____ and technology have changed our everyday lives dramatically.
   b Many _____ believe that climate change will lead to more extreme weather conditions.
2 biology – biologists – biological
   a New technological devices help _____ to follow the movements of animals.
   b Ageing can be described as a _____ process.
3 physics – physicist – physical
   a _____ states that energy cannot be created or destroyed.
   b Basic science is about better understanding the _____ world and how it works.
4 chemistry – chemists – chemical
   a To speed up the _____ reaction, it is necessary to carry out the experiment at high temperatures.
   b Across the world, _____ use the same symbols to refer to the elements; H for hydrogen, O for oxygen, etc.
5 experiments – experimented – experimental
   a Recent _____ work has provided support for this theory.
   b He investigated this problem using a series of laboratory _____ .

b Identify the part of speech (noun or adjective) of the keyword in each sentence in 6a.

1 a __   2 a __   3 a __   4 a __   5 a __
  b __   b __   b __   b __   b __

7 Write a short paragraph (two or three sentences) about one of the following. Try to use some of the words from the unit.
   • A famous scientist   • An area of science you are interested in

11 Academic writing

Words to learn

assessment (n) AWL	draft (n) AWL	introduction (n)	summary (n) AWL
assignment (n) AWL	edit (v) AWL	report (n)	support (n)
conclusion (n) AWL	essay (n)	style (n) AWL	word count (n)
deadline (n)	feedback (n)	submit (v) AWL	

Academic assignments

A During your course, you'll be asked by your tutors to **submit** a number of written **assignments**. Some assignments will be quite short, such as a description or an explanation of a key idea. You'll need to write **reports** of work that you do in the lab. And sometimes you'll be asked to write an **essay** on a particular topic.

For each assignment, you'll be a given a **word count**: how many words you should write. It's important that you always check your word count before you submit your work. If you go over the maximum number of words, you could lose marks. And you must make sure that you submit any assignments before the **deadline** your tutor gives you. Again, you can lose marks if you submit work late.

At the end of the year, you'll write a longer essay on a topic of your choice. For this, you'll need to use information from your lecture notes and from the reading you've done through the year. You'll submit the first **draft** of your essay to your tutor at the end of May. They'll give you **feedback** on your writing, then you'll have another four weeks to **edit** your writing and to make any changes before you submit your final draft for **assessment** at the end of June.

1 Match the students' questions, 1–5, to the tutor's answers, a–e.

1 What's the **word count** for this assignment?
2 When's the **deadline** for the essay?
3 What's a lab **report**?
4 How much do we have to write for the first **draft**?
5 Is the extended essay part of our final **assessment**?

a You need to submit your whole essay to your tutor for feedback.
b It's a short description of the work you do in the laboratory, including your results.
c Yes, it's 25% of your final grade for the year.
d You should write between 450 and 500 words.
e You need to submit your essay before Friday the 20th.

2 Complete the sentences using the best verb from the box. Not all the verbs are needed.

    edit   give   make   submit   write

1 You must complete and _____ your **assignment** before the deadline.
2 After we do an experiment in the lab, we have to _____ a lab **report**.
3 Our tutors _____ us **feedback** on our first draft.
4 Based on your tutor's feedback, you should _____ your first **draft**: make any changes and improve it.

Feedback on writing

> **B** The overall structure of your essay is good and you make some interesting points.
>
> Introduction:
> You introduce the topic very well, but be careful about the **style** of your writing. Sometimes your language is rather informal.
>
> Main body:
> Your ideas are generally well organized, and you have included some good **support** for your arguments.
> • Make sure you only have one main point in each paragraph.
> • Remember to include references for any information you use from your reading.
>
> Conclusion:
> This is the weakest part of your essay: it's a bit too short. You should include:
> • a brief **summary** of the main points in the essay, in one or two sentences
> • a clear statement of your main argument again
> • some closing comments – Why is this issue important? Who does it affect? How might the problem be solved?

3 **Read text B, the feedback on a student's essay. Which of these parts of the essay were generally good (✔) and which need more work (✘)?**

1 The overall structure __
2 The style of writing __
3 The introduction __

4 The main body __
5 The conclusion __
6 Summary of the main points __

4 **Complete the descriptions of different parts of an essay using highlighted words from text B.**

1 The _____ briefly repeats the main ideas and the main argument and includes some final comments.
2 A _____ should include just the main points, not the details.
3 In the _____ , you explain the main topic of the essay and give some background information.
4 In the main body, you present your main points and include _____ in the form of examples and references.

5 **Choose the correct word to complete the sentences. Use the glossary on pp.127–141 to check any new words.**

1 He *conclusion / concludes* the essay by suggesting that the two approaches could be used together.
2 See the university website for more information about exams and *assessment / assess*.
3 The next section *summaries / summarizes* the results of the research.
4 Include definitions of any key terms in the *introduction / introduce*.
5 Allow some time to check and *edit / editor* your work before you submit it to your tutor.
6 Each student in the group is *assigned / assignment* a different task.

6 **Write a short paragraph (two or three sentences) describing the academic writing you have already done at school or at university. Try to use some of the words from the unit.**

• What type of academic texts (essays, reports, etc.) have you written?
• What is the average word count for your writing?
• Do you write on paper or on a computer?
• Do you have to submit your work by a deadline?
• Do you get feedback on your first draft?
• Do you have to edit your work?

Words to learn

author (n) AWL   date of publication (n)   index (n) AWL   reference (n)
bullet point (n)   glossary (n)   page number (n)   term (n)
chapter (n) AWL   heading (n)   paragraph (n) AWL   textbook (n)
contents (n)   illustration (n) AWL   reading list (n)   title (n)

Deciding what to read

A textbook

title — **business economics**
Andrew Gillespie
author —
2ND EDITION
OXFORD

B contents

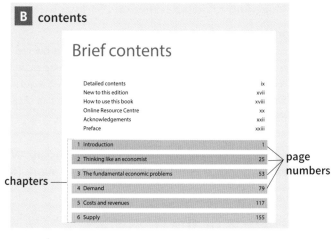

Brief contents

chapters —   → page numbers

1 Answer the questions about pages A and B from a textbook.

1 What is the title of the textbook? _____
2 Who is the author? _____
3 Where can you find information about the contents of the book? _____
4 What is the topic of chapter 2? _____
5 How many pages long is chapter 3? _____

2 Complete the explanation using words from the box.

author   chapters   contents   page numbers   textbook   title

On the front cover of a ¹_____ , you can usually find the ²_____ of the book and the
name of the ³_____ . You can use the ⁴_____ page to find a list of ⁵_____ , and the
⁶_____ show where each one starts.

C

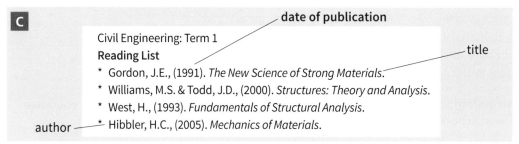

date of publication

Civil Engineering: Term 1
Reading List
* Gordon, J.E., (1991). *The New Science of Strong Materials.*   title
* Williams, M.S. & Todd, J.D., (2000). *Structures: Theory and Analysis.*
* West, H., (1993). *Fundamentals of Structural Analysis.*
author —* Hibbler, H.C., (2005). *Mechanics of Materials.*

3 Complete the comments using one word in each gap.

1 Do we need to buy all the books on the _____ list?
2 The number in brackets is the date of _____ , isn't it?
3 Do you know who the _____ of *Mechanics of Materials* is?
4 There's a really good book by Gordon with a green cover, but I can't remember the _____ .

Reading texts

D

1 _____

Survival in hot, dry climates

2 _____

DRY CLIMATES are often also hot climates – like deserts. Deserts are very difficult places for animals to live. There is scorching heat during the day, followed by bitter cold at night.

The biggest challenges if you live in a desert are:

- coping with the lack of water
- stopping body temperature from getting too high
- finding supplies of water.

3 _____

Many desert animals are adapted to need little or nothing to drink. They get the water they need from the food they eat. Mammals keep their body temperature the same all the time. So as the environment gets hotter, they have to find ways of keeping cool.

4 _____

4 Complete the labels using words from the box.

bullet points   heading   illustration   paragraph

5 Answer the questions about text D.

1 What type of book is the text from? _____
2 What is the heading of this section? _____
3 How many paragraphs are there? _____
4 What does the illustration show? _____

At the back of the book

E **Glossary of terms**

public debts: the amount of money owed by the state
public goods theory: a branch of economics that studies how voters, politicians and government officials behave

F **References**

Bourne, A.K., (2003). The impact of European integration on regional power. *Journal of Common Market Studies*, 41(4), pp.597–620.

Breyer, S.G., (1982). *Regulation and its reform*. Cambridge, MA: Harvard University Press.

Brown, L. and Kennedy, T., (2000). *The Court of Justice of the European Community*. 5th ed. London: Sweet & Maxwell.

G **Index**

P
Paris Treaty 2, 16
parliamentary model of democracy 365
participation 368, 369
partnership 300, 301
party systems 417

6 Complete the three explanations using highlighted words from texts E–G.

- You use the ¹_____ if you want to find information about a particular topic in the book. For example, if you want to read about 'party systems', you can go to page 417.
- The ²_____ contains definitions of ³_____ used in the book. You can use this to check the meaning of important words or phrases.
- You will find a list of all the sources (books or articles) mentioned in the book in the ⁴_____. You can use this if you want to do further reading.

7 Do the academic reading quiz.

1 What is another word for the writer of a book? _____
2 Where can you find a list of the chapters in a textbook? _____
3 Which three pieces of information about a book can you find on a reading list? _____
4 Where can you find full details of all the sources mentioned in a book? _____
5 If you don't understand a term (such as 'public debts'), where can you find a definition? _____
6 If you want to read about a particular topic, how can you find it in a textbook? _____

13 Academic speaking and listening

Words to learn

argument (n)	interrupt (v)	question (n)	tutorial (n)
debate (n) AWL	lecture (n) AWL	seminar (n)	
discuss (v)	lecturer (n) AWL	take notes (phr)	
discussion (n)	presentation (n)	tutor (n)	

Academic speaking

A **Seminars** usually include a group **discussion** of lecture topics or reading texts. Students give **presentations** which develop communication skills. Seminars encourage students to work independently and in teams. Some students may feel unsure about giving their opinions or presenting **arguments**. However, seminars provide a supportive group where you can ask and answer **questions** and **discuss** key ideas from the course. During seminars, students should also listen carefully and **take notes** on others' opinions. When students speak they should try to be clear and concise. Remember not to **interrupt** other speakers. Taking turns in a discussion is an important aspect of successful communication.

Glossary
concise (adj): giving only information that is necessary and important, using few words

1 **Read text A about how seminars help students. Tick the reasons mentioned in the text.**

a Seminars help students to work better on their own and as part of a group. __
b Seminars give students the chance to give presentations. __
c Seminars give students a place where they can discuss ideas and ask questions about lectures. __
d Seminars can help with ideas for writing essays. __

2 **Complete the diary extracts using words from the box to make collocations.**

answer ask discuss give interrupt present take

1 At the beginning of term, all the students were asked to _____ **presentations** on their learning goals. During the presentations, the students who were listening had to _____ **notes** on key points. They used these notes to _____ the speaker **questions** and get more information.

2 In later seminars, students were asked to summarize reading texts and _____ **ideas** from the lectures. This meant that they had to _____ **arguments** from the textbooks and _____ **questions** that anyone had on the topic. There was often a lot of disagreement in the discussions, and it was sometimes hard not to _____ **speakers**.

Usage note collocations with *question*

ask/answer a question:
• *It is important to ask questions if something is not clear.*
• *Try to answer any questions another student might have.*
take/put questions:
• *Remember to tell your audience when you will be taking questions.*
• *You can put questions to the speaker at the end of the presentation.*

3 **Choose the best word or phrase to complete the student's suggestions.**

1 Remember that seminars are a really good place to *ask / answer / ask and answer* questions about key ideas from lectures and reading texts. Don't be afraid to give opinions.
2 If you've got to *give presentations / take notes / discuss ideas*, be prepared. Practise what you're going to say, and make sure you have relevant and interesting visuals.
3 Let people finish what they are trying to say, and don't *ask questions / discuss ideas / interrupt speakers*.
4 Think of the best way to *take notes / ask questions / discuss ideas*. For example, if you are thinking about arguments for and against something, you could divide your notebook into two columns.

Academic listening

4 Complete the sentences using highlighted words from texts B and C.

1 The _____ is going to discuss the positive effect of new materials on the environment.
2 If you want to have some background information before the _____ , you should read the suggested text.
3 There is a _____ on Thursday the 17th. The _____ is Catherine Harvey.
4 During the _____ , students have to present their arguments for and against the environmental importance of new materials.

5 Match the pictures to the words and phrases in the box.

ask questions   lecture   presentation   take notes   tutorial

1 _____

2 _____

3 _____

4 _____

5 _____

6 Complete the student blog post with words or phrases from the unit.

Going to ¹_____ is a really important part of your coursework. Although you can always read key ideas and ²_____ in textbooks, ³_____ can often provide details about the latest research – before it has been published. Some lecturers provide detailed handouts, but it is still very useful to ⁴_____ on the main ideas and the points that support them. If you get the chance to ⁵_____ at the end of the lecture, then do. This gives you the opportunity to ⁶_____ and check your understanding of the topic. And remember to read over any notes, highlighting key information. This is always useful if you have to give ⁷_____ in a follow-up ⁸_____ .

14 Learning and technology

Words to learn

access (n) AWL
access (v) AWL
administration (n) AWL
catalogue (n)
communicate (v) AWL

communication (n) AWL
connection (n)
delete (v)
document (n) AWL
insert (v) AWL

keyword search (n)
link (n) AWL
log on (phrasal v)
on screen (adv)
print out (phrasal v)

register (v) AWL
slide (n)

Online learning systems

A What is UniWeb?

UniWeb is the university's online learning environment. It has a range of tools for **communication** between university staff and students. It can be used at any time of day, from any location that has internet **access**.

Why use UniWeb?

- To **access** course materials such as reading lists, **slides** from lectures and **links** to useful information.
- To **communicate** with staff and other students.
- To reduce time spent on **administration**. You can find important information about your course all in one place, such as term dates, lecture schedules, news and messages from your department.

How can I start using UniWeb?

To access UniWeb, you need to **register** using your student number. You will get a username and password. Then you can **log on** from anywhere with an internet **connection**.

---

1 **Read the information from a university website, text A. According to the website, which of these things can students do using UniWeb?**

a Contact tutors or lecturers __
b Find the reading list for their course __
c Watch video recordings of lectures __
d Find information about their courses __

2 **Complete the comments using words from the box.**

> access   administration   communicate   connection   links   log on   registered   slides

1 As a tutor, I use UniWeb to _____ with my students; I can post messages or send an email to a whole class.
2 I mostly use the system to _____ information about my course; for example, I can check lecture timetables.
3 Most of our lecturers put their _____ online. It means you can focus on listening during the lecture because you don't have to write everything down.
4 For office staff, the system makes _____ much easier – there's much less paperwork because students can fill in forms, etc. online.
5 Once you've _____ , you can use your username and password to _____ from any computer.
6 You can use the system anywhere – you just need a laptop and an internet _____ .
7 The page for each course has a list of useful _____ , such as online journals and other websites.

Using technology to study

B Students don't have to come to the library to access our resources. They can search the library **catalogue** online. If they do a **keyword search** for a topic they're interested in, they can find both physical books and digital resources, such as online academic journals. (University librarian)

C I do all my writing on my laptop. It's much easier to edit your work **on screen**; you can easily **delete** something or **insert** an extra sentence. You can use tools like the spellchecker and word count as well. It's really important to save your **documents** regularly, though, so you don't lose anything. (Student)

D Research shows that students don't remember information they read on screen as well as information on paper. When we read online, we tend to read more quickly. Also, we don't read the whole text; instead we move around looking for key information and we usually only read once. Several recent studies have found that university students like to search for information online. However, they actually prefer to **print out** documents in order to read them carefully. (University tutor)

3 Read comments B, C and D. Answer the questions, yes (Y) or no (N).

1 Can you search for books and online sources using the library catalogue? __
2 Is it easy to edit your writing on screen? __
3 Do students remember information better when they read it on screen? __
4 Do people usually read information more quickly on screen than on paper? __

4 Match the sentence halves. Use the highlighted words to help you.

1 I find it difficult to read **on**
2 The easiest way to **communicate**
3 You can search the **library**
4 There's free Wi-fi **internet**
5 You need a password to **log**
6 On the website, there are **links**
7 You could **insert**
8 In the library, you can **print**

a **catalogue** by author, by title or by keyword.
b **on** and check your university email.
c **to** several online dictionaries.
d another **heading** before the third paragraph.
e **out** copies of articles you want to read.
f **screen** for a long time.
g **access** in the coffee bar.
h **with** your tutors is via email.

5 Match the words and phrases in the box to the pictures.

a document   a link   a slide   keyword search   log on   print out

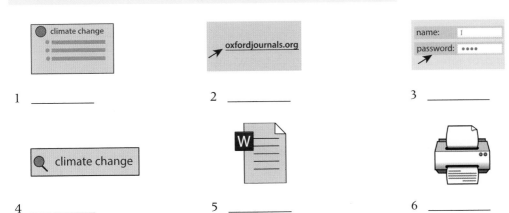

1 _____

2 _____

3 _____

4 _____

5 _____

6 _____

6 Write a short paragraph (two or three sentences) about how you use technology to study. Try to use some of the words from the unit.

Student writing: writing a report

When writing a report, we usually describe the main stages in the research project. Typically, these include stating the aims and purpose of the research, explaining the research methods and presenting the results.

A **1**
The aim of this **report** is to look at the challenges faced by **international students** in **higher education**.

2 150 **undergraduates** from several **departments** and **faculties** were contacted by email; 123 students responded. They were interviewed by email and completed an online questionnaire.

3 The results suggest that most students are likely to have difficulty with the following:
- **taking notes** in **lectures**
- understanding **lecturers**
- contributing to **discussions** and asking **questions** in **tutorials**.

The responses also suggest that around half of students also have problems in the following areas:
- giving **presentations** • **submitting** essays by the **deadlines**.

However, in spite of any problems, the majority of the students (79%) said that they were happy with their **courses**. The study also asked students what advice was the most helpful. Popular responses included:
- use **bullet points** to keep your notes concise
- pay attention to **feedback** on the first **draft** of your **assignments**
- make sure that **references** are accurate and complete.

---

1 What methods were used to collect information for the research? _____

2 Match the headings below to sections 1–3 of the text. Two headings are not needed.

1 Methodology __   3 Conclusions and   4 Findings __
2 Research aims __   recommendations __   5 Glossary __

Focus on collocation

3 Complete the sentences using verbs from the box in an appropriate form. Use the report to help you and/or refer back to Units 8–14.

> access   contribute   give   meet   submit   take

1 There will be a talk this afternoon about how to _____ materials in the university library.
2 Before you _____ the first draft of your essay, make sure to check your word count and your references.
3 In seminars all students are expected to _____ to discussions, but you should not interrupt other students when they are discussing their ideas.
4 I'm _____ a short presentation on how to access the library catalogue and how to conduct keyword searches.
5 One of the biggest challenges I faced in my first year was _____ the essay deadlines.
6 Ancient history is a new subject for me, so I always try to _____ some notes in lectures and seminars.

Student writing: writing definitions

Academic writing needs to be very precise. For this reason, you will often have to write definitions as part of an essay. Examples of definitions in academic writing might include: defining which types of people answered questions in a study (e.g. men, women, elderly people, students, etc.), defining the aims of a study, defining the meaning of a complex term.

> **B** Engineering is an **applied science** which looks at the design, building and use of engines, machines and structures. Students learn by **observing** and designing **experiments** to test the **physical** properties of the materials they are using. On this **programme**, engineering students often work in **teams** on practical projects and **assignments**. Students also take part in regular **seminars** where they can **discuss** their ideas and listen to **arguments** from other students and **tutors**.

4 Read text B. Mark the statements true (T) or false (F) according to the text.

1 The engineering course involves lots of practical work. __
2 Students on the engineering course always work on practical projects alone. __
3 Seminars mostly involve listening to tutors and taking notes. __

5 Match the sentence halves to complete the definitions. Use Units 8–14 and the glossary on pp.127–141 to help you if necessary.

1 A **link** is a place in an electronic document which
2 A **glossary** is a list which
3 A **perspective** is
4 An **objective** is something
5 A **summary** is a short statement that

a an attitude or way of thinking about something.
b explains the meanings of technical or special terms.
c gives only the main points of something, not the details.
d is connected to another electronic document or another part of the same document.
e which you are trying to achieve.

Focus on prepositions

6 Complete the sentences using an appropriate preposition. Use the definition above and Units 8–14 to help you if necessary.

Sociology is a social science which looks [1]_____ the development, structure and functioning [2]_____ human society. Students on the degree course will study a number of different topics and must submit an assignment [3]_____ their tutor at the end of each topic. Undergraduates are able to discuss social issues such as crime, technology and the family [4]_____ other students and tutors in regular tutorials and seminars, while lectures give an opportunity for them to learn [5]_____ the key ideas and themes that help us understand the way humans live in modern society.

Writing task

7 Write a short definition (two or three sentences) of your academic subject or course of study.

15 Structure

Words to learn

attached to (*adj*) AWL	contain (*v*)	include (*v*)	specific (*adj*) AWL
category (*n*) AWL	describe (*v*)	item (*n*) AWL	structure (*n*) AWL
complex (*adj*) AWL	element (*n*) AWL	pattern (*n*)	type (*n*)
consist of (*phrasal v*) AWL	exist (*v*)	section (*n*) AWL	version (*n*) AWL

Physical structures

A In very basic terms, a building is defined as a **structure** which is used to provide shelter to humans. However, a building has an important cultural and social role, which can often change during the building process. Architects and construction teams look at buildings in **specific** stages. The building 'envelope' is the skeleton of the building which **contains** columns, beams, floors and the roof, without any internal fittings. These are the first parts of a building which are **attached to** outer walls. In modern methods of construction, many **sections** of a building are prefabricated. This means that **elements** of the structure are made in a factory, and then assembled on-site. With more **complex** designs, different **items** such as glasswork or heating and lighting systems need to be carefully fitted into the build.

Both builders and architects use computer-generated **versions** of the design to ensure that the final building matches their plans.

Source: Adapted from Gorse, C. *et al.* (2012). 'building.' 'building system.' *A Dictionary of Construction, Surveying and Civil Engineering.* Oxford: Oxford University Press. p.237.

Glossary
assemble (*v*): build or make

1 a Read text A. Mark the statements true (T) or false (F) according to the text.

1 Buildings are only important because they provide shelter. __
2 Architects and builders think about buildings as complete structures. __
3 During the first part of the building process, the basic structure of the building is connected to the walls. __
4 Modern methods mean that parts of buildings can be made in factories. __
5 Builders tend not to use technology in their work. __

b Rewrite the false statements so that they are true according to the text.

2 Complete the sentences using words and phrases from the box.

attached to   complex   contain   elements   item   section   specific   structure   version

1 Many food products _____ added sugar and salt.
2 The first _____ on the list is sugar.
3 The next _____ of the book looks at different features of academic writing.
4 There is a lot of information on the best _____ for argument-led essays.
5 In diamond, each carbon atom is _____ four other carbon atoms.
6 Applying to study abroad can be a very _____ process, with many different steps.
7 Large windows and high ceilings were key _____ in the design of his house.
8 The programme was made for a _____ age group, but seemed popular with most children.
9 The latest _____ of the software is available on all new laptops.

3 Replace the highlighted words in the sentences with one of the keywords or phrases from text A.

▶ EXAMPLE: There are two ways of playing *versions of* the game, one long and one short.

1 There are particular _____ differences between the two species.
2 I found this part _____ of the story very boring – not much happened.
3 People with serious allergies should avoid eating foods that include _____ additives.
4 Research into the form _____ of DNA molecules has helped our understanding of genetics.
5 Maintaining good customer relations is an important aspect _____ of business success.

Organizing systems and structures

B Scientific research suggests that between three and 30 million different species **exist** in the world. So far, over two million different **types** of organism have been **described** and identified. To do this, scientists look at **patterns** of similarity and difference between them. In this way, plants, animals and fungi are classified – put into a **category** that **includes** the key information needed to describe them. For example, all mammals have a very similar limb structure which **consists of** one upper bone, two lower bones and five digits. By studying this structure, biologists were able to see the similarity between very different species, like humans, bats and dolphins.

Source: Adapted from Williams, G. (2016). *GCSE Biology For You.* (5th ed.). Oxford: Oxford University Press. p.237.

Glossary
digit (*n*): a finger, thumb or toe
limb (*n*): an arm or leg, or similar part of an animal
organism (*n*): a living thing

4 Read text B and choose the best summary.

a By studying the similarities and differences of various organisms, scientists can better classify them. __
b By identifying the key information needed to describe organisms, scientists can understand how change happens. __

5 Choose the correct word to match the definitions.

1 *exist / consist of* – to be formed from things or people mentioned
2 *exist / include* – to be real; to be present in a place or situation
3 *category / pattern* – a group of people or things with particular features in common
4 *category / pattern* – a regular arrangement of lines, shapes, colours or features
5 *pattern / type* – a specific example of a class or group of things or people
6 *consist of / include* – to have a second thing as one of its parts

Usage note verb/noun + preposition

When you are reading, note the prepositions that follow verbs and nouns: *consists of attached to patterns of types of elements of* Recording these words together will help you to remember how to use them.
For more about prepositions, see Unit 6.

6 Complete the sentences using the correct form of the highlighted words in text B.

1 Global weather _____ have changed in recent years, causing flooding in Northern Europe.
2 A number of different causes _____ for the illness, but smoking has the biggest impact.
3 The study focused on the learning experiences of people in different age _____ .
4 The final chapter of the textbook _____ a case study on the development of materials science.
5 The information _____ detailed descriptions of new organic compounds.
6 There are two _____ of drugs commonly used during the treatment.

16 Processes

Words to learn

constant (*adj*) AWL	previous (*adj*) AWL	remove (*v*) AWL	task (*n*) AWL
finally (*adv*) AWL	procedure (*n*) AWL	series (*n*) AWL	transfer (*v*) AWL
involve (*v*) AWL	process (*n*) AWL	stage (*n*)	while (*conj*)
last (*det*)	regularly (*adv*)	step (*n*)	

Describing a process

A All the planets absorb heat from the sun in a **process** known as solar radiation. However, for life on our planet to continue, Earth must stay at an average surface temperature of around 15°C. For the Earth to stay at a **constant** temperature, it needs to absorb and emit radiation at the same rates.

As solar radiation travels to Earth, there is a **series** of **steps** which reduce the amount of radiation that reaches the surface:

- Firstly, some is **removed** as it enters the atmosphere – the mixture of gases that surround our planet. Around 25% is then reflected by the upper atmosphere and clouds, **while** a further 20% is absorbed by them.
- 5% of the radiation is reflected from the surface of the Earth – by deserts or ice.
- **Finally**, 50% is absorbed by the Earth's surface.
- Around 10% of this heat radiates from the surface, and the remaining 40% moves to the clouds and the atmosphere. This heat is then radiated back out into space, completing the cycle.

Source: Adapted from Johnson, K. (2016). *GCSE Physics For You*. (5th ed.). Oxford: Oxford University Press. p.214.

Glossary
absorb (*v*): to take in and keep heat, light, or other forms of energy
emit (*v*): to send out light or heat
radiate (*v*): to send out light, heat or energy
reflect (*v*): to throw back light or heat

Usage note sequence in a process

There are a number of different ways to talk about events in a process.
You can use adverbs: *firstly, then, next, after that, finally*
- ***Firstly***, *some energy is removed by the clouds.*
You can also use words like *after, as, as soon as, once* and *when* to show how two events relate to each other:
- ***As soon as*** *sunlight hits the flower, its petals open.*
The phrase *at this stage* is used to help create a clear sequence:
- *The temperature reaches 100°C.* ***At this stage***, *the water in the container begins to boil.*

1 Complete the student's summary of text A using sequencing words and phrases from the box.

as   at this stage   finally   firstly   then

[1]_____ solar radiation enters the Earth's atmosphere there are a number of steps that reduce it. [2]_____ , approximately 25% is reflected by clouds and the upper atmosphere. [3]_____ , a further 20% is absorbed by them. [4]_____ , 5% is reflected back from the Earth's surface. 50% is absorbed by the Earth's surface. 10% of this heat radiates directly from the surface and 40% is transferred back to the upper atmosphere and clouds. [5]_____ , this remaining amount radiates back into space.

2 Complete the sentences using words from the box.

constant   process   removed   series   steps

1 During the interview, he was asked a _____ of questions about his work experience.
2 Child psychologists are interested in the _____ of learning among children.
3 The number of students in higher education has remained _____ .
4 Following a large landslide, many trees and plants are _____ from the surface layer.
5 The discovery of DNA was one of the first _____ in understanding how to cure genetic conditions.

Important processes

B A blood culture **involves** taking a sample of blood from a patient and **transferring** the blood into a blood culture bottle. The bottle is then transported to the laboratory for processing. The **procedure** has three main **stages**: sample taking, transport and processing.

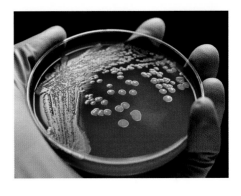

Glossary
culture (*n*): a group of cells grown in the laboratory for a medical or scientific study
sample (*n*): a small amount of a substance, often taken to be tested

C Many companies who use internet-based questionnaires now include 'progress indicators'. These tell the person who is completing the questionnaire how many questions they have answered. They also often say how much more information needs to be given to complete the **task**. **Previous** research suggested that the indicators could have a negative effect on how many people answer questionnaires. However, people who **regularly** answer these kinds of questionnaires report that if they know how long the process will be, they will answer more honestly and completely. It is also important that the **last** question in the process allows respondents to give their own opinions.

Glossary
indicator (*n*): a sign that shows what something is like or how it is changing
respondent (*n*): a person who answers questions in a questionnaire or survey

3 Read texts B and C. Match the content to the correct subject.

1 business studies __   2 medicine __

4 Choose the correct word to complete the definitions.

1 *last / previous* – happening or existing before an event that you are talking about now
2 *stage / task* – a piece of work that has to be done
3 *procedure / stage* – a point, period or step in a process
4 *procedure / task* – a series of actions done in a particular order or way
5 *previously / regularly* – often
6 *involve / transfer* – to move from one place to another

5 Complete the sentences using the correct form of the highlighted words in texts B and C. Use the glossary on pp.127–141 to help you.

1 To stay fit and healthy it is important to get _____ exercise.
2 The final _____ of the experiment involved heating the materials to 1,000°C.
3 The _____ major change to the economy began with the banking crisis in 2008.
4 The current energy minister has _____ worked for a major oil and gas company.
5 The writing exam _____ describing a graph, and then writing an essay.
6 The oesophagus _____ food from the mouth to the stomach.

6 Write a short paragraph (two or three sentences) about one of the topics below. Try to use some of the words from the unit.

• Describe a process or cycle that you are familiar with.
• Explain which processes are important in your area of study.

17 Time

Words to learn

annual (*adj*) AWL	currently (*adv*)	period (*n*) AWL	short-term (*adj*)
brief (*adj*) AWL	decade (*n*) AWL	permanent (*adj*)	temporary (*adj*) AWL
century (*n*)	duration (*n*) AWL	present (*adj*)	
contemporary (*adj*) AWL	long-term (*adj*)	recent (*adj*)	
current (*adj*)	ongoing (*adj*) AWL	recently (*adv*)	

The time we live in

A At the **present** time, the population of China is around 1.3 billion. That is about one-fifth of the world's **current** population. During the **period** from 1950 to 1990 the population increased from half a billion to over one billion. **Recent** predictions, based on **annual** birth rates, suggest that there will be a continued growth in population. By 2030, the Chinese population will be 1.5 billion. However, this growth will not be **permanent**. **Ongoing** studies show that after 2030 the population will begin to fall.

India's population has also grown very quickly. In the five **decades** from 1950 to 2000, the population more than doubled. Although there has been a **temporary** slowdown in the number of people born each year, by the middle of the 21st **century** India's population will also be more than 1.5 billion.

Glossary
double (*v*): to increase by twice as many
slowdown (*n*): a reduction in speed or activity

Usage note *current*, *present* and *recent*

Current and *present* mean 'existing or happening now':
- *The current economic crisis was caused by many failures in the banking system.*
- *The present situation is very difficult, but we hope it improves.*

In academic writing, *current* and *present* are used to mean 'being considered now':
- *the current/present study*

Present is used with a wider range of nouns:
- *present article/chapter/paper/review*

Recent means 'that happened or began only a short time ago':
- *Two recent studies had very different results.*

Note: *Actual* means 'existing in fact; real' and does not relate to time.

1 Choose the correct word to complete the sentences.

1 *Present / Recent* changes to the rules mean that fewer foreign students are going to the UK.
2 The *annual / current* sales of smartphones for 2015 were greater than in previous years.
3 After the floods, the family were moved to *permanent / temporary* accommodation until they could return home.
4 The *current / recent* government has announced changes to the laws on voting age.
5 There are five questions in the *present / recent* exercise.

2 Replace the highlighted words in the sentences with one of the keywords or phrases from text A. Make any other changes to the sentence as required.

▶ EXAMPLE: During the eclipse, observers noted changes which didn't last long <u>temporary changes</u>.
1 The government is working on a long-lasting _____ solution to youth unemployment.
2 In the time _____ from 1985 to 1990, many traditional businesses closed down.
3 After a period of ten years _____, the war finally ended.
4 It took more than one hundred years _____ for the effects of mass immigration to be felt.
5 There are continuing _____ problems with student attendance.

Usage note time expressions

In academic writing, time expressions are important for expressing time accurately.
Common expressions are as follows: *for 50 years* ***over a period of*** *20/30 years* ***over a*** *short/long/ten-year* **period** ***over the past*** *five years/decade/few months* ***for a period of*** … ***since*** *1958/this January* ***in the*** *medieval/post-war period* ***in recent*** *years/decades* ***during the*** *past/last ten years* ***during this*** *period/time*

3 Find similar time expressions in text A.

_____ / _____ / _____ / _____ / _____

Thoughts in time

B The **contemporary** view of human memory is quite complex. **Currently**, psychologists describe memory as a set of systems with various different, but connected, functions. **Short-term** memory is used to store information only for **brief** periods. **Long-term** memory enables us to store information for a longer **duration**. We also have memory for information about how to do certain actions, and memory for factual information about the world.

Recently there have been more detailed descriptions of how we store thoughts. Understanding the different systems is important when considering the long-term effects of age on memory, and also how to improve memory for short-term gain.

4 Read text B, an extract from a textbook. Decide which student summary, a or b, is most accurate.

a The current psychological view of memory is as a series of connected systems which have different functions. People use long-term and short-term memory to store important information for different lengths of time. __

b Memory is best described as a series of connected systems that each have different functions. Psychologists divide these systems into two categories. Of these, long-term memory is the most important as it is used to store factual information about the world. __

5 Complete the sentences using words and phrases from the box.

brief   contemporary   currently   duration   long-term   recently   short-term

1 Researchers have understood the _____ effects of smoking since the 1950s.
2 The online promotion led to a _____ improvement in sales.
3 We stopped the meeting for a _____ lunch, and started again 15 minutes later.
4 The situation has got worse _____ , leading to the UN becoming involved.
5 Their candidate is _____ the most popular, but unlikely to become president.
6 The new library is extremely modern. It won an award for its _____ design.
7 The building was used as a hospital for the _____ of the war.

6 Complete the sentences using the correct form of the word in CAPITALS. Use the glossary on pp.127–141 to help you.

1 Last year, the US dollar was worth 20% more than its _____ value. CURRENT
2 _____ , wages are growing slower than the rest of the economy. PRESENT
3 After many years of job losses, the company was _____ closed in 2015. PERMANENT
4 I'll _____ summarize the results of the experiment before going on to discuss methods in more detail. BRIEF

18 Place

Words to learn

area (n) AWL   global (adj) AWL   location (n) AWL   region (n) AWL   urban (adj)
country (n)   international (adj)   nation (n)   rural (adj)   worldwide (adj)
foreign (adj)   local (adj)   national (adj)   site (n) AWL

Our modern world

A In recent years, the term *globalization* has been used to describe how people's life experiences **worldwide** have become increasingly similar. Although people live in a variety of different **locations** and each have their own **national** interests, they often recognize the same brands, listen to the same music, drink the same soft drinks, support the same football teams, and agree on what is culturally important.

However, while this process has removed many **international** differences, it is not always a positive change. In this modern **global** way of life, more people are moving to cities from the countryside. **Urban** areas grow, while **rural** communities are slowly disappearing. As the city becomes the most important **site** for business and education, many old ways of living and **local** customs will disappear. As a result, our world may lose a lot of what makes it interesting.

1 Read text A. Mark the statements true (T) or false (F) according to the text.

1 In today's world, people in different countries do very different things. __
2 As people move to cities, the countryside is negatively affected. __
3 The writer thinks that the world will become a less interesting place. __

2 Match the words, 1–3, with their opposites, a–c.

1 international   a rural
2 urban   b local
3 global   c national

> **Usage note** *global*, *international* and *worldwide*
> These are all adjectives that usually go before nouns.
> **Global** means covering or affecting the whole world: • *The global economy has slowed down recently.*
> **International** means connected with, or involving, two or more countries: • *The film was made by an international team.*
> **Worldwide** is very similar to *global*, and means affecting all parts of the world: • *There was a worldwide effort to end child poverty.*

3 Replace the highlighted words in the sentences with a word from the box. Change any other words if required.

> global   international   locations   national   rural   site   urban   ~~worldwide~~

▸ EXAMPLE: Researchers have been studying opinion from around the world _worldwide opinion_.
1 The government has suggested lots of different places _____ to build the nuclear power station.
2 There was a football match between two countries _____ this weekend.
3 The UN said that countries affected by the floods needed support from the whole world _____.
4 People in the capital city earn more than the average for the country _____.
5 Living costs in areas with towns and cities _____ are usually quite high.
6 It took emergency services several hours to remove cars from the place _____ of the accident.
7 Countryside _____ living can be difficult because people live so far from important services.

Foreign aid

B In recent years, there has been a lot of discussion about the importance of foreign aid and whether it helps developing **countries** to grow. Foreign aid is usually money which is sent overseas by one **nation** to support another less-developed **region** of the world. Critics say that sending money to **foreign** countries stops them developing. **Local** people find it hard to run businesses successfully because charity money or loans make goods and services cheaper. In some rural **areas**, farmers cannot sell their produce because cheap food, which was given as foreign aid, has lowered prices. In urban areas, there might be higher levels of unemployment.

4 Read text B, an extract from a textbook. Decide which paragraph comes next.

a However, foreign aid may not reach the people who need it the most. Sometimes the money which should be used for development is taken by local politicians and used to support projects which help their supporters. __

b However, supporters of foreign aid say that it can be extremely beneficial. Many projects supported by foreign aid improve health and living standards overseas. Foreign aid which encourages industrial development can also create jobs and improve transport links. __

5 Match the sentence halves. Use the highlighted words to help you.

1 In many countries, young people are leaving rural
2 She visited lots of **foreign**
3 World leaders met to discuss how to help developing
4 People who live in **developed**

a **countries** during her gap year.
b **areas** in large numbers.
c **regions** usually live longer lives.
d **countries** affected by climate change.

6 Choose the correct words to complete the pairs of sentences. Use the glossary on pp.127–141 to help you.

1 international – national
   a Both governments decided to close their _____ borders until the migrant crisis ended.
   b The _____ average income in the UK is higher than in many other European countries.
2 local – location
   a It took developers a long time to find a suitable _____ for the new hospital.
   b _____ people complained that the plans for the new railway would affect their lives.
3 nation – national
   a The USA's _____ debt has grown in the last decade.
   b Poland became an independent _____ in 1918.
4 regions – regional
   a Most coastal _____ have a lot of rainfall each year.
   b There are big _____ differences between rural and urban areas.
5 foreign – foreigner
   a Being a _____ in China can be difficult because of language and cultural differences.
   b The number of _____ students at the university is increasing every year.

7 Write a short paragraph (two or three sentences) discussing one of the following. Try to use some of the words from the unit.

• How developed countries should help less developed countries
• A country or place in a country that you know well

19 People and groups

Words to learn

adolescence (n)   family member (n)   in relation to (phr)   relationship (n)
adult (n) AWL   gender (n) AWL   occupation (n) AWL   resident (n) AWL
colleague (n) AWL   identity (n) AWL   peer group (n)   role (n) AWL
ethnicity (n) AWL   individual (n) AWL   position (n)

Social groups and identity

A The different social groups we belong to influence our sense of **identity** in terms of social class, **gender**, **ethnicity** and age. Family, **peer groups**, education, religion, the media and the workplace all play a **role** in shaping the way we see ourselves.

Peer groups:
Our peer groups become a significant source of our identity and status during **adolescence**. **Relationships** with our peer group are quite different from the relationships we have with **family members**. They are likely to be more equal, involving an exchange of problems and advice. It is through interaction with our peer group that we begin to develop an understanding of ourselves and our identity.

Source: Adapted from Newbold, Peace, Swain & Wright. (2014). *AQA Sociology AS.* Oxford: Oxford University Press. p.26.

Glossary
interaction (n): the way that people communicate with each other and spend time together

1 Match the terms in the box to the examples of groups of people.

> adolescence   ethnicity   family members   gender   peer group

1 your friends at school or college _____
2 parents, brothers and sisters _____
3 women and girls _____
4 children in their early teens _____
5 Berber people from North Africa _____

2 Replace the highlighted words in the sentences with one of the keywords or phrases from text A.

▶ EXAMPLE: Researchers observed how each child interacted with their friends and schoolmates
peer group.

1 Participants complete a form giving their name, age and whether they are male or female
_____.

2 The psychologist asks patients about how they get on _____ with their family and friends.

3 Parents also play an important part _____ in children's experience of education.

4 In some communities, religion is a key factor in shaping people's idea of who they are as a person _____.

5 During the period from around age 12 to 15 _____, young people typically want more freedom.

Individual roles

B 'So last week we were discussing the influences on us as we grow up – the role of our family and peer group in shaping our identity. But what about the different roles we play as **adults**? As **individuals**, what different groups are you a part of that define who you are?'

'I think your **occupation** is a really important part of your identity. When you meet someone, the first question you ask is "What do you do?" And it's not just your job; your **position** in the company is quite important too. You're aware of how junior or senior you are **in relation to** your **colleagues**.'

'You have a role within the place where you live, too. You can be part of a community of local **residents**. So I say hello to my neighbours and I know the local shopkeepers and such like.'

3 Read the extracts from a seminar discussion in text B. Complete the statements using highlighted words from the text. Add any other words that are needed.

▶ EXAMPLE: The tutor mentions influences on our identity in childhood and moves on to ask about <u>the roles we play as adults</u>.
1 The tutor asks the students about groups they are part of _____ .
2 The first student mentions the importance of _____ .
3 He talks about a person's status at work in relation to _____ .
4 The second student says she is part of _____ .

4 Choose the best preposition to complete the sentences.

1 Teenagers can sometimes have a difficult **relationship** *to* / *with* their parents.
2 Schools can play a significant **role** *in* / *to* encouraging healthy behaviours.
3 A person's job title indicates their **position** *in* / *of* an organization.
4 We assess a child's development in **relation** *to* / *with* other children of the same age.

5 a Choose the best words to complete the pairs of sentences. Use the glossary on pp.127–141 to check any unknown words.

1 **adolescence – adolescents**
   a Poor eating habits that develop during _____ may affect long-term health.
   b Children and _____ are increasingly consuming foods high in fat and sugar.
2 **ethnicity – ethnic**
   a Some local _____ groups continue to use their own languages.
   b The group included 15 eighth-grade students of mixed gender and _____ .
3 **residents – residential**
   a The company arranged a meeting with local _____ to discuss the plans.
   b The school is in a quiet, _____ area in the north of the city.

b Identify the part of speech of the keyword (noun, verb or adjective) in each sentence in 5a.

1 a __   2 a __   3 a __
  b __   b __   b __

6 Write a short paragraph (two or three sentences) describing one of the following. Try to use some of the vocabulary from the unit.
  • A group of people within your community (e.g. teenagers, the elderly)
  • The different roles you play (e.g. student, family member, neighbour)

20 Quantity

Words to learn

amount (n)	estimate (v) AWL	maximum (adj) AWL	quantity (n)
approximately (adv) AWL	figure (n)	minimum (adj) AWL	significantly (adv) AWL
capacity (n) AWL	level (n)	moderate (adj)	
considerably (adv) AWL	limit (n	numerous (adj)	

Expressing quantity

A A recent UK study notes that the **amount** of housework done by women has not decreased **significantly** in recent decades. It **estimates** that if housework was paid, it would be worth £700 billion to the economy (ONS: 2002).

B There are **approximately** 688,000 people who are deaf in the UK, and 840 children who are born deaf each year (RNID: 2011). It is clear from these **figures** that there is a large community of people who are deaf in the UK alone.

C Statistics from the National Health Service (2010) highlight that cardiovascular disease (CVD) is the main cause of early death in the UK. CVD is caused by a complex combination of genetic and environmental factors. The **numerous** possible causes of CVD present a problem when attempting to reduce the risk. Evidence suggests, however, that increasing the **quantity** of fruit and vegetables in your diet can lower the risk **considerably**.

Source: student essays

Glossary
cardiovascular (adj): connected with the heart and blood flow
genetic (adj): connected with genes; the DNA which is passed from parents to children

1 Read texts A–C from student essays. Do these pairs of words from the essays have a similar meaning (S) or a completely different meaning (D)?

1 amount – quantity __
2 numerous – main __
3 figures – statistics __

4 estimated – approximately __
5 considerably – significantly __

Usage note number, amount and quantity

Number, amount and **quantity** all express how much of something there is. Remember to use:
- **number of** + a countable noun: *the number of people/cases/factors/reasons*
- **amount of** + an uncountable noun: *the amount of housework/time/information*
- **quantity of** + a countable or an uncountable noun: *the quantity of products/resources/water/information*
For more about countable and uncountable nouns, see Unit 2.

2 Choose the best word to complete the sentences.

1 Companies spend huge *amounts / numbers* of money on advertising.
2 The region has large *amounts / quantities* of natural resources.
3 Recent *figures / quantities* show that half the population are now in non-manual jobs.
4 There are *considerable / numerous* examples of online political campaigns.
5 The number of cases has *approximately / considerably* doubled in the last ten years.
6 We can use these statistics to *estimate / figure* future health care costs.
7 The students' scores were *approximately / significantly* higher than expected.
8 As the two designs differ *considerably / numerously*, it is difficult to compare the results.

Describing limits

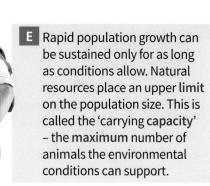

D Physical inactivity is an important public health problem in many modern societies. In Switzerland, 64% of the adult population does not achieve the recommended levels of physical activity: a **minimum** length of 30 minutes of **moderate** physical activity five days per week.

E Rapid population growth can be sustained only for as long as conditions allow. Natural resources place an upper **limit** on the population size. This is called the 'carrying **capacity**' – the **maximum** number of animals the environmental conditions can support.

Glossary
inactivity (*n*): not being active or doing exercise

3 **Read texts D and E. Mark the statements true (T) or false (F) according to the texts.**

1 Over half of Swiss adults do less exercise than recommended by doctors. __
2 Experts say you should do not more than 30 minutes of exercise five times a week. __
3 The number of animals that can live in an area is limited by the natural resources available. __
4 The 'carrying capacity' is the number of animals which live in an area. __

> **Usage note** collocations with *level* and *limit*
>
> someone or something ***reaches/achieves a level***: • *Pollution reaches its highest level in August.*
> something ***has high/low levels of something***: • *The area has a high level of crime.*
> someone ***sets/places a limit on something***: • *The manager must set limits on the time spent on each task.*
> ***the upper/lower limit (of something)***: • *the lower limit of the temperature range*
> ***time/speed/age limit***: • *There is a time limit of seven days to reply.*

4 **Match the sentence halves. Use the highlighted words to help you.**

1 There is no upper
2 A company wants to reach the **maximum**
3 Union membership reached
4 The airport has an annual **capacity**
5 The law sets a **minimum**
6 The guidelines define **moderate** physical

a its lowest **level** since the 1950s.
b activity as fast walking or cycling.
c age of 16 for factory workers.
d of 30 million passengers.
e number of customers.
f age **limit** for the course.

5 **Rewrite the sentences using the word in CAPITALS.**

▶ EXAMPLE: Volunteers work for a period of at least three months.
 MINIMUM *Volunteers work for a minimum period of three months.*

1 The adult birds reach about 35 cm in length.
 APPROXIMATELY _____
2 The male birds are quite a bit larger than the females.
 SIGNIFICANTLY _____
3 People were asked to make a guess about the number of hours they spend online each day.
 ESTIMATE _____
4 There have been quite a few studies into the effects of computer games on behaviour.
 NUMEROUS _____
5 Students were given no more than 30 minutes to complete the task.
 LIMIT _____
6 The government published the latest information about the number of unemployed people.
 FIGURE _____

21 Statistics

Words to learn

average (n)   fraction (n)   per cent (n) AWL   total (n)
calculate (v)   majority (n) AWL   percentage (n) AWL   value (n)
divide by (phrasal v) mean (n)   proportion (n) AWL
formula (n) AWL   minority (n) AWL   statistics (n)

Describing proportions

A The study found that the **majority** (56%) of those questioned were non-smokers. These **statistics** show that the number of smokers varies significantly by city. The highest **percentage** of smokers was found in Naples (49.5%).

B According to one study of Italian smoking habits, Naples has the highest **proportion** of smokers (Ficarra et al. 2011).

C Today only two **per cent** of the US population works on farms, while another three per cent works in the food processing and food service industries. This small **fraction** of the population (five per cent) is able to grow, process and serve enough food to meet the needs of the whole country.

D Perhaps surprisingly, only a small **minority** of US workers (around 5%) are employed in food production, yet they produce enough food for the whole population (Bowles et al. 2005).

1 **Match the phrases from the academic texts, A and C, to phrases with the same meaning from the student citations, B and D.**

1 the highest percentage of smokers _____
2 this small fraction of the population _____

2 **Do the underlined phrases refer to a large quantity (L) or a small quantity (S)?**

1 This type of treatment is appropriate in only a **minority** of cases. ___
2 Fuel costs make up a tiny **fraction** of the firm's total operating costs. ___
3 The **majority** of students at the college speak English as a second language. ___
4 A high **proportion** of their income is spent on food and accommodation. ___
5 This disease affects a relatively small **percentage** of the population. ___

Usage note *per cent, percentage* and *proportion*

Use *per cent* or *%* after a number:
  five per cent of the population
  inflation rose by two per cent
Use *percentage* or *proportion* to talk more generally about a quantity:
  *the **highest percentage of** smokers*   *only a **small percentage of** students*
  *a **high/large proportion of** patients*   *a relatively **small proportion of** total spending*

3 **Complete the sentences using the word in CAPITALS. Add any other words needed.**

▶ EXAMPLE: _A high percentage_ of employees (74%) work more than 45 hours. PERCENTAGE
1 These examples represent only _____ the total number of cases (less than 4%). FRACTION
2 The survey found that _____ customers (82%) are satisfied with the service. MAJORITY
3 _____ patients (approximately 10%) suffer more severe symptoms. PROPORTION
4 In 1900, only 20 _____ American women worked outside the home. PER CENT
5 In _____ people (less than 3%), the problem may continue into adulthood. MINORITY

Talking about averages

E When looking at data, it is useful to have some idea of a typical **value** for the data. This is usually called an **average**. When you know the average for a set of data, you have some idea of what value or values you might expect from other data from the same source. If the data is from a sample, you can use the average of the sample to estimate the average for the whole population.

When people talk about averages they are usually talking about the **mean**. The mean is obtained by **calculating** the **total** of all the data values and then **dividing by** the number of data values. This can be shown in a **formula**:

$$\text{mean} = \frac{\text{total of all the data values}}{\text{number of data values}}$$

Source: Adapted from Procter-Green & Winters. (2009). *AQA Statistics GCSE.* Cheltenham: Nelson Thornes.

4 Read text E and complete the statements using words from the box.

> average   calculate   divide   formula   mean   total   value

1 You can use an _____ to represent a typical _____ for a set of data.
2 The most common way of measuring an average is called the _____ .
3 You can _____ the mean using the _____ shown in the text.
4 You work out the _____ of all the values, then you _____ that by the number of values in the set.

5 Label the pictures using words from the box.

> divide by   formula   majority   minority   percentage   total

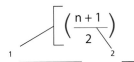

1 _____   2 _____

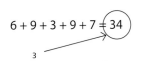

3 _____

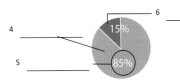

4 _____   5 _____   6 _____

6 Complete the text describing the table.

If we look at the table showing the weather conditions for the island of Madeira, we can see that October to March are the wettest months. To ¹_____ the ²_____ rainfall for this whole period, we first work out the ³_____ ₅of the rainfall ⁴_____ for these six months: 76 + 89 + 84 + 64 + 74 + 79 = 466. Then we _____ this by the number of months: 466 ÷ 6 = 77.66. So 77.66 mm is the ⁶_____ amount of rain during the winter months. Looking at these ⁷_____ , we can also say that throughout the year, the ⁸_____ of wet days each month is relatively low. The table also shows that for the ⁹_____ of the year, the maximum temperature is above 19°C and for a large ₁₀_____ of the year, the temperature does not drop below 15°C.

	Jan	Feb	Mar	Apr	May	Jun	July	Aug	Sept	Oct	Nov	Dec
Rain (mm)	64	74	79	33	18	5	0	0	25	76	89	84
Wet days	6	6	7	4	2	0	0	0	3	7	6	7
Max temp	19	18	19	19	21	22	24	24	24	23	22	19
Min temp	13	13	13	14	16	17	19	19	19	18	16	14

Figure 1: Weather conditions in Madeira

22 Trends

Words to learn

decline (n) AWL	fall (v)	increase (v)	rapid (adj)	rise (v)
decrease (v)	grow (v)	increasingly (adv)	rate (n)	trend (n) AWL
dramatic (adj) AWL	growth (n)	peak (v)	reduce (v)	variable (adj) AWL

Upward trends

A In 2011 the world's population reached seven billion people. Since about 1900 the world's population has **grown** exponentially. This means that the **rate of growth** has become **increasingly rapid**. Between AD 1 and AD 1000 growth was slow, but in the last thousand years it has been **dramatic**. By 2000, there were ten times as many people living as there had been 300 years before in 1700. Not only is population **increasing**, but the rate of increase is becoming greater.

Growth is predicted to continue, but now the rate is slowing down. Population is likely to **rise** to 8.92 billion by 2050 and finally **peak** at 10.8 billion a century later in 2150.

Exponential growth curve

Source: Durman & Ross. (2014). *AQA Certificate in Geography (iGCSE)*.
Oxford: Oxford University Press.

Glossary
exponentially (*adv*): used to say that a rate of increase is getting faster and faster

1 Read text A. Tick the paraphrases which are correct according to the text.

a Since 1900, the global population has increased very rapidly. __
b Between 1900 and 2011, the population continued to grow at the same rate. __
c During the period from 1000 to 2000, the population grew dramatically. __
d In the future, experts believe that the global population will increase more quickly. __
e After 2150, the world's population is expected to stop increasing. __

Usage note describing trends

Verb + adverb: *increase dramatically   rise rapidly*
Adjective + noun: *rapid growth   a dramatic increase   growth was slow*
Adverb + adjective: *increasingly rapid*
Describing rates: *the rate of growth   the rate is slowing down*
Describing levels: *the population reached seven billion   population is likely to peak*

2 Match the sentence halves.

1 The population has **grown**	a was relatively slow.
2 During the summer, there is a **dramatic**	b **rapidly** over the past hundred years.
3 The number of hospital admissions **rose**	c at around 32°C in July.
4 The **increase** in temperature over the period	d large proportion of the population.
5 There are several ways to measure the **rate**	e of **growth** of a country's economy.
6 People over 65 make up an **increasingly**	f **dramatically** last month.
7 Daytime temperatures **peak**	g **increase** in the number of visitors.

Downward trends

B Many freshwater plants and animals are particularly sensitive to low pH (i.e. high levels of acid in the water). Studies generally show that as pH levels **fall**, there is a **decline** in species diversity. Within a single site, acidification of water can significantly **reduce** the number of species present.

C Analysing the long-term **trends** of precipitation (i.e. the amount of rain and snow) and temperature can help in understanding climate patterns. According to records for the past century, temperatures in this region have varied considerably, showing no clear overall trend. The long-term trend of precipitation is less **variable** than temperature. A few years of heavy snowfall occurred in the early 1990s, but otherwise annual precipitation **decreased** slightly during the 20th century.

Glossary
pH (*n*): a measure of the level of acid in a substance; a substance with a low pH value contains more acid
diversity (*n*): a range of different things, e.g. different types of animals

3 Tick which things the writer talks about in terms of a downward trend in texts B and C.

a pH levels __   b the number of species __   c average temperatures __   d rain and snowfall __

4 a Complete the table using the correct verb and noun forms. Use the language reference section on pp.108–114 to help you.

Verb: infinitive	Verb: past simple	Verb: past participle	Noun
to decrease	decreased	decreased	a decrease
to grow	grew	grown	a growth
to fall	1 _____	2 _____	a fall
to rise	3 _____	4 _____	a rise
to reduce	reduced	reduced	5 _____
to decline	declined	6 _____	a decline

b Complete the sentences using the best form of the word in CAPITALS.

1 The value of the dollar _____ dramatically after yesterday's announcement. FALL
2 Wages and prices have _____ at roughly the same rate in recent years. RISE
3 There has been a long-term _____ in electoral participation across many countries. DECLINE
4 A factor behind the _____ of international trade is improved transport methods. GROW
5 Trends indicate a significant _____ in the number of people smoking since 1980. REDUCE

Usage note using prepositions to describe trends

increase/decrease + *to* + level: *population is likely to **rise to** 8.92 billion*
increase/decrease + *by* + size of change: *costs **fell by** 6%*
an increase/a decrease + *in* + the thing being measured: *a **decline in** species diversity*
reach + a level (no preposition):   *the world's population **reached** seven billion*

5 Choose the best preposition to complete the sentences. Choose '–' if no preposition is needed.

1 The latest figures show a decrease *in / to* the unemployment rate.
2 China's economy grew *by / in* 6.9% last year.
3 The new charge led directly to a reduction *in / –* the number of car journeys.
4 At the last election, the proportion of women in the parliament fell *by / to* 33%, from 45 to 30.

Words to learn

become (v)	develop (v)	innovation (n) AWL	progress (n)	revise (v) AWL
change (n)	disrupt (v)	invention (n)	reverse (v) AWL	trigger (v) AWL
create (v) AWL	improve (v)	occur (v) AWL	review (v)	vary (v) AWL

Changes that happen

Glossary
lungs (n): the organs inside the chest that are used for breathing
inflamed (adj): red, painful and swollen
admission (n): when someone goes into hospital

Asthma is a chronic lung condition where the air passages in the lungs **become** inflamed. This results in breathing problems for the patient. It is not known exactly what causes asthma, but we do know that certain conditions make a person more likely to **develop** it.

An important area of research for medical scientists is finding out what can **trigger** an asthma attack. Asthma attacks **vary** according to the time of year and are sometimes caused by sudden **changes** in the weather. Autumn, for example, is known to be a bad time for sufferers. Findings show an increase in the number of hospital admissions in October. It seems likely that asthma attacks **occur** more frequently at this time of year because it is the season when people catch colds and flu most often.

Source: Adapted from Allot, A. (2012). *IB Biology: Course Companion.* Oxford: Oxford University Press. p.351.

1 Read text A. Why do asthma sufferers have more attacks in the autumn, according to the text?

a Because the weather is colder. _____

b Because colds and flu are more common. _____

c Because there are more hospital admissions. _____

2 Read text A and match the verbs in the box to the type of change they describe.

become   develop   occur   trigger   vary

1 _____ – to change gradually over time
2 _____ – to be different at different times
3 _____ – to cause something to start
4 _____ – to happen
5 _____ – to begin to have a disease or a problem

3 Choose the correct verb to complete the sentences. Think about meaning and grammar.

1 Earthquakes *occur / trigger* frequently along Sumatra's coastline.
2 The events in New York *became / triggered* a strong public reaction.
3 Only about 5% of humans who are infected with tuberculosis *develop / occur* the disease.
4 Infection rates *become / vary* considerably according to geographic region.

Usage note types of verb

Remember that some verbs cannot be followed by an object; they are **intransitive**:
• *asthma attacks* **occur**
Some verbs are always followed by an object; they are **transitive**:
• *what can* **trigger** *an asthma attack*
Some verbs can be used with or without an object:
• *Certain conditions make a person likely to* **develop** *asthma.* ('develop' is transitive)
• *Symptoms* **develop** *gradually.* ('develop' is intransitive)
Note that passive verb forms are only possible with transitive verbs:
• *His asthma attacks are triggered by grass pollen.*
For more about types of verbs, see Unit 3.

Making changes

B According to Schumpeter, for **progress** to occur, old methods of doing business must be **disrupted**. He suggests that old ways must be destroyed to **create** the basis for new leaps forward.

C New technological **innovations** often pose legal challenges. The **invention** of the video recorder (VCR) in the 1970s, for example, raised questions about copyright law. In 1976, several film companies sued the makers of video recorders because they argued that any machine that could record copyrighted material broke the copyright laws. In 1979, a US federal judge declared that recording and viewing television material in the home were 'fair use'. However, an appeals court **reversed** this decision. It was not until 1984 that the Supreme Court **reviewed** the situation and ruled that home recording is in fact legal.

D One example of how campaign groups can bring about change is by publicly 'naming and shaming' particular organizations. Several multinational companies were heavily criticized by human rights groups for their use of cheap labour, for instance, and as a result, a number of them **revised** their code of ethics and **improved** the working conditions in their factories.

Glossary
copyright (*n*): if a person or organization has the copyright of a piece of writing, film, etc. they are the only people who have the legal right to publish or broadcast it
name and shame (*phr*): to publish the names of people or organizations who have done something wrong or illegal

4 a Read texts B–D. Are the highlighted change words used as nouns or verbs?

1 Nouns: _____
2 Verbs: _____

b Complete the verb and noun pairs. Use the glossary on pp.127–141 to help you.

▶ EXAMPLE: *disruption* (*n*) – disrupt (*v*)

1 progress (*n*) – _____ (*v*)
2 _____ (*n*) – create (*v*)
3 innovation (*n*) – _____ (*v*)
4 invention (*n*) – _____ (*v*)
5 _____ (*n*) – reverse (*v*)
6 _____ (*n*) – review (*v*)
7 _____ (*n*) – revise (*v*)
8 _____ (*n*) – improve (*v*)

c Complete the sentences using the best noun or verb form of the word in CAPITALS.

1 The new government _____ the policy of the previous administration. REVERSE
2 Repair work should be planned to cause minimum _____ to customers. DISRUPT
3 This latest document is a _____ of the previous regulations. REVISE
4 How can we _____ the quality of life for older people? IMPROVE
5 The _____ of public health systems in the late 19th century had a huge impact on life expectancy. CREATE
6 Firms often _____ new technologies in order to make new products. INVENT
7 We have clearly made significant _____ in understanding the basic causes of aging. PROGRESS
8 A number of new _____ have emerged recently that should reduce production costs. INNOVATE
9 Each case is carefully _____ by two independent doctors. REVIEW

5 Write a short paragraph (two or three sentences) about recent changes in one of the areas below. Try to use some of the change words from the unit.

- The way people use mobile phones
- Shopping habits

Student writing: describing a chart

In many subjects, students have to refer to statistical information in their writing. It is important to decide on the clearest way of presenting and describing such information. Often, charts and graphs are used to include a lot of information in a clear way. You may then need to write a description of what the data shows.

A [A] This chart shows average life expectancy in a number of countries **worldwide** in 1970 and 2013. [B] Fourteen countries are shown, and almost 50 **per cent** of these are in the developed world. It can be seen that life expectancy has **increased significantly** in most countries shown, although the **rate** of this **change** has been more **rapid** in some countries than others. [C] The biggest rise in life expectancy over the four **decades** was in Turkey, where it **grew** by 23 years. Next was South Korea, with an increase of 20 years. [D] The **changes** in more developed countries such as the United States and Sweden were less **dramatic**. Life expectancy did not **decrease** in any country. However, in the Russian Federation it increased by only three years. It can also be seen that while the **long-term trend** is for life expectancy to increase during the **period**, globally it still **varies considerably**. It remains much lower in the poorer countries such as South Africa (57 years) than in rich nations such as Japan (83 years).

1 Match the sentences below to sections A–D of the text.

1 Gives a summary of the information in the chart. __
2 Describes the most important information given in the chart. __
3 Defines the topic of the chart. __
4 Describes other information shown in the chart. __

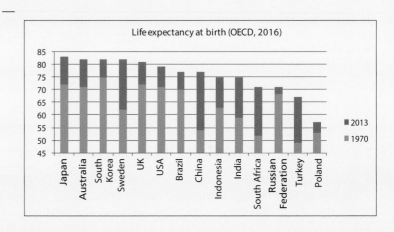

Life expectancy at birth (OECD, 2016)

Focus on word form

2 a Complete the table with the missing information. Use text A, Units 15–23 and the glossary on pp.127–141 to help you if necessary.

Noun	Verb
1 _____	increase
2 _____	grow
change	3 _____
4 _____ / _____	vary
rise	5 _____
6 _____	decrease

b Do the same with the table below.

Adjective	Adverb
rapid	1 _____
2 _____	significantly
3 _____	considerably
dramatic	4 _____

3 Complete the paraphrases of information in text A using an appropriate adjective + noun or verb + adverb pair.

1 There was a _____ _____ in life expectancy in almost all of the countries in the chart.
2 There are still _____ international _____ in life expectancy.
3 Life expectancy in developed countries such as the UK did not _____ as _____ as in countries such as India or Indonesia.

Student writing: describing a process

B A wood-burning stove **consists of** three main **elements**: the flue, the main chamber and the pan. The pan sits underneath a metal grill at the bottom of the chamber, and the flue is **attached to** the top of the stove to take smoke up the chimney. The **process** of lighting a fire is simple. First, a small amount of paper or wood is placed on the grill and lit. At this **stage**, the fire needs plenty of oxygen, so the door of the chamber and the vents should be left open. In the next **step**, larger pieces of wood can be added to the fire, and once it is burning strongly, the door can be closed. **Finally**, the bottom vent can also be closed. The top vent is left open so that air can pass into the chamber and smoke can be pulled out into the flue.

flue
top vent
main chamber
bottom vent
grill
pan

4 Put the following stages describing how to use the stove into the correct order.

1 Light the fire _____
2 Open the top and bottom vents _____
3 Add large pieces of wood _____
4 Add small pieces of wood to the chamber _____
5 Close the door _____
6 Shut the bottom vent _____

Focus on types of verb

5 In each sentence below, is the verb transitive (T) or intransitive (I)? Look at the usage note in Unit 23 for help if necessary.

1 A wood-burning stove consists of three main elements. __
2 The flue is attached to the top of the stove. __
3 The door can be closed. __

6 Complete the sentences using an appropriate form of the verb in CAPITALS.

1 The region _____ a number of important religious sites. CONTAIN
2 Next year, four new versions of the machine _____ for different markets. CREATE
3 During the floods, residents _____ by helicopter to temporary accommodation. TRANSFER
4 The operation takes four hours and _____ a series of complex procedures. INVOLVE
5 The number of hours needed should _____ before the project begins. CALCULATE

Writing task

7 Write a few sentences describing one of the following:

• The process of applying to a university in your country • A graph or chart that is relevant to your subject

Words to learn

affect (v) AWL	cause (v)	ineffective (adj)	reason (n)
as a result (phr)	consequence (n) AWL	lead to (phrasal v)	risk (n)
associated with (adj)	effect (n)	link (n) AWL	so as to (phr)
cause (n)	factor (n) AWL	mean (v)	

Cause and effect

A Antibiotic resistance

Antibiotics are drugs that kill bacteria, but do not damage your body. They have no **effect** on viruses. Bacterial infections have been treated with antibiotics ever since penicillin was discovered and developed. Since then, antibiotics have saved millions of lives.

However, unfortunately, bacteria can mutate, and these mutations can **lead to** some types becoming resistant to antibiotics. This **means** that many types of antibiotic will no longer kill them. These bacteria are often referred to as 'superbugs'. When antibiotics are used to treat an infection, they will kill individual bacteria that do not have antibiotic resistance. However, resistant bacteria will survive. They then reproduce and **as a result**, the population of resistant bacteria increases.

In the past, doctors would prescribe antibiotics to treat minor illnesses, such as coughs and colds. However, antibiotics have no effect on the viruses that are the **cause** of these conditions. This widespread use of antibiotics is one **factor** that has increased the development of antibiotic-resistant bacteria.

Source: Adapted from Hayward, Locke & Thomas. (2011). *AQA GCSE Science*. Oxford: Oxford University Press. pp.166–167.

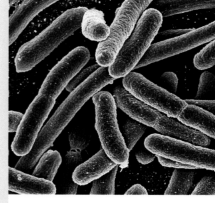

Glossary
bacteria (n): very small living things that can cause disease
mutate (v): to develop a new form
prescribe (v): to say what medicine someone should have
resistant (adj): not affected by something

1 Read text A. Mark the statements true (T) or false (F) according to the text.

1 Antibiotics kill bacteria and viruses. __
2 Bacteria can change in a way that means they are no longer affected by antibiotics. __
3 Antibiotics kill some bacteria but allow resistant bacteria to survive and increase. __
4 Bacteria are the cause of coughs and colds. __

2 Match the sentence halves to make a short description. Think about meaning and grammar.

1 El Niño **causes**
2 This rise in ocean temperature often **leads**
3 Heavy rain and flooding can have a particular
4 This can reduce food production and **as a result,**
5 What's more, wetter conditions in the Americas often **mean**
6 El Niño is also a **factor**

a **effect** on agriculture in these regions.
b that influences weather patterns in Europe and Africa.
c **to** heavy rain and other extreme weather across the continent.
d the economy can suffer.
e that there is less rain on the other side of the Pacific in Asia and Australia.
f warm water from the Pacific to move eastwards towards North and South America.

Connections

B There is a clear **link** between doctors overprescribing antibiotics and the increase in antibiotic resistance. However, doctors continue to prescribe antibiotics for coughs and colds, even though they know the drugs will be **ineffective**. The **reason** for this is largely pressure from patients. Doctors give out antibiotics **so as to** keep their patients happy.

C The **consequences** of antibiotic resistance are serious. From a medical perspective, it is more difficult to treat people who are **affected** by 'superbugs'. Thus, increased antibiotic resistance is **associated with** higher death rates in hospital. The problem has a serious financial impact, too. Extra hygiene procedures are needed to reduce the **risk** of hospital infections. And more money is spent on research into new drugs.

Glossary
overprescribe (*v*): to prescribe a medicine too often, especially when it is not necessary
hygiene (*n*): the practice of keeping everything clean to prevent illness

3 **Read the two paragraphs, B and C, from a student essay about antibiotic resistance. Choose the best simple summary of each paragraph.**

1 The consequences of antibiotic resistance ___
2 The link between antibiotic use and antibiotic resistance ___
3 The reasons why doctors overprescribe antibiotics ___
4 The effects of antibiotic resistance on patients ___

> **Usage note** *effect* and *affect*
>
> **effect** is a noun: *they **have no effect on** viruses   the negative **effects of** age **on** memory*
> **affect** is a verb: *people who are **affected by** 'superbugs'   severe cold weather especially **affects** farmers*
> **effective** (opposite = **ineffective**) is an adjective: *an **effective** method*

4 **Complete the sentences using the correct form of *effect*, *affect* or *effective*.**

1 We need to find more _____ ways to reduce pollution.
2 The research showed the negative _____ of stress on overall health.
3 Diabetes _____ approximately 9% of the US population.
4 The changes in teaching methods had no _____ on the children's test results.

5 **Choose a word or phrase to complete the statements.**

> associated with   consequences   link   reason   risk

1 If the factory closes, many people will lose their jobs; it will have serious _____ .
2 Many people move to the city in order to find work; that is the main _____ .
3 Older people are more likely to have hearing problems; there's a _____ between age and hearing loss.
4 People who are overweight are more likely to develop diabetes; they are at high _____ .
5 Malaria is a particular problem in tropical countries; the disease is _____ hot climates.

6 **Choose the correct word to complete the sentences. Look at how the highlighted words are used in texts A–C to help you. See Unit 6 for more about prepositions.**

1 They found that public protests had little **effect** *on / to* political decisions.
2 There are several **reasons** *for / why* this difference.
3 Metals such as gold are very rare and *as / in* **a result**, they are extremely valuable.
4 Firms invest in research and development **so as** *for / to* create new products.
5 Not drinking enough water can **lead** *on / to* headaches and tiredness.
6 Politicians have to consider the possible **consequences** *for / of* the decisions they take.

25 Similarities and differences

Words to learn

a great deal (*phr*)
alternative (*adj*) AWL
as well as (*phr*)
by far (*phr*)

compare (*v*)
equally (*adv*)
resemble (*v*)
separate (*adj*)

similarly (*adv*) AWL
similar to (*adj*) AWL
to some extent (*phr*)
unique (*adj*) AWL

unlike (*prep*)
various (*adj*)

Comparing two approaches

A Lam *et al.* (2009) completed research into how different approaches in the classroom can affect educational outcomes. The research involved video recording the classes of two **separate** teachers in a Hong Kong secondary school. They then analysed and **compared** the different teaching styles. They found that the learning outcomes were **a great deal** better when the teachers used more motivating strategies and less discipline. This may indicate that a positive learning environment can help learning. It must be noted that this was a small study in just one school. Learners of **various** ages and in different cultures may respond differently to **alternative** teaching styles. However, the findings are **similar to** those in other studies.

Source: student essay

1 **Read the paragraph from a student essay, text A. Choose the best option, a or b, to complete the statements.**

1 The researchers recorded lessons …
  a by the same teacher with two different groups of students. __
  b by two different teachers in the same school. __
2 The research found that students learned more when the teacher …
  a tried to motivate them in a positive way. __
  b carefully controlled classroom discipline. __

2 **Match the sentence halves.**

1 Identifying the problem was **a great deal**
2 It is difficult for customers to **compare**
3 There are several **different**
4 The style of the buildings is **similar**
5 Individuals often respond

a **to** those found in Southern Europe.
b **differently** to the same problem.
c easier than finding a solution.
d the costs of different phone companies.
e ways of contacting your tutor.

3 a **Replace *different* in the sentences with the correct adjective from the box. Use the glossary on pp.127–141 to help you.**

> alternative   separate   various

1 Psychologists from different _____ countries around the world presented papers at the conference.
2 Fish can be divided into two different _____ groups; marine and freshwater species.
3 Users can choose between two different _____ screen formats, as shown below.

b **Complete the text using the words from the box in 3a.**

These words all describe things which are **different**. ¹_____ describes a range of people or things. ²_____ describes people or things which are not the same and not connected. ³_____ describes one thing which is used instead of another.

Describing similarities and differences

B Human intelligence is **to some extent** genetic. Children are likely to **resemble** their parents in terms of their mental abilities. However, we also know that environmental factors can reduce intelligence (for example, brain injuries) or increase intelligence (for example, education).

C One of the most spectacular discoveries in recent years has been the existence of extremely hot springs deep under the ocean. **Unlike** other parts of the ocean, the water here can reach temperatures of 350°C – **by far** the hottest environment on Earth to support life. These extreme environments contain **unique** ecosystems of animals found nowhere else.

D Good timekeeping is essential for a presenter. An audience might be unhappy if a presentation is too long. **Similarly**, they may feel dissatisfied if it is shorter than expected. **As well as** the overall length of the presentation, the timing of stages within the session is **equally** important.

4 Read the short extracts, B–D. Do they describe similarities (S) or differences (D) between these things?

1 Intelligence in children and their parents. __
2 Ecosystems in hot springs and other ecosystems. __
3 The importance of the timing of a whole presentation and the timing of each stage. __

5 Choose the correct word or phrase to complete the sentences.

1 Our model has three *unlike / unique* features compared with the existing theories.
2 For some people, work and family life are *by far / equally* important.
3 The heartrate monitor *compares / resembles* a normal watch.
4 Children learn through observation *as well as / equally* through discussion.
5 Today, *unique / unlike* in the recent past, more children are driven to school than walk or cycle.
6 Cloud forests make up only about 1% of the world's forests. *Similarly / As well as*, coral reefs cover less than 1% of the ocean floor.

6 Which of the sentences describes the greatest difference? Number the sentences so that 1 is the greatest difference and 3 is the smallest difference.

1 All the courses differ **to some extent** in terms of student numbers. __
2 Business Studies is **by far** the most popular course out of all those available at the college. __
3 Some courses are always **a great deal** more popular than others. __

7 Replace the highlighted words in the sentences using the word in CAPITALS. Make any other changes necessary.

▶ EXAMPLE: Each type of material has its own properties that are different from others *own unique properties*. UNIQUE

1 The two organizations differ in several different _____ ways. VARIOUS
2 Early humans were genetically a lot like _____ humans today. SIMILAR

8 Write a short paragraph (two or three sentences) describing differences and similarities between one of the pairs below. Try to use some of the words and phrases from the unit.

• City life and life in the countryside
• Traditional books and information online
• Studying in your own country and studying abroad

26 Problems and solutions

Words to learn

accident (n)	emergency (n)	problem (n)	suffer (v)
address (v)	enforce (v) AWL	quality (n)	take into account (phr)
aim to (v)	issue (n) AWL	regulation (n) AWL	
disaster (n)	lack of (n)	solution (n)	
disposal (n) AWL	minimize (v) AWL	successfully (adv)	

Describing problems

A Environmental disasters

During the early hours of 3 December 1984, the world's worst industrial **accident** happened in the Indian city of Bhopal. Poisonous gas escaped from a chemical plant and killed at least 3,000 people who lived close to the plant. Around 50,000 **suffered** permanent disabilities. This is one example of how rapid urbanization and industrialization can lead to environmental **disasters** in poorer parts of the world. Expanding cities lead to **problems** of air and water pollution and **disposal** of waste. Poor **regulations** and a **lack of** planning for an environmental **emergency** make problems worse.

Source: Durman & Ross. (2014). *AQA Certificate in Geography.* Oxford: Oxford University Press. p.134.

Glossary
poisonous (adj): causing death or illness if you take it into your body
urbanization (n): the process by which people move from the country to live in cities
industrialization (n): the process by which a place develops more industry

1 **Read text A. Complete the sentences about the text using words from the box.**

disposal   lack   problem   regulations   suffered

1 Many thousands of people _____ serious health problems as a result of the Bhopal accident.
2 When there is a _____ of planning for emergencies, the authorities cannot deal with a disaster.
3 With a growing number of people living in cities, the _____ of waste has become a major _____ .
4 In many countries, the _____ to control pollution are not good enough.

2 a **Complete the notes using three nouns from text A. The three nouns have a similar meaning.**

1 An <u>accident</u> is an event that happens suddenly and is not expected. It often causes injury or damage: a traffic / road / car <u>accident</u>, an industrial <u>accident</u>.
2 A _____ is an unexpected event that kills a lot of people or causes a lot of damage. It can be caused by man or by nature: a natural / environmental _____ .
3 An _____ is a sudden serious or dangerous situation which needs immediate action: a medical / health _____ , the _____ services; police, fire and ambulance.

b **Complete the sentences using the best nouns from 2a.**

1 If the person has stopped breathing, it is a medical _____ and requires urgent attention.
2 The Red Cross also provide help after earthquakes, storms and other natural _____ .
3 Road traffic _____ were the most common cause of injuries.

Describing solutions

B Reducing the problems: finding solutions

In order to **address** the environmental problems resulting from rapid urbanization and industrialization, there need to be guidelines to indicate what is allowed and what is not. Air and water pollution are a major **issue** in many industrial cities. There is a need to encourage the use of new technologies that can **minimize** pollution. Limits on pollution also need to be **enforced** so that air and water **quality** can be improved. For example, in 1986, the Ganga Action Plan **aimed to** introduce water treatment works on the River Ganges in India, which it did **successfully**. However, the increasing population was not **taken into account** and the quality of the water has since deteriorated.

Source: Adapted from Durman & Ross. (2014). *AQA Certificate in Geography.* Oxford: Oxford University Press. pp.135–136.

Glossary
deteriorate (*v*): to become worse

3 **Read text B. Complete the student's notes about the text using the keywords.**

Ways to ¹_____ environmental problems – e.g. ²_____ such as air and water pollution
- New technologies > can ³_____ pollution
- Regulations > need to ⁴_____ limits on pollution
- Actions such as Ganga Action Plan
    - it ⁵_____ to introduce water treatment works on River Ganges
    - at first, it ⁶_____ improved water ⁷_____
    - but didn't take into ⁸_____ population growth > water quality got worse again

Usage note *problem* and *solution* collocations (verbs)

have/face/experience a problem: • *Many countries are facing this problem.*
cause/create a problem: • *Extreme weather can cause major problems for transport networks.*
address/solve a problem: • *This problem can be solved in two different ways.*
find/provide/offer a solution: • *New technology may provide solutions to some of these problems.*

4 **Choose the best verb to complete the sentences.**

1 One way to *face / solve* this problem is to use stronger materials.
2 Certain chemicals can *cause / offer* serious health problems.
3 City councils need to find ways of *addressing / facing* the issue of household waste.
4 It is never easy to *address / find* simple solutions to complex social problems.
5 Several customers *addressed / experienced* problems accessing the company's website.
6 Most countries *provide / face* the same issues in finding ways to regulate the internet.

5 a **Match the problems and possible solutions below.**

1 traffic problems in a city   a improve public transport
2 damage to the environment from waste plastic   b reduce the focus on exams
3 stress among young people   c charge for plastic bags in shops

b **Choose one of the problem-solution situations from 5a. Write a short paragraph (two or three sentences) explaining the problem and describing a solution. You could describe a real solution that has been tried in a place you know, or a possible solution.**

▶ EXAMPLE: The city of Bristol has a traffic problem. The congestion makes it difficult to get around and the pollution from cars can cause serious health issues. The council has introduced regulations, such as stricter limits on parking in the city centre.

27 Information and evidence

Words to learn

assume (v) AWL	evidence (n) AWL	in detail (phr)	knowledge (n)
available (adj) AWL	expert (n) AWL	in fact (phr)	obtain (v) AWL
collect (v)	explain (v)	in the form of (phr)	source (n) AWL
definition (n) AWL	for example (phrase)	item (n) AWL	terminology (n)

Talking about information

A The 'information gap' is the difference between what you know as the writer of a text and the **knowledge** of your reader. You need to give enough information in your text so that your reader understands your message. To do this effectively, you need to know your 'audience' – the people who will read your text. If you are writing for other **experts** in your field, you can **assume** they already know quite a lot about the topic. However, if you are writing for a more general audience, you may need to **explain** your ideas **in more detail**. You also need to give clear **definitions** of any specialist **terminology**.

1 Read text A. Mark the statements true (T) or false (F) according to the text.

1 The 'information gap' is the gap between what the writer knows and what the reader knows. __
2 You need to explain things in more detail for an expert audience. __
3 You need to explain any specialist language for a general audience. __

2 Complete the tutor's feedback comments using words from the box.

assume   definitions   detail   experts   explain   knowledge   terminology

- You need to ¹_____ your key points in more ²_____ – some ideas are not clear.
- Your readers may not be ³_____ in mobile phone technology, so you can't ⁴_____ they have any background ⁵_____ about how mobile networks operate.
- Remember to give ⁶_____ of key ⁷_____ (5G, base station, radio frequency, etc.) at the start of your essay.

3 a Complete the table using the correct form of the words. Use the word families in the glossary on pp.127–141 to help you.

Verb	Noun
assume	1 _____
2 _____	definition
explain	3 _____
4 _____	knowledge

b Complete the sentences using words from the table.

1 Below, we _____ the key terms: 'social capital' and 'civil society'.
2 See Section 2.3 for an _____ of the methods used.
3 Designers have to make _____ about how a product might be used.
4 The doctor carefully _____ the process to the patient.
5 Laboratory staff require detailed _____ of the components used in each experiment.

Collecting evidence

B When you set out to study something, you need to **collect evidence**. This will form the basis of your understanding. What type of evidence is **available** will depend on the area of study.

'Quantitative data' is **in the form of** numbers and measurements. These data will often be the results of experiments, either from your own research or from published **sources**, such as academic journals. 'Qualitative data' is information in the form of words. These **items** of information are generally **obtained** directly from the people being studied, using questionnaires or interviews.

We often associate quantitative data with scientific disciplines, and qualitative data with the arts and social sciences. **In fact**, both types of evidence are used across disciplines. **For example**, a biologist might observe animal behaviour (qualitative data) and a social scientist might use statistics about population, employment figures, etc. (quantitative data).

4 a **Read text B. Mark the types of evidence as quantitative (QN) or qualitative (QL).**

1 Interviews with language learners about how they record vocabulary __
2 A questionnaire about diet and exercise __
3 Statistics about average incomes in different countries __
4 Feedback from users about the design of a new mobile phone __
5 Measurements of air pollution in a city at different times of year __

b **Which disciplines (e.g. economics, engineering, etc.) do you think the examples in 4a are from?**

1 _____   2 _____   3 _____   4 _____   5 _____

Usage note *a piece/an item* of information

Information and *evidence* are uncountable nouns, so they have no plural form and cannot be used after *a/an* or *one*. You can talk about *a piece* or **an *item* of information/evidence.**
  • Each new **piece of information** on this topic changes our perspective.
  • This idea is based on several **pieces of evidence**.
Data is a plural noun. The singular form is *datum*, but it is rarely used. You can also talk about **an item of data**.
  • Dates of birth are clearly **items** of personal **data**.

5 **Complete the sentences using the best form of the word in CAPITALS. Add *piece of/item of* where necessary.**

1 There is strong _____ of the health benefits of physical activity. EVIDENCE
2 One more _____ is needed to calculate the size of the building. INFORMATION
3 His analysis did not take into account several important _____ . FACT
4 There are thousands of individual _____ stored in the database. DATA
5 We assume that students on science courses have some basic _____ of statistics. KNOWLEDGE
6 More _____ are available on the university website. DETAIL

6 **Choose the best words or phrases to complete this paragraph from a report on a student project.**

We set out to investigate how much time people in different age groups spend online. Because this was a small-scale project, it was not possible to ¹*collect / know* data ourselves, so we ²*assumed / obtained* most of our evidence from published ³*experts / sources*. A lot of information about internet usage is ⁴*available / in fact* online ⁵*in the form of / in detail* news reports. However, these reports generally do not ⁶*define / explain* how statistics were calculated, so we chose to use data primarily from the Office for National Statistics. The ONS website gives clear ⁷*details / knowledge* about how the data was collected. It also includes much of the specific information we needed; ⁸*for example / in fact*, it shows internet usage by age group.

28 Research

Words to learn

activity (n)	method (n) AWL	research (n) AWL	show (v)
analysis (n) AWL	organize (v)	researcher (n) AWL	study (n)
conduct (v) AWL	project (n) AWL	respond (v) AWL	suggest (v)
findings (n)	record (v)	results	survey (n) AWL

Doing research

A Doing **research** means different things depending on your academic discipline. We focus on two different kinds of research here: what you do in the library or on your computer, and what you do in the lab. Although these types of research may seem very different, they have a great deal in common. The goal of any research **project** is to answer a question that you have set yourself.

No matter what kind of research project you are working on, you will go through the same three stages: obtaining information, **organizing** that information and presenting the information to an audience.

If you are writing an essay, you will obtain your information from a variety of sources, either in print or online. If you are in the laboratory, you may be **conducting** an experiment as well as doing some background reading. Although these are quite different **activities**, one thing they share is the need for organization.

If you are doing a lot of reading, you will need to take notes in a way that they can be easily

rearranged, depending on how you decide to organize your essay. If you do an experiment in a lab, you want to **record** your **results** in a way that makes it easy to organize your **analysis** and the final write-up of your lab report.

Source: Adapted from Northey & Timney. (2015). *Making Sense: A Student's Guide to Research and Writing Psychology.* Ontario: OUP. pp.13–14.

1 Complete the summary of text A using the correct form of keywords from the text.

Different types of academic ¹_____ involve different ²_____ . If you are in the lab, you might have to ³_____ an experiment and also do some background reading. Other research ⁴_____ mostly involve reading sources, either online or in the library. In both cases, though, you need to ⁵_____ the information you collect so that you can use it effectively later on. That might be the way you take notes to use in an essay or the way you ⁶_____ the ⁷_____ of your experiments for later ⁸_____ .

2 a Are the words nouns (N) or verbs (V) in text A?

1 research __   2 organize __   3 record __   4 analysis __

b Write the other form (noun or verb) of the words in 2a. Use the glossary on pp.127–141 to help you if necessary.

1 _____   2 _____   3 _____   4 _____

c Complete the sentences using an appropriate form of a noun or verb from 2a and 2b.

1 Researchers then _____ the interview data.
2 Her course involves _____ the development of health care over the last decade.
3 Patients are asked to _____ everything they eat during the day.
4 Statistical _____ of the data found no significant differences between the two groups.
5 As head of department, she is responsible for the management and _____ of various projects.

Research findings

B Several **researchers** have questioned Hofman's **findings**. There has also been criticism of his **method** of data collection.

C A 2002 national **survey** in Japan found that 73.7% of people who **responded** owned a mobile phone. By 2016, that figure had reached 82.8%, and three quarters of those were smartphone users.

D There is no evidence to **suggest** that the low proportion of women in leadership roles in medicine is due to lower academic ability. If anything, females tend to do better than males in academic examinations. **Studies** have also **shown** that women are good team leaders. So the situation is clearly not down to a lack of leadership skills.

3 **Read texts B–D. Mark the statements true (T) or false (F) according to the texts.**

1 Some researchers do not think that the results of Hofman's research are correct. __
2 They disagree with his analysis of the data. __
3 The research into mobile phone use in Japan was based on sales of mobile phones. __
4 Women do not get senior medical jobs because they lack the academic qualifications. __
5 According to research, women have good leadership skills. __

Usage note *research* and *study*

Remember that *research* is an uncountable noun; it has no plural form and it is not used with *a* or *one*. *Research* can describe a particular project or all the projects to find out about a particular topic.
- More **research** (in general) *is needed in this area.*
- *The* **research** (this particular project) *showed a strong* link.
- *In total, 12 people are working on the current* **research project.**
- *This is a very important* **piece of research.**

A *study* is a particular research project. *Study* is a countable noun.
- *Several* **studies** *have shown that health screening programmes are effective.*

4 **Do the pairs of words and phrases have a similar meaning (S) or a different meaning (D)?**

1 results – findings __
2 a study – a piece of research __
3 method – analysis __
4 respond – answer __
5 suggest – show __

5 **Complete the sentences using words from the box. Not all the words are needed.**

> conducted   do   further   of   on   projects   recent   scientific   shown   suggest

1 The authors _____ the research using a structured interview approach.
2 She is currently involved in three major research _____ .
3 Research has _____ that about 50% of all print adverts fail to gain the reader's attention.
4 Studies _____ that there may be an association between healthy behaviour and mental health.
5 The findings of _____ research have provided new evidence for this theory.
6 It is a national centre for research _____ climate change.
7 A number of recent _____ studies have investigated the effects of rising sea levels.
8 However, _____ research is needed to fully assess the effectiveness of the technique.

6 **Write a short paragraph (two or three sentences) about the type of research that happens in one of these academic areas or in your own discipline. Try to use some of the words from the unit.**

- medicine   • psychology   • economics   • engineering

▶ EXAMPLE: *Medical researchers conduct research into human diseases. They analyse their findings to understand the causes of the diseases. Some medical research projects help to develop new drugs.*

Words to learn

approve of (*phrasal v*)	believe (*v*)	in terms of (*phr*)	point of view (*n*)
argue (*v*)	consider (*v*)	in turn (*phr*)	presume (*v*) AWL
attitude (*n*) AWL	critic (*n*)	justify (*v*) AWL	public opinion (*n*)
belief (*n*)	definitely (*adv*) AWL	opinion (*n*)	view (*n*)

Opinions

A Journalists are expected to report the news openly and honestly, providing facts which can be attributed to the sources. This means that while the media may encourage discussion, debate and varying **points of view**, they should avoid presenting **opinions** where possible when reporting the events of the day. Journalism training emphasizes the separation of fact and opinion in news articles. However, in practice these are often mixed. Some kinds of journalism might try to support a particular **view**, for example a political **belief**, in order to affect **public opinion**. In many tabloid newspapers, writers include comments on behaviour which they perhaps do not **approve of**. The journalists writing such stories might **argue** that they can **justify** including their opinion as it adds to public interest, but it often means that the facts are lost somewhere in the storytelling.

Glossary
tabloid newpaper (*n*): a small-size newspaper which often has short articles about famous people – often thought of as less serious than other media

1 **Read text A. Choose the best summary of the text.**

a People expect to read both fact and opinion in news articles. __
b The role of the media is to present facts, and not opinion, when publishing news articles. __
c The role of the media is to present opinions when they can change public attitudes. __

2 **Choose the best word or phrase to complete the sentences.**

1 I'm interested in your *point of view / belief* – what do you think?
2 There were many *beliefs / opinions* about the best way to proceed.
3 Recent evidence seems to support the *view / public opinion* that blue light affects sleep patterns.
4 Traditional *beliefs / opinions* and skills were passed down over many years.
5 It is important for governments to *argue / justify* their spending plans.
6 Some historians *argue that / approve of* the Cold War period was one of global stability.
7 The university *approved of / believed in* his academic achievements.

3 **Complete the sentences using the correct form of words and phrases from the box.**

approve   argue   belief   justify   opinion   point of view   view

1 His parents' _____ is that he should attend a smaller school.
2 There isn't much evidence supporting the _____ that memory is located in one place in the brain.
3 He resigned, as he didn't _____ of the approach the company was taking.
4 Many immigrants find that their cultural _____ seem strange to their new neighbours.
5 One could _____ that the rich deserve to be wealthy due to their hard work.
6 Bankers' pay rises were hard to _____ during the financial crisis.
7 Advertising can often influence _____ about the quality of a product.

Perspectives

B All countries are different. Some are rich and have a high standard of living, while others are poor and have a lower standard of living. Countries that differ in this way are said to be at different stages of development. From a financial perspective, most people would **definitely** agree that a country like India is rich and becoming increasingly successful. The economy of India is the seventh largest in the world, and the third largest when purchasing power is taken into account. Many forecasters **believe** that it will grow in strength over the next decade. However, **in terms of** living standards, there is evidence that this development is not obvious in many parts of the country. While economic analysis will often **consider** factors like growth, it does not look at many important issues that have an effect on daily life. Studies which are concerned with money **presume** this is the best way to measure how well a country is doing. They may not take into account the fact that there are difficulties in accessing clean drinking water, or that education levels in rural areas are low. **Critics** argue that reporting or highlighting the economic success of countries which still face development challenges could influence the **attitudes** of people in other countries. **In turn**, this might affect whether they help to fund development projects.

4 **Read text B, an extract from a student's essay. Decide which essay title it answers, a or b.**

   a 'The success of a country is best measured through its economy.' Discuss whether you agree with this opinion, providing examples and evidence. __

   b 'The development of a country can only be understood in economic terms.' Provide evidence for this opinion. __

5 **Match the sentence halves.**

1 People should not just **presume**
2 The drugs have been classified **in**
3 Despite what many **critics**
4 Their supporters **definitely**
5 When making a choice, it is important to
6 Geologists **believe**
7 Many people seem to worry about the **attitudes**

a **argue**, he is doing nothing wrong.
b that there are oil reserves nearby.
c **terms of** their harmful effects.
d of others more than their own.
e agree on the way the club is going.
f that they know all the facts.
g **consider** all possible outcomes.

6 **Replace the highlighted words in the sentences with keywords or phrases from this unit. Make any other changes to the sentence as required.**

  ▶ EXAMPLE: His opinion was, _His point of view was that_ technology can benefit many pupils.

1 People who disagree with _____ their policies have been writing letters to the government.
2 It is important to think about _____ the impact our actions have on the environment.
3 I'm afraid that you are clearly _____ wrong in your opinion.
4 Studies show that teenagers often feel strongly _____ that animal rights are an important social issue.
5 I strongly disagree with his attitude towards _____ immigration.
6 A lot of academics suppose _____ that their readers understand all the key terms in their texts.
7 She made a lot of mistakes during the interview. Following that _____, she lost a lot of support.

7 **Write a short paragraph (two or three sentences) about one of the following. Try to use some of the words from the unit.**

  • Give your opinion on a story from the news today.
  • Explain why it is often hard to change somebody's opinion.
  • Discuss whether all beliefs are equally important.

30 Theory

Words to learn

based on (adj)	persuade (v)	propose (v)	set out (phrasal v)
concept (n) AWL	predict (v) AWL	prove (v)	theory (n) AWL
explain (v)	prediction (n) AWL	put forward (phrasal v)	
model (n)	principle (n) AWL	relationship (n)	

Theories

A A **theory** is defined as 'a formal set of ideas that **explains** why something happens or exists'. Theories help us to understand and organize **concepts**, or 'big ideas', about the world in a systematic way. For example, we might be able to agree on a statistical **relationship** between education and life expectancy and use this to make **predictions** about how long people will live. But to explain the relationship we need to **set out** a number of theories. These could include ideas about what makes people live more healthily, or the social meanings attached to a higher level of education. Theories can also be used to explain how society is organized in a way that leaves some people less well-educated. Using this approach helps society to **prove** connections between different situations and **propose** changes to improve our quality of life.

Glossary
systematic (adj): done according to a system or plan

1 Read the paraphrases, 1–4, of ideas in text A. Do they paraphrase the ideas accurately (✔) or do they change the meaning (✘)?

1 Theories take into account more than facts and figures. __
2 We can use statistics to make predictions about why better-educated people live longer. __
3 The way society is organized can be described by different theories. __
4 Theories about society rarely have a practical use. __

2 Choose the correct word to complete the sentences.

1 According to the latest *concept / theory*, you should aim to eat fruit and vegetables of different colours.
2 We were asked to explain the *relationship / theory* between smoking and lung disease.
3 The board of directors *predicted / proposed* plans to reduce spending on marketing.
4 It is a very difficult idea to *explain / prove* to non-professional people.
5 Students were asked to create a demonstration to *explain / prove* that CO_2 is heavier than air.
6 It is important to have all the data available before making *concepts / predictions* about change.
7 Doctors need to understand the *concept / relationship* of risk when they work in emergency wards.
8 The architects *predicted / set out* their plans for an eco-city.

3 Match the sentence halves. Focus especially on the highlighted words.

1 We used our earlier observations to make
2 The article highlighted how current **theories**
3 After so many students failed, the university **proposed**
4 There is a lack of any **proven**
5 They used a diagram to **explain**
6 The model helps researchers to organize

a **relationships** between different species.
b **explain** patterns of population growth.
c connection between diet and crime.
d **concepts** clearly.
e changes to the marking guidelines.
f **predictions** about their behaviour.

Models

B There are many theories of ageing. Biological **models** tend to describe it as a negative process. As the body and mind become weaker, older people lose the ability to do certain things. These models focus on physical changes and **put forward** the idea that old age means inevitable decline. Critics say these models **persuade** people to have negative perceptions of the ageing process and of the elderly.

The continuity theory of ageing provides a different approach. This theory is built on the **principle** that older people should make their own choices about their lives as they get older. It suggests that, wherever possible, continuity of behaviour, activities and environment has a positive impact. Studies which are **based on** the continuity theory **predict** that an ageing person will show less physical and mental decline if they can control the changes in their lives.

4 Read text B. Use it to complete the student notes.

> Ageing
> Biological ¹_____
> Understand ageing as ²_____ process
> Ageing = ³_____ – body and mind become weaker
> Contributes to negative ⁴_____ of ageing
> Continuity ⁵_____
> The elderly make own ⁶_____ – behaviour, activities, environment Studies show more
> control = ⁷_____

5 Complete the sentences with the correct forms of words and phrases from the box.

> based on   model   persuade   predict   principle   put forward

1 Different academics offer alternative _____ to describe the process of ageing.
2 Studies _____ that the global population will stabilize at one billion by the middle of the 22nd century.
3 Once they had seen the sales figures, it was easy to _____ them to invest in our business.
4 In his final book he _____ arguments that changed the way people viewed the human mind.
5 The basic _____ of his theory was that most human behaviour follows rules like a game.
6 His ideas are _____ the work of several different academics.

6 Replace the highlighted words in the sentences with one of the keywords or phrases from the texts. Make any other changes to the sentence as required.

▶ EXAMPLE: The European Union is a way of describing _model for_ shared ideals across borders.
1 The council drew up _____ proposals to increase local taxes.
2 It was hard to tell in advance _____ where the earthquake would cause the most damage.
3 The right to vote is an essential idea _____ that makes democracies work.
4 The results clearly show _____ that better sanitation leads to an increase in life expectancy.
5 The salesman tried to convince _____ us to buy a new laptop, but we wanted a PC.

7 Write a short paragraph (two or three sentences) about one of the following. Try to use some of the words from the unit.

- Describe an important theory from your area of study.
- Discuss why it is important that theories sometimes change.
- Explain an important concept from your area of study, e.g. the law of supply and demand.

31 Positive evaluation

Words to learn

accurate (*adj*) AWL
achieve (*v*) AWL
advantage (*n*)
appropriate (*adj*) AWL

benefit (*n*) AWL
convincing (*adj*) AWL
effective (*adj*)
efficient (*adj*)

goal (*n*)
interesting (*adj*)
popular (*adj*)
positive (*adj*) AWL

precise (*adj*) AWL
successful (*adj*)

Achieving success

A Achieving a **goal**, or being **successful** in something that you do, has many **benefits**. Research shows that the **positive** feelings created by success can have important mental and physical effects. For athletes, success means the difference between winning and losing. There are a number of different ways that they can try to increase their chances of performing well.

Visualization, also known as imaging, is an **effective** method for athletes to prepare for performing a physical activity. As they do this, they create an **accurate** picture in their mind of themselves **achieving** success. This could be imagining themselves running a race in **precise** detail – thinking about the physical and external circumstances.

Psychologists believe that visualization establishes neural pathways in the brain that act as a model to be followed in an actual performance. By creating a **convincing** version of success in their head, the athlete is more likely to achieve this on the sports field.

Glossary
neural pathways (*noun*): systems of nerves that send messages in the brain

1 Choose the correct word or phrase to complete the sentences.

1 This argument isn't very *effective / convincing* – there isn't enough evidence to support your view.
2 Their report gave a highly *accurate / precise* picture of the current situation.
3 We don't know the *accurate / precise* details yet, but we hope to have more information soon.
4 Their company was *effective / successful* in winning the contract to supply IT to the college.
5 It was important for the industry to take *accurate / positive* action to reduce job losses.
6 Scientists are exploring *accurate / effective* ways of preventing the Zika virus.
7 The health *benefits / goals* of regular exercise are hard to ignore.

2 Match the sentence halves. Use the highlighted words to help you.

1 Learners who have clear goals will often **be**
2 The report didn't give an **accurate**
3 Botanists are studying whether compounds in fruit **have**
4 Washing your hands carefully is one of the most **effective**
5 Although she's new to the piano, she can play a **convincing**
6 He described in **precise**

a **methods** of preventing illness spreading.
b **detail** the effects of the storm.
c version of the piece.
d **picture** of what we felt was happening.
e **benefits** as anti-ageing treatments.
f more **successful** at acquiring language.

Measuring popularity

B When companies set up websites for commercial purposes, they want to know how many people are visiting the page, and how long they are staying on it. Having accurate data can help a company greatly grow its online presence. This data can then be used to either improve the experience for users, or to assess ways that internet traffic could be increased. This might be by adding more **interesting** content, or ensuring that navigation of the site is clear and **appropriate**.

Page popularity is a basic measure of how **popular** a web page is with end-users. This is calculated by counting the number of links to a specific page from pages on other websites. Page popularity is used by a number of search engines when ordering the results of a search query made by a user. One **advantage** of this method is that it shows where connections are made and how people are drawn to a particular website. However, it may not be the most **efficient** way of calculating popularity, as often links are not followed from one site to another.

Source: Ince, D. (2013). 'page popularity.' *A Dictionary of the Internet.* (3rd ed.). Oxford: Oxford University Press.

Glossary
hits (*n*): visits to a website
search engine (*n*): a computer program that searches the internet for information, especially by looking for a word or group of words

3 a Read text B. Mark the statements true (T) or false (F) according to the text.

1 Knowing exactly who is visiting their website can help a business succeed. __
2 Page popularity is a very complex way of measuring internet use. __
3 Page popularity is worked out by counting individual hits on a website. __
4 Many search engines use page popularity to organize search results. __
5 Page popularity sometimes gives the wrong information about how popular a site is. __

b Rewrite the false statements so that they are true according to the text.

4 Complete the sentences using words from the box.

advantage   appropriate   efficient   interesting   popular

1 The newest film in the series was extremely _____ – earning more money than predicted.
2 The main _____ of the approach is that it allows materials to be produced at lower cost.
3 The Grand Canyon is an _____ example of this geological feature, and is often photographed.
4 Counting hits is an _____ but fairly simple way of measuring internet traffic.
5 Plants and animals survive best in the most _____ environment.

5 Replace the highlighted words in the sentences with one of the keywords or phrases from this unit. Make any other changes to the sentence as required.

1 They designed the most effective _____ car engine possible.
2 Although the essay was enjoyable to read _____, it failed to answer the question completely.
3 Working in technology still seems to be the number one _____ choice for most graduates.
4 Now the problem has been identified, we'll take suitable _____ action.
5 One good point about _____ globalization is that the same products are available in most countries.
6 Which definition is the correct _____ description of 'neural pathway'?

6 Write a short paragraph (two or three sentences) about one of the following. Try to use some of the words from the unit.

- Describe how success is defined in your culture or a culture you know about.
- Give a positive evaluation of a product or brand you know well.
- Discuss whether it is important to be successful or popular.

32 Negative evaluation

Words to learn

absent (*adj*)	challenging (*adj*) AWL	false (*adj*)	pressure (*n*)
avoid (*v*)	criticism (*n*)	harmful (*adj*)	risk (*n*)
blame (*n*)	disadvantage (*n*)	mistake (*n*)	threat (*n*)
blame (*v*)	effort (*n*)	negative (*adj*) AWL	weakness (*n*)

Motivation

A Motivation to succeed in life is important, as it shows that individuals have a willingness to continue to work hard in the face of **challenging** situations. Psychologists consider motivation as having two aspects – intensity and direction. Intensity focuses on how much **effort** is made to reach a goal. Direction is concerned with movement towards the goal. When describing direction, psychologists often talk about people approaching a task or **avoiding** behaviour which they may see as having **harmful** effects. If a person lacks motivation, they may try to avoid **risks**. However, in doing this there may be several **disadvantages** to personal development. Success often occurs when people are pushed into a position which forces them to make difficult choices. If the **pressure** to succeed is **absent** from a person's plans, then there may be a lower intensity, and less direction in life goals.

Source: Adapted from Kent, M. (2006). 'motivation.' *The Oxford Dictionary of Sports Science & Medicine*. (3rd ed.). Oxford: Oxford University Press.

1 Read the paraphrases of ideas from text A. Do they paraphrase the ideas accurately (✔) or do they change the meaning (✗)?

1 Having a strong sense of motivation shows that people can succeed in difficult times. __
2 In terms of motivation, *intensity* refers to how hard a person tries to achieve a goal. __
3 In terms of motivation, *direction* describes how people avoid doing things. __
4 Without pressure to be successful, people's lives will have more direction. __

> **Usage note** *disadvantage* (*of*, *in* and *to*)
>
> **disadvantage + of/in/to sth**: • *The main disadvantage of a nuclear power plant is potential risk.*
> • *Turek (2005) outlines a number of disadvantages to this model.*
> **disadvantage + of/in/to + -ing**: • *Individuals in rural communities may be at a disadvantage in accessing health care.*

2 Choose the correct word to complete the sentences.

1 The popular Wi-fi technology was *absent / challenging* from the latest version of the product.
2 There are a number of *pressures / risks* associated with smoking in pregnancy.
3 Burning the waste released large clouds of *challenging / harmful* smoke into the atmosphere.
4 The greatest *pressure / disadvantage* of building with new materials is their cost.
5 A lack of jobs is one of many *pressures / risks* on young people today.
6 During the interview he was asked some *challenging / harmful* questions about immigration.

3 Match the sentence halves. Use the highlighted words to help you.

1 It is important that children **take**
2 Food producers increasingly **face**
3 People's behaviour can change greatly in **challenging**
4 There are many **disadvantages**
5 If eaten in large quantities, the plant has **harmful**
6 The gene is completely **absent**

a competitive **pressures** to keep costs low.
b **to** leaving school with no qualifications.
c **effects** on young children and pets.
d **risks** when they are developing.
e **from** male fruit flies.
f **situations** where life is in danger.

Criticism

B Modern working environments are often challenging places, with increased pressures and the **threat** of job losses. In such situations, **mistakes** are often made. For managers in such companies, there are choices which can be made about how these mistakes are dealt with.

A recent development in work theory is 'no **blame** culture'. This describes how organizations should be tolerant of mistakes, as long as the people who make them learn from the experience. Instead of **blaming** employees for making mistakes, and creating a **negative** way of communicating, employers are encouraged to avoid giving **criticism**. In a no blame culture, employees are responsible for making their own decisions. If they make mistakes, they have to evaluate these and discuss the issues with colleagues.

However, this can be a time-consuming process, and it can create a **false** sense that there are no difficulties in working practices. Many traditional managers may also feel that not criticizing errors is odd and could be considered a **weakness** in their management.

Source: Adapted from Heery, E. & Noon, M. (2008). 'no blame culture.' *A Dictionary of Human Resource Management.* Oxford: Oxford University Press.

4 Read text B. Use it to complete the student notes.

No ^{1}_____ culture = recent development in ^{2}_____
Organization: should be tolerant of employees' ^{3}_____
Employees: should be willing to learn from experience, evaluate + ^{4}_____ with colleagues
Bosses: withhold blame = + workers more responsible for actions = – time-consuming process;
creates a ^{5}_____ of no probs; not criticizing feels like a ^{6}_____

5 Complete the sentences using words from the box.

blame   criticism   false   mistake   negative   threat   weakness

1 It is _____ to say that single parents cannot raise a child.
2 Teachers often _____ themselves if things go wrong in the classroom.
3 The study looked at people's _____ attitudes towards the long-term unemployed.
4 The _____ of job losses worries many skilled workers in Europe.
5 Following the earthquake, geologists identified a _____ in the Earth's crust.
6 There was a lot of _____ of their attitude.
7 Perhaps his biggest _____ was agreeing to appear in the debate.

6 Replace the highlighted words or phrases in the sentences with keywords from the unit. Make any other changes necessary.

▶ EXAMPLE: He was asked to leave after making harmful _negative_ comments about his colleagues.
1 I wonder why the source is missing _____ from this quote.
2 Smoking has well-documented dangerous _____ effects.
3 We checked the facts again and discovered that their story was not true _____.
4 Perhaps his greatest fault _____ is his lack of self-confidence.
5 The company faced criticism after it failed to take warnings _____ of strike action seriously.
6 Many people say bankers are responsible _____ for starting the 2008 financial crisis.

7 Write a short paragraph (two or three sentences) about one of the following. Try to use some of the words from the unit.

• Describe the most challenging situation you have been in and what you did.
• Describe a situation where you wish you had done something better.
• Discuss whether it is important to be given encouragement in life or in your studies.

Student writing: discussing problems and solutions

Academic research often focuses on trying to find solutions to problems. When you write about this, you will have to look at the causes and effects of the problems, and discuss the evidence for your solutions.

> **A** One recent **study** has **suggested** that simple changes in city planning could have a significant impact on the environment. **Researchers** looked at a number of **models** and have **put forward** several key proposals. Firstly, they considered the **issue** of flooding. They found that one **factor** which has increased the **risk** of flooding is the decline in green space in cities. Many people have replaced gardens with hard surfaces for car parking, which **means** that it is more difficult for rainwater to drain away. The researchers also **believe** that there is a **link** between urban development and pollution. They suggest that building new homes on land in the middle of cities can have environmental **benefits, compared** with building on new sites in the suburbs. It **leads to** a decrease in pollution, because people do not need to drive into the city centre for work.

1 Match each cause, 1–3, to two effects, a–f.

1 replacing gardens with hard surfaces
2 building new suburbs around cities
3 building on land in the city centre

a water can't drain away
b less traffic driving into city centre
c lower air pollution
d more air pollution
e more flooding in cities
f more use of cars

Focus on cause and effect

2 Match the sentence halves to show the cause and effect relationships. Use text A and Units 24–32 to help you if necessary.

1 Taking the bus instead of driving leads to
2 There is a link between pollution of rivers and oceans
3 Burning coal and gas increases the risk of
4 Our failure to look after the environment may have serious consequences
5 The use of chemicals on crops may be one reason

a global warming.
b and the use of too much packaging.
c for the decline of the honey bee.
d less traffic on the roads.
e for future generations.

3 Complete the sentences using the correct form of words from the box.

associated believe mean minimize predict suggest

1 Researchers have _____ that eating too much red meat can lead to heart problems.
2 Our project is looking at some of the problems _____ with studying abroad.
3 We _____ that the findings of this study will help us to put forward some solutions to the problem of poor air quality.
4 Mistakes in the application _____ that he was unable to get a visa to study abroad.
5 Gardeners can _____ the amount of tap water they use by collecting rainwater.
6 Scientists _____ that sea levels may rise by 90 cm by 2100 because of global warming.

Student writing: comparing

The analysis of data often involves making comparisons. This might mean describing statistics in the form of charts or tables. In other fields, you may also need to compare different arguments about a topic before evaluating them for yourself.

B **To some extent**, class size influences parents' choice of school. Smaller class sizes are generally more **popular** because they allow teachers to spend more time with each student. Many people therefore **assume** that small classes lead to higher performance. **In fact**, in highly **successful** education systems, the average class size differs **a great deal**. Countries such as Denmark and Finland have 20 students or fewer per class, **compared** with more than 34 students in South Korea and up to 50 students in China. Since students in all of these countries are successful in achieving high scores, it is difficult to **argue** that large class sizes are always **harmful**.

4 **Mark the statements true (T) or false (F) according to the text.**

1 Parents often believe that children do better in small classes. __
2 Children in countries with small classes get higher scores than children in countries with big classes. __
3 Denmark and Finland resemble each other in terms of class size. __

Focus on comparison

5 **Choose the best word or expression to complete the sentences.**

1 *To some extent / A great deal*, the company's failure is due to the recession.
2 Children who read with their parents from a young age are *a great deal / highly* more likely to be strong readers at school.
3 More students passed the exams with top marks, making this year the most *successful / popular* ever.
4 Although the business has had a good year, the company should not *argue / assume* that this success will continue in these difficult economic times.
5 Exercising in very polluted air can be more *harmful / successful* to health than doing nothing.

6 **Match the sentence halves. Use the highlighted words, Units 12–32 and the glossary on pp.127–141 to help you.**

1 The researchers **set**
2 Critics **blamed** the government
3 My predictions are **based**
4 The study did not **take** the latest data

a **for** the poor economic situation.
b **on** a detailed analysis of the results.
c **out** their findings in a brief presentation.
d **into account**.

Writing task

7 **Write a short paragraph (two or three sentences) for one of the following.**

- Describe a problem you have faced in your studies. What caused it and what solutions did you find?
- Compare the systems of government in two countries you are familiar with.

33 Emphasis

Words to learn

absolutely (adv)	draw attention to (phr)	essential (adj)	major (adj) AWL
actually (adv)	emphasize (v) AWL	highlight (v) AWL	obvious (adj) AWL
central (adj)	entirely (adv)	importance (n)	stress (v) AWL
completely (adv)	especially (adv)	important (adj)	

Emphasizing what is important

A The French naturalist Charles-Georges Le Roy **emphasized** the **importance** of field observations. He **stressed** that watching animals in the wild was **central** to understanding their natural behaviour.

B It is **absolutely essential** that any questionnaire is piloted before sending it out to a particular audience. While all the questions might seem **entirely** logical and appropriate to the researcher, there may be a few that will cause confusion or attract answers that the research team were not expecting. A pilot study can be carried out at low cost with a small sample, and any changes can be made as a result.

C We all have biases, however objective we try to be. It is very easy indeed to have an idea of what result 'should be obtained' before an experiment is **actually** conducted. It is **especially important** that you guard against errors of this type.

Glossary
pilot (v): to test something on a few people before it is used everywhere
bias (n): a feeling or belief that influences your decisions in an unfair way
objective (adj): not influenced by personal feelings or opinions
guard against (phrasal v): to take care to prevent something

1 Read texts A–C about research methods. Identify the main emphasis in each text. Not all the answers are needed.

1 How important it is to observe natural behaviour __
2 How difficult it is to design a clear questionnaire __
3 How important it is to start research with an open mind __
4 How useful it is to test your research methods on a small sample before you begin __

2 Choose the best word to complete the sentences.

1 It is not *actual / entirely* clear whether the two events are linked.
2 Growth hormone is *central / essential* for the growth of humans and other mammals after birth.
3 Doctors emphasize the *importance / important* of regular exercise.
4 Shared meals were *central / essential* to family life.
5 The job of the court is to establish what *actually / entirely* happened, based on the evidence.
6 This method is *especially / absolutely* useful for studying larger groups.
7 The guidelines *emphasis / stress* the importance of regular hand-washing for all hospital staff.
8 We cannot be *absolutely / indeed* certain that a finding based on a sample will be true for the whole population.

Emphasizing differences and similarities

D While comparisons to the US system of government may be helpful, it is also important to **draw attention to** some very **obvious** differences between the two systems.

E A central question relates to differences between men and women entrepreneurs. The next two sections will **highlight** the **major** areas of similarity and difference.

F In computer programming, two **completely** different sets of code can produce programs that perform almost identical functions.

3 Match the student paraphrases to texts D–F.

1 The author is going to draw attention to some key ways in which the groups differ and are similar. __
2 The author emphasizes that there are clear differences between the two systems. __
3 It is possible for two pieces of software to achieve the same result using very different approaches. __

Usage note adverb + adjective

Gradable adjectives (*important, useful, difficult, strong*) can be used with certain adverbs to add emphasis: *very/especially/extremely/particularly important/useful*
Limit adjectives that already describe something extreme (*essential, certain, central*) are used with different adverbs: *absolutely essential/certain*
Some adverbs have a meaning that only logically fits with certain adjectives. *Completely, entirely* and *totally* mean 'in every possible way': *completely/entirely/totally different/new/absent*

4 Match the sentence halves. Use the highlighted words to help you.

1 Bilingual dictionaries are **especially**
2 Strong personal relationships are **absolutely**
3 We compared the findings of two **completely**
4 Knowledge of human biology is **particularly**

a important in making health decisions.
b essential to doing business.
c useful for lower-level students.
d separate studies.

5 Complete the sentences with the correct form of the word in CAPITALS. Use the glossary on pp.127–141 to help you.

1 We present an overview of the issues, with a particular _____ on practical solutions. EMPHASIZE
2 The report has _____ the need for a more active approach. HIGHLIGHT
3 The exact details are _____ different for each individual project. OBVIOUS
4 It is very difficult to calculate the _____ number of insects in any location. ACTUALLY
5 The company changed its policy after activists _____ attention to human rights issues. DRAW
6 This equipment can be used to find and, more _____ , to remove blockages. IMPORTANT
7 New forms of communication have been _____ to the process of globalization. CENTRE

6 Rewrite the sentences to add emphasis. Add or substitute a word from this unit and make any other changes needed. More than one option may be possible.

▶ EXAMPLE: In terms of climate, the two regions are different.
In terms of climate, the two regions are completely different.

1 The paper explains a new method for identifying the age of samples.

2 There are differences between print books and online information.

3 The authors say that the findings only apply to this specific environment.

4 Working as a team is a part of nursing.

34 Hedging

Words to learn

appear (*v*)
indicate (*v*) AWL
likely (*adj*)
more or less (*phr*)

normally (*adv*) AWL
on the whole (*phr*)
overall (*adv*) AWL
perhaps (*adv*)

possible (*adj*)
potentially (*adv*) AWL
relatively (*adv*)
seem (*v*)

somewhat (*adv*) AWL
tend to (*v*)
typically (*adv*)

Expressing possibilities

A Patients with memory problems often have trouble remembering something that happened a few minutes ago. However, old memories from their childhood **appear** to be intact. This **perhaps indicates** that different types of memories are stored in different parts of the brain.

B Patients with memory problems **seem** to remember events from their childhood, but they may be unable to recall something from a few minutes ago. **Potentially**, this suggests that older and more recent memories are **likely** to be stored in different parts of the brain.

C Memory problems **tend to** affect short-term and long-term memory differently. One **possible** explanation for this is that these two types of memory are stored in different areas of the brain.

Glossary
intact (*adj*): complete and not damaged
recall (*v*): to remember sth

1 Read texts A–C, which all describe the same idea. Mark the statements true (T) or false (F) according to the texts.

1 It is difficult to prove that these patients clearly remember events from their childhood. __
2 There is clear evidence that older and recent memories are stored in different parts of the brain. __

Usage note hedging (1)

In academic writing, it is important to show the difference between proven facts and ideas which *may be* true. We use hedging language to show that an idea may be true, based on the evidence we have.
• Adverbs: *perhaps   potentially   possibly*
• Adjectives: *likely   possible   potential*
• Verbs: *appear to   seem to   tend to   indicate   suggest*
Note: We use *appear/seem/tend + to do sth*:   • They **seem to remember** *events from childhood.*
We also use *appear/seem + adjective*:   • *Unrelated species can* **appear** *very* **similar**.
For more about hedging, see the language reference section on pp.108–114.

2 Find words in texts A–C that have a similar meaning to the words below.

1 appear to – _____
2 potentially – _____

3 suggest – _____
4 likely – _____

3 Choose the best word or form to complete the sentences. Think about meaning and grammar.

1 The following factors all appear *have / to have* an impact on student choices.
2 These findings *potential / perhaps* explain the decrease in bee numbers in recent years.
3 These problems tend *occurring / to occur* during childhood.
4 Some of these drugs are more *likely / possible* to have side effects.
5 Students should bookmark *potentially / perhaps* useful sources to read later.
6 In this case, no other explanation *seems / seems to* possible.
7 Research *indicates / seems* that 50% of people read consumer reviews before making a purchase.

Expressing general ideas

D China has a **relatively** dispersed pattern of industry and therefore its cities are **typically** less specialized. Basic goods such as clothes, bicycles and watches are produced in all cities, not just a few. There are no single-industry towns. However, this situation is **somewhat** countered by investment policies that favour the largest cities. Thus, while most cities have a mixture of industrial activities, industrial activity **overall** is concentrated in a few relatively large cities.

E Consumers, **on the whole,** tend to be not particularly interested in the make-up of the products they buy. Buying decisions **normally** depend on factors such as price or brand. Most shoppers buy **more or less** the same goods each week, without checking the label. However, there is a trend that consumers are becoming increasingly interested in what makes up their products and how they are produced; for example, whether products are grown organically or produced ethically.

Glossary
dispersed (*adj*): spread over a wide area
counter sth (*v*): to have the opposite effect
make-up (*n*): the different things that something is made of

4 **Read texts D and E. Choose the best option to complete the statements so that they are true according to the texts.**

1 Industry is *very equally / quite equally* spread across China.
2 However, *there is generally more industry / industrial activity occurs only* in a few large cities.
3 Consumers *do not know about / are mostly not very interested in* how products are made.
4 Shoppers *buy exactly the same things / often buy many of the same things* every week.

5 **Complete the sentences using the best word or phrase from the box.**

more or less   normally   overall   relatively   somewhat   typically

1 The exact measurements varied from region to region, but _____ , the trend was upwards.
2 The farms in this region are _____ small, and _____ they are family-run.
3 The three studies were conducted using _____ identical methods.
4 The two writers take a _____ different view of the situation.
5 A microscope is _____ used to examine the samples.

35 Citation

Words to learn

according to (*prep*)   explain (*v*)   quote (*v*) AWL   source (*n*) AWL
citation (*n*) AWL   plagiarize (*v*)   reference (*v*)   state (*v*)
discuss (*v*)   quotation (*n*) AWL report (*v*)

Citing materials in an essay

A Part of the academic process at university involves referring to material from other written **sources** in your own writing. This shows that you have read texts which **explain** the same situations, problems, solutions and arguments you want to **discuss** in more detail. Using published academic writing to support your position makes it stronger, and also shows tutors that you can understand and evaluate content. This process is referred to as **citation**.

The most common forms of citation are summary, paraphrase and **quotation**:
- summary – a shorter version of the source text, written in your own words and including main points
- paraphrase – a new version of the source text, keeping the meaning, but using mostly your own language. Key terms or technical definitions do not need to change.
- quotation – a sentence or short paragraph taken directly from the source material, with no words changed. When you **quote** from a source, you have to use quotation marks, and you have to include a clear reference to the author and date of publication.

1 **a Read text A. Mark the statements true (T) or false (F) according to the texts.**

1 Good academic writing does not require references to other work. __
2 Using references shows that the writer does not have many ideas of their own. __
3 There are two main ways to refer to other academic writing in your essays. __
4 A summary includes the main points of a text but often simplifies the language. __
5 When you paraphrase a text, you change the words but keep the meaning. __
6 A quotation should have no changes to the original words in the text. __

b Rewrite the false statements so that they are true according to the texts.

B There are several mechanisms by which the water we have on Earth might have got here. One popular theory is that it came through the impacts of 'wet' bodies such as comets, which contain large amounts of frozen water.

Source: O'Shea, M. (2015). *Water: A Very Short Introduction*. Oxford: Oxford University Press. p.3.

C O'Shea (2015) suggests that there are a number of ways water probably arrived on Earth. Many people believe it may have come from comets, which are mostly made of ice.

2 **Read the source material, text B and essay extract, text C. Decide if the extract uses a summary, a paraphrase or a quotation.**

a summary __   b paraphrase __   c quotation __

3 Complete the sentences with the correct form of the words from the box.

citation   discuss   explain   quotation   quote   source

1 My tutor often _____ Benjamin Franklin: 'Tell me and I forget. Teach me and I remember. Involve me and I learn.'

2 Which speech is that _____ from? I can't find it anywhere.

3 Economic changes happened after the Wall Street Crash, which is _____ in detail in Chapter 3.

4 Her grade was lower than expected because she had forgotten to provide a list of the _____ she had used.

5 These factors _____ the situation shown in the data.

6 A dissertation usually contains a large number of _____ , as writers refer to lots of different sources.

Referencing

D When you have decided which approach to take, you need to **reference** the material which you have read. Good writers **state** where their ideas have come from. This acknowledges the fact that you are using other people's ideas to support your work, and shows that you are taking part in the academic process of extending ideas. It also prevents you from being accused of plagiarism (copying other people's work and saying it is your own). Students who **plagiarize** will lose marks, have their grades lowered, and may even be asked to leave the university. To avoid any doubt, you must use clear referencing.

Within your essay, you should give the name of the author of the book you are referring to and the year of publication. For example:

"**According to** Dasgupta (2007), we cannot truly understand personal success and failure if we do not consider the important impact of economics on our life choices."

You then need to include this information in the reference list, or bibliography, at the end of your essay. This is the section where you **report** to the reader all the books or articles you have mentioned in your writing. The format is as follows:

References:
Dasgupta, G. (2007). *Economics: A Very Short Introduction*. Oxford: Oxford University Press.

4 Complete the advice using the correct form of the highlighted words in text D. Use the glossary on pp.127–141 to help you.

[1]_____ a number of studies, writing extended essays is one of the biggest challenges for most undergraduates – so take time to plan. Once you have completed your work, include a detailed list of [2]_____ . This shows readers which sources you have used. Make sure that the sources you use are [3]_____ clearly and are accurate. Remember, [4]_____ someone else's academic work is considered a serious offence.

5 Write a short paragraph (two or three sentences) about one of the following. Try to use some of the words from the unit.

- Explain why it is important to provide references in academic work.
- Discuss where the best sources for academic writing can be found – online or offline. Say why.
- Find a quotation from a text you are familiar with. Write a citation using paraphrase, summary or quotation.

Words to learn

although (*conj*)	contrast (*v*) AWL	even though (*conj*)	since (*conj*)
as a result of (*prep*)	despite (*prep*) AWL	however (*adv*)	therefore (*adv*)
because of (*prep*)	due to (*prep*)	owing to (*prep*)	whereas (*conj*) AWL

Expressing reasons

A Tourism can often have a positive social impact. For example, local people may find opportunities for sport and entertainment, **since** new leisure facilities are often created in tourist destinations. These kinds of facilities also create more jobs and **therefore** can improve the quality of life for local people. In addition, it is possible for tourists and locals to learn from each other, **as a result of** meeting people from different places and cultures.

Due to the growth of tourism, however, there may be disruption to the traditional way of life. Many local people leave farming in the countryside. These are often younger adults, who move to cities or tourist resorts to work. **Because of** this, often only the older population remains, and traditional communities in the countryside may disappear. **Owing to** these kinds of changes, many tourist destinations are now encouraging travellers to visit

traditional communities and spend money there as well as in modern resorts.

Source: Adapted from Rickerby,S. (2009). *Leisure and Tourism GCSE.* Cheltenham: Nelson Thornes. pp.86–87.

Glossary
disruption (*n*): a situation when it is difficult for sth to continue in the normal way

1 Read text A. According to the text, which two sentences, a, b or c, describe positive effects of tourism?

a Tourism creates new jobs and brings money to communities. __

b Tourism creates the opportunity for people to share cultural ideas. __

c Tourism helps people to move from the countryside to cities. __

Usage note linking reasons

You can use verbs to express reasons and causes (e.g. *cause, produce, create*):
• *The rules were changed and this caused fewer students to pass the exam.*
You can also use a range of phrases. These can go at the beginning or in the middle of a sentence:
• *Because of changes to the rules, fewer students are passing the exam.*
• *Fewer students are passing the exam as a result of changes to the rules.*
• *Due to changes to the rules, fewer students are passing the exam.*

2 Complete the text with the correct prepositions.

Due ¹_____ the ingredients it contains, green tea is considered an extremely healthy drink. As a result ²_____ recent studies, researchers now know that the drink increases energy use and can help in burning fat. Furthermore, some compounds in green tea have been shown to protect brain cells. Owing ³_____ this fact, it is predicted that drinking green tea could help brain functions.

Because ⁴_____ the high levels of caffeine in coffee, many studies link it to anxiety and sleep loss. Caffeine makes the brain more active as a result ⁵_____ blocking the chemical adenosine, which usually slows brain function. Owing ⁶_____ this effect, coffee reduces tiredness and makes drinkers feel more alert.

Showing contrast

B Tourist spending has increased in the UK, **whereas** it has declined in many other parts of Europe. **Although** the cost of foreign travel has decreased, many people are choosing not to go on holiday abroad. One reason is that people are working longer hours, and may not want to travel long distances when they have free time. **However**, there can be some disadvantages to being a tourist in your own country. **Even though** you have saved money on travel, you are likely to spend more on meals or entertainment. Another disadvantage is the weather. **Despite** a small rise in temperatures, it has been much wetter in the UK in recent years. This **contrasts** with the rest of Europe, which has been much warmer and drier.

3 **Choose the best summary, a or b, of the ideas from text B.**

1 a Tourists are spending more money in the UK but less in the rest of Europe. __
   b Even though tourist spending is low in the UK, it is high in Europe. __
2 a People are not travelling abroad despite lower costs. __
   b People are travelling abroad due to lower costs. __
3 a Although the UK may be a popular destination, the weather is often poor. __
   b Despite the poor weather, the UK is warmer than other holiday destinations. __

Usage note expressing contrast

However can be used at the beginning, in the middle or at the end of a sentence. Note the use of commas:
- *The hotel was modernized.* **However**, *visitor numbers stayed down.*
- *The hotel was modernized. Visitor numbers,* **however**, *stayed down.*
- *The hotel was modernized. Visitor numbers stayed down,* **however**.

Despite is followed by:
- a noun phrase: *It's still a popular destination,* **despite** <u>the bad weather</u>.
- a gerund (-ing) clause: **Despite** <u>having crowded resorts</u>, *it is still a popular tourist destination.*
- the fact that + clause: **Despite** <u>the fact that</u> *many hotels fail to make money, tourism is a growth industry.*

4 **Complete the sentences using words from the box to express contrast. More than one option may be possible.**

   although   despite   even though   however   whereas

1 Local people welcome tourists to the islands, _____ the fact that tourism has changed their traditional ways of life.
2 _____ most of the income leaves the country, there are some economic benefits from tourism.
3 The number of people in work increased last year. _____ , this figure has fallen in the last month.
4 _____ closing many of its branch offices, the bank is still financially successful.
5 More and more people get their news from online sources, _____ newspapers are less popular.

5 **Choose one of the topics below. Write a short paragraph (two or three sentences) about which option you prefer, a or b. Include some reasons and contrasts.**

- Where to live   a In the city   b In the countryside
- Where to study   a At home   b Abroad
- Where to shop   a Online   b In stores

37 Linking 2

Words to learn

after that (*prep*)	at last (*phr*)	initial (*adj*) AWL	in the past (*phr*)
afterwards (*adv*)	at the same time (*phr*)	initially (*adv*) AWL	subsequently (*adv*) AWL
as soon as (*phr*)	by the time (*phr*)	in recent years (*phr*)	whenever (*conj*)
at first (*phr*)	eventually (*adv*) AWL	in the meantime (*phr*)	

Expressing time

A In many parts of the UK, the autumn of 2012 was the wettest since official records began in 1766. Major flooding affected many towns and cities, **eventually** costing the economy £600 million. York, a city with a population of around 200,000, has often been affected by floods **in the past**. However, the flooding has occurred more frequently and more seriously **in recent years**. The Environment Agency has carried out studies to highlight the ways that urban development has affected this process. **At first**, they considered the natural causes. **Initial** reports showed that in the days before the city flooded, a month's rain fell in 24 hours. Soon **after that**, the ground became full of water and could no longer absorb falling rain. **As soon as** this water moved downstream, rivers burst their banks, flooding the surrounding area. However, the study also showed that there were a number of human factors involved **at the same time**. As the population around the city had grown, trees were cleared from slopes, allowing more housing to be built. **Subsequently**, housing estates were built on existing flood plains. This meant that the areas which had been designed specifically to hold flood water now had property on them. **By the time** the water levels increased, these properties were at risk.

Source: Adapted from Waugh, D. & Bushell, T. (2014). *Nelson Key Geography: Foundations.* Cheltenham: Nelson Thornes. pp.38–39.

Usage note *at first*, *firstly* and *first (of all)*

At first is used to talk about the situation at the beginning of a period of time, especially when it is compared to a different situation at a later period:
• *The sales of the smartphones were high **at first**. Now demand has decreased.*
Firstly and **first (of all)** are used to introduce a series of facts, reasons or opinions. They can assist in ordering points in spoken or written work:
• ***Firstly/First of all**, we need to discuss the issue of overspending, **then/next** we will consider interest rate changes.*
Note that when we use phrases to show sequence or series (e.g. **First of all**, **Subsequently**), we use commas immediately afterwards.

1 Choose the best word or phrase to complete the sentences.

1 There have been many changes to the law *in the past / in recent years* which affect the way businesses operate.
2 *At first / As soon as*, the management team was surprised by the results.
3 *As soon as / At the same time* they heard the news, investors began to sell their shares.
4 The company lost its most important customer in 2015 and *eventually / subsequently* went bankrupt.
5 *By the time / At the same time* the figures were published, the company had lost 50% of its value.
6 After months of bad publicity, the company *eventually / afterwards* agreed to pay its tax bill.
7 The *eventual / initial* payment for the house is due at the start of the month.
8 First, you add a small amount of sulphur. *After that / Initially*, you should light the Bunsen burner.

Expressing sequence

B The area near the station was bought by a property investment company which did not have an immediate use for the land, although eventually it would be used for housing. **In the meantime,** the company **initially** allowed walkers access to the land. This agreement would end **whenever** the building project began. However, the company soon reported that people were on the site without permission, and **afterwards** placed large fences around the area. Local residents protested, and **at last** sought legal advice.

2 Choose the best summary of the issues discussed in text B, an extract from a student essay.

a A company bought the land, which they let local residents use. When they started building they tried to stop local residents using the land. The residents asked lawyers to help them. __

b A company bought the land, and refused to let residents use it. They built fences to keep them off. Residents protested, and the company contacted the police. __

3 Complete the sentences using words and phrases from the box.

> at last   in the meantime   initially   whenever

1 I note down the source of an idea _____ I use one in my writing.
2 It was _____ thought that there were no more mammals to be discovered in the rainforests.
3 They waited for three months, then _____ the exam results arrived.
4 He has applied to study abroad and won't hear if he's been successful for a while. _____ , he's taking a language course.

Usage note *lastly* and *at last*

Lastly is used to introduce the last in a list of things, or the final point you are making:
• *Lastly, I want to discuss the role of private business in national growth.*
At last is used when something happens after a long time, especially when there has been a difficulty or delay:
• *At last, the convoy of aid supplies reached the refugee camp.*
You can also use *finally*, *eventually* or *in the end* with this meaning, but not *lastly*.

---

4 Choose the correct word or phrase to complete the sentences.

1 firstly – at first
  a _____ , the government refused to get involved in the dispute.
  b There are two important factors to consider – _____ climate change and secondly population growth.
2 eventual – eventually
  a The _____ goal of the team was to identify new materials that could function in space.
  b There were a number of problems during the experiment, so we _____ gave up.
3 initial – initially
  a Following the _____ investigation, doctors identified the cause of his pain.
  b The rock formations were _____ created by ice moving through the valley.
4 lastly – at last
  a _____ , after many years of campaigning, women were given the right to vote.
  b _____ , I would like to thank the team at Anglia University for their cooperation in this study.
5 subsequent – subsequently
  a After the surgery, there were _____ improvements in his overall health.
  b She became a member of parliament at the age of 20 and _____ went on to lead her party.

Student writing: hedging

Using hedging language makes your arguments more cautious. This shows that you have thought about other possible arguments before reaching a conclusion. It also helps the reader to see the difference between facts and opinions. If you do not use any hedging language, an academic reader will probably think that your text is not reliable.

> **A** It **appears** that the problems of adjusting to life in a new country **typically** fall into three main categories. Firstly, it is **possible** that there will be language problems, **although** these **tend to** become fewer as language ability improves. Research also **indicates** that many new immigrants have problems adjusting to a new culture. Simple activities such as shopping, visiting the doctor or knowing where to find help are **potentially** very stressful in a new environment. **At first**, new immigrants are also **likely** to have financial concerns, such as paying for accommodation before they start working.

1 Which three types of problem are mentioned by the writer?

1 _____   2 _____   3 _____

Focus on hedging language

2 Choose the correct word to complete each sentence.

1 It *appears / possible* that this new fuel can help to reduce air pollution.
2 Research indicates that this pill can help with heart problems, *although / despite* more research is needed.
3 At first many new students found it difficult to make friends, but this *tended to / typically* improve with time.
4 The building work is *tend / likely* to be delayed owing to poor weather.

3 Make the following sentences more cautious using the words in CAPITALS. You may need to make other changes in the sentences.

1 Air travel is less expensive than ten years ago.
   TENDS _____
2 Women earn less than men.
   TYPICALLY _____
3 This vaccine will change people's lives in the developing world.
   POTENTIALLY _____
4 There is a mistake in that data.
   APPEARS _____
5 The research proves that inflation contributes to poverty.
   INDICATES _____
6 Violent crime will increase if guns are more available.
   LIKELY _____

Student writing: linking your ideas together

The main aim of all writing is to communicate your ideas clearly to your reader. One of the ways that we do this is by making use of linking language to show the reader the relationships between the ideas in a text. These may be cause-effect relationships; time sequences; comparisons or other connections. You should attempt to make these as clear as possible in your writing.

> **B** The Apple computer company was launched in 1976 by Steve Jobs and Stephen Wozniak. **Initially,** they had a third partner, Ronald Wayne, but he dropped out almost **as soon as** the business began. The first Apple computer was produced in 1978 . This was mostly used in schools and businesses, and **by the time** IBM introduced their first personal computer in 1981, Apple already had 1,000 employees. **However,** it was not until 1984 that Apple launched its first real home computer, the Macintosh. **Despite** fierce competition and financial problems, the company continued to introduce new computer products throughout the 1980s and 1990s. **In recent years,** however, Apple has made most of its money from the mobile phone and music markets.

4 Put the following events into the correct chronological (time) order.

1 Introduction of IBM's first personal computer _____
2 Apple has 1,000 employees _____
3 Foundation of the Apple computer company _____
4 Moves into new markets such as mobile phones _____
5 Launch of the Macintosh computer _____
6 The third partner drops out of the business _____
7 Launch of the first Apple computer _____

Focus on linking expressions

5 Choose one of the words or expressions in CAPITALS and link the pairs of sentences to show the relationship between them. Make any other changes necessary.

> ▶ EXAMPLE: She applied to the university three times. The third time she was successful.
> AT LAST/BY THE TIME *She applied to the university three times and at last she was successful.*
> 1 The researchers wanted to continue with the research project. There was not enough money.
>   AS SOON AS/HOWEVER _____
> 2 An earthquake struck the city. Almost immediately, the electricity supply was cut.
>   HOWEVER/AS SOON AS _____
> 3 The company launched the new vaccine. Ten thousand people had already died.
>   DESPITE/BY THE TIME _____
> 4 There was a risk of failure. The team decided to go ahead with the operation.
>   DESPITE/AT LAST _____

Writing task

6 Read the following text and try to improve the style by adding some hedging language to make it more cautious and joining some of the ideas using linking language.

> There are studies of deforestation in the Himalayas. They say that deforestation leads to a number of problems. People cut down trees for agriculture. There are fewer trees and there is less rain. Crops need rain. This is bad for agriculture. Farmers are negatively affected. Local people also use wood to build houses. But now there is deforestation and there is no wood for building.

> ▶ EXAMPLE: *Studies of deforestation in the Himalayas indicate that it can lead to a number of problems ...*

38 Business

Words to learn

business (n)	consumer (n) AWL	firm (n)	job (n) AWL	purchase (v) AWL
career (n)	customer (n)	fund (v) AWL	organization (n)	service (n)
commercial (adj)	employee (n)	guarantee (v) AWL	product (n)	set up (phrasal v)
company (n)	employer (n)	industry (n)	professional (n) AWL	

Business organizations

A Location is very important for a **business** and can have a big effect on a **company's** success. **Employers** have to consider where to place their **organization** to make sure that they can compete with other businesses in the **industry**. They have to think about the costs of **setting up** a business, and also how much it will cost them in the future. **Employees** have higher salaries in some places than others. For example, in the UK, a **firm** will have to pay employees a higher salary in London than for the same **job** outside the capital. **Professionals**, such as teachers, medical staff or lawyers, are paid more to have a **career** in the city instead of studying there and then moving away. Any business that wants to be based in the city needs to have money in place to **fund** this choice.

1 Read text A. Mark the statements true (T) or false (F) according to the text.

1 The location of a business does not affect its success. __
2 Businesses pay their workers the same amount of money in different locations. __
3 Employees in London often earn more than their colleagues. __
4 Lawyers and teachers can be described as professionals. __

Usage note talking about businesses

Business, **company** and **firm** all describe organizations that make money by selling goods or services.
A **company** is a business organization that exists independently of its owners and employees:
• *Walmart is one of the world's largest companies, with shops in most countries.*
Business often refers to a small company that is owned by an individual or a family:
• *The family business has operated since 1985.*
Firm means a company that provides a particular professional service: • *The accountancy firm employs 35 people.*
An **industry** describes all the people and activities involved in producing a particular thing or providing a particular service: *the automobile/manufacturing/chemical industry*

2 Complete the sets of sentences using the correct form of the words provided.

1 employee – employer – professional
   a As more people become self-employed, there is a growth in businesses with just one _____ .
   b Graduate job fairs at universities help _____ find future staff.
   c Employing a marketing _____ helps a business grow as they focus on ways to sell products.
2 job – career
   a She's worked for several different companies throughout her _____ as an accountant.
   b As the economy slowed down, around 25% of graduates could not find a _____ .
3 organization – industry
   a Sales in the car _____ have fallen by more than 10% since 2008.
   b Many international _____ have moved their businesses to areas where staff costs are lower.

Customers and products

> **B** In recent times, **consumer** choice has increased due to the growth of global markets and the internet. Greater access to information on **products** and **services** has given consumers greater choice. It has also given them greater power. A business which wants **commercial** success has to focus on the needs of **customers** and their experiences when they **purchase** goods. They have to be able to **guarantee** quality goods and service. Consequently, marketing has become an industry which has greater importance to modern businesses.
>
> Source: Adapted from *A Dictionary of Marketing*. (3rd ed.). (2011). Oxford: Oxford University Press.

3 Read text B. Do the paraphrases have roughly the same meaning as the original text (S) or do they have a different meaning (D)?

1 '... **consumer** choice has increased due to the growth of global markets and the internet.'
   Globalization and online shopping mean that people can buy things cheaper than before. __

2 'Greater access to information on **products** and **services** has given consumers greater choice.'
   People are in a better position because they can find out more about what they want to buy. __

> **Usage note** *customer* and *consumer*
>
> A *customer* buys a product and a *consumer* uses a product. When a parent buys a toy, they are the *customer*. A child uses the toy, so they are the *consumer*.
>   *customer services/support/care*   *consumer goods/choice/spending*

4 Complete each description with a word from the box.

> consumer   customer   guarantee   product   purchase   service

1 Sony's new smartphone is one of the most popular on the market. It is a bestselling _____ .
2 Sam is eight years old. He wants his parents to buy an Xbox for his next birthday. He is a

   _____ .
3 The Anderson Company offer advice on how to do business in Asia. This is their _____ .
4 He bought the latest game on the day it was released. He's a repeat _____ at the store.
5 The factory buys large amounts of electricity to use when producing goods. They _____ more than their competitors.
6 The company promises to keep prices low. They _____ it.

5 Match the sentence halves.

1 Large websites such as Amazon have increased **consumer**
2 Customers often use the internet to compare **product**
3 By increasing their focus on **customer**
4 Having a good reputation plays an important role in **commercial**
5 The company's promise to its customers **guarantees**

a success, as companies which are trusted tend to have more repeat customers.
b needs, their business became more competitive.
c choice, but have had a negative effect on small businesses.
d information before making an offline purchase.
e quality at low prices.

6 Write a short paragraph (two or three sentences) about one of the following. Try to use some of the words and phrases from the unit.

• Describe a business that has been successful/unsuccessful.   • Describe a business you know well.

39 Economics

Words to learn

borrow (*v*)	economics (*n*) AWL	financial (*adj*) AWL	lend (*v*)	profit (*n*)
currency (*n*) AWL	economy (*n*) AWL	income (*n*) AWL	loan (*n*)	
earn (*v*)	fee (*n*) AWL	invest (*v*) AWL	loss (*n*)	
economic (*adj*) AWL	finance (*n*) AWL	investment (*n*) AWL	owe (*v*)	

The economy

A **Economics** involves the study of how a country organizes its **finance**, trade and industry. A common way to assess the strength of a country's **economy** is by calculating gross domestic product (GDP) per person. GDP is a **financial** term which is defined as 'the total value of all the goods and services produced by a country in one year'. One way to work out GDP is by adding together everyone's **income**. This includes wages and **profits** made from **investments**. To calculate GDP per person, you divide the country's total GDP by its population. A strong GDP generally indicates a good **economic** situation. It usually also means that a country's **currency** will be strong, and as a result, goods from other countries are cheap to buy.

1 Complete the definitions with the correct part of speech – *n* (noun) or *adj* (adjective).

1 **economy** /ɪˈkɒnəmi/ (___) the relationship between production, trade and the supply of money in a country or region
2 **economic** /ˌiːkəˈnɒmɪk/ (___) connected with the trade, industry and development of wealth in a country or region
3 **finance** /ˈfaɪnæns/ (___) the activity of managing money
4 **financial** /faɪˈnænʃl/ (___) connected with money

2 Complete the sentences with the words and phrases from the box.

> currency   economy   finance   financial   income   investment

1 Although many areas were affected by the financial crisis, the _____ here is improving.
2 There are often limits on the amount of foreign _____ you can take into a country.
3 If you have a higher _____ , you normally pay more tax.
4 London has become a global centre for banking and _____ .
5 Over the last few years there has been more _____ in technology companies.
6 _____ services is one of the most important industries in the UK.

3 a Complete the table with the correct form of the words. Use the glossary on pp.127–141.

Noun	Adjective	Verb
1 _____	–	invest
finance	2 _____	finance
economy, economics	3 _____	economize
4 _____	profitable	profit

b Complete the sentences with the correct words. Use the table in exercise 3a to help.

1 Business owners tend to _____ money to make more money.
2 If you want to improve your personal wealth you could take some _____ advice.
3 Analysts predict that China's _____ growth will rapidly decline over the next two decades.
4 Many companies now find online business more _____ than traditional models.

Finance

B People often need to **borrow** money from a bank. They may want to **invest** in a business or to buy a property, but they do not have or **earn** enough money. Banks provide **loans** to make this possible. When someone applies for a loan, the bank looks at their income and decides how much they can afford. If the loan is agreed, the bank **lends** the money and sets an interest rate. The borrower has to repay the original loan and an additional percentage **fee**. This is how the bank makes a profit. If the borrower cannot repay what they **owe**, the bank may make a **loss**.

Usage note *borrow, lend* and *owe*

Borrow means to *take* an item or amount of money from someone and agree to pay it back:
- *Many students borrow money from the government so they can pay university fees.*

Lend means to *give* an item or amount of money to someone but they have to give it back to you:
- *Banks prefer to lend money to companies which have clear business plans.*

Owe means that you have to pay for something that you have already received:
- *Their business owes £1.4 million in unpaid taxes to the authorities.*

Note the use of prepositions with the terms: **borrow** from, **lend** to, **owe** to.

---

4 **Choose the correct word to complete the sentences.**

1 When the economy is performing well, banks usually *borrow / lend / owe* more money to businesses.
2 If you plan to *borrow / lend / owe* large sums of money, you should consider how you will pay it back.
3 A large proportion of the UK population *borrows / lends / owes* money to credit card companies.
4 It is usual to *borrow / lend / owe* money from banks when making a large purchase, such as buying a house.
5 The World Bank can *borrow / lend / owe* money to countries which are trying to build their economy.

5 **Read the text. Complete the sentences using words from the box.**

> earn   income   invest   profits

On average, men ¹_____ more than women in most companies. Many people feel that businesses should reduce the pay gap because they are making large ²_____ from the ideas and efforts of their female employees. Statistics from the USA also show that a woman's ³_____ is likely to be 75% of a man's, even if the woman has similar qualifications. This level rises to around 80% if the woman has a PhD. There is growing support for businesses to ⁴_____ more in female talent to reduce the pay gap and help generate economic growth.

6 **Decide whether each situation describes a profit (P) or a loss (L).**

1 A small business buys cotton T-shirts from Turkey at €3 per item and then sells them to a department store for €4.50 each. Packaging and transporting the T-shirts costs ten cents per item. __
2 A company has a value of $1.5 billion. After making bad investments, it is sold by its owners for $1.2 billion. __
3 A house is bought for £250,000 in 2008, and sold for £240,000 three years later. __
4 A trader buys shares at a price of £1.25. Due to currency changes, the value of the share is £1.30 by the end of the day. __

7 **Write a short paragraph (two or three sentences) about one of the following. Try to use some of the words from the unit.**

- The economy in your country, or a country you know about
- A company which has been financially successful/unsuccessful
- Any differences between the financial position of men and women in your country
- How the global economy has changed in the last few years

40 Technology

Words to learn

application (*n*)	design (*v*) AWL	equipment (*n*) AWL	store (*v*)
automatically (*adv*) AWL	device (*n*) AWL	input (*v*) AWL	system (*n*)
code (*n*) AWL	digital (*adj*)	security (*n*) AWL	technical (*adj*) AWL
data (*n*) AWL	electrical (*adj*)	software (*n*)	technology (*n*) AWL
design (*n*) AWL	electronic (*adj*)	storage (*n*)	

Useful technology

A Ajay Bhatt is an Indian inventor and computer architect who studied in the USA. In 1990, he began working at the **technology** company Intel. At Intel, he **designed** different computer technologies and has become famous for co-inventing USB (Universal Serial Bus) technology. Before its invention, computer **devices** were connected in many different ways, but this could often cause **technical** problems. When computer **systems** had lots of connections, they needed more **software** to get them to communicate. This meant that devices took longer to exchange **data**. The USB invention solved the problem. Nowadays, nearly all **digital** devices use this piece of **equipment**.

Glossary
computer architect (*n*): a person who decides the rules and methods which organize and run computer systems

1 Read text A, an extract from a student's essay. Decide which essay question it answers, a, b or c.

a Write a paragraph about an inventor, discussing their reasons for becoming an inventor. __

b Write a paragraph about an inventor, outlining the technology they invented. __

c Write a paragraph about an invention that has changed the way we live. __

2 Choose the correct word to complete the sentences.

1 The company's system was affected by a virus. It lost lots of important *data / devices*.

2 Having a strong Wi-fi signal means you can be online on several *technologies / devices* at once.

3 There were some problems with the *software / technologies*, but engineers have fixed the bug.

4 Engineers are available to offer *digital / technical* support when needed.

5 Architects used a *data / design* program to help them plan the new buildings.

6 Moodle and other *digital / technical* learning platforms are becoming increasingly popular online tools.

7 Many students chose to study information *technical / technology* following the growth in dotcom businesses.

8 You need a lot of *equipment / system* to set up a home office, and it can be expensive.

9 It took a long time for engineers to install the new telephone *system / technology*.

3 Replace the highlighted words in the sentences with the correct form of words from the box. Make any other changes necessary.

data   design   device   ~~digital~~   software   technical   technology

▶ EXAMPLE: Computer-based ᴅɪɢɪᴛᴀʟ media are becoming more popular as people use the internet for news.

1 The company invented and produced _____ the system used for online banking.

2 Machines and computers are _____ changing the way that children learn.

3 The job required a lot of knowledge about machines _____, so he decided not to apply.

4 The cost of electronic equipment _____ such as smartphones and laptops has decreased rapidly.

5 Antivirus programs _____ can keep computers working efficiently.

6 Researchers used computer models to analyse the information _____ they gathered in their tests.

Encoding and storing data

B When a large amount of data needs to be entered into a computer system, it makes sense to encode it. Encoding means putting the data into a **code** (the program instructions) and reducing its size. There are several key reasons to put data into a code before **storing** it. Firstly, coded data is quicker to **input**. Although there are many systems and **applications** which can enter data **automatically**, it is often still done by hand. Secondly, coded data takes up less **storage** space and can be transferred more quickly over a network. Large amounts of information can then be sent by **electronic** means. There is also greater **security** if data is coded. This is because the information remains protected unless you have knowledge of the code or the passwords. However, data stored in this way is not 100% safe. For example, without a constant **electrical** supply or an online database or cloud, it can be lost.

Source: Adapted from Doyle, S. (2010). *Essential ICT GCSE.* Oxford: Oxford University Press. pp.2–3.

4 Read text B. Choose the reasons mentioned by the writer for encoding information.

a It reduces the size of data. __

b It speeds up the process of entering data. __

c It is cheaper to store. __

d It is more secure than other forms of data storage. __

5 Choose the best option to complete the sentences. Use the glossary on pp.127–141 to help you.

1 The software has *automatic / automatically* updates to make sure that it runs without problems.

2 There are a number of useful vocabulary recording *appliances / applications* available on the internet.

3 There is enough memory on the smartphone to *store / storage* over 5,000 images.

4 While studying computing at university, he learned to use several different *codes / coding* languages

5 It took programmers hours to *input / secure* the data. They had to type it in by hand.

6 Match the processes, 1–4, with the word that best describes them, a or b. Use the glossary on pp.127–141 to help you.

1 The information is recorded and put on a sound file so it can be emailed as an attachment.

    a digital __   b electrical __

2 A signal is sent from the power source to the router.

    a digital __   b electrical __

3 When the components reach a temperature of 70°C, they switch off.

    a automatic __   b electrical __

4 Employees at the call centre can offer advice on fixing errors in the software.

    a digital __   b technical __

7 Read the extract from a student essay. Complete it using words from the box.

> applications data design device electronic security store

'Product design' refers to part of the [1]_____ process where the focus is on the style, look and feel of an object or component rather than the engineering principles. When engineers are making a new [2]_____ , for example a laptop or smartphone, they have to consider how it will work with the user. As more day-to-day activity (such as banking and communications) uses [3]_____ methods, new products need to be designed in a way that makes them user-friendly and accessible. Size is an important factor. Many new [4]_____ need a lot of memory to [5]_____ all the [6]_____ they use, but this should not mean that objects become larger. It is also important to consider additional [7]_____ features, too – the device can be protected internally with software, but designers also have to think about what happens if it is dropped.

Words to learn

conservation (*n*)
conserve (*v*)
energy (*n*) **AWL**
environment (*n*) **AWL**
environmental (*adj*) **AWL**

habitat (*n*)
natural (*adj*)
pollution (*n*)
protect (*v*)
protection (*n*)

recycle (*v*)
recycling (*n*)
renewable (*adj*)
renewables (*n*)
resource (*n*) **AWL**

species (*n*)
waste (*adj*)
waste (*n*)
wild (*adj*)

Environmental protection

A Governments can help to **protect** the **environment** by using more **renewables**. These are types of **energy** from sources that will not end. Examples of **renewable** energy sources include moving water (hydroelectric power, tidal power and wave power), solar energy and wind energy. This energy supply contrasts with commonly used **resources** such as fossil fuels (coal, oil and gas), which will eventually run out. Burning fossil fuels creates high levels of **pollution**.

Individuals can also protect the environment by trying to reuse and **recycle** as much as possible. The **recycling of waste** materials means that they can be used again. For

example, **waste** such as used plastic bottles can be made into fibres for clothing. Although it is important to recycle, the process still causes some level of pollution because it involves collection, sorting and processing before the waste is used in the production of new products.

Glossary
hydroelectric (*adj*): referring to power generated by falling or flowing water
solar (*adj*): of or connected to the sun
tidal (*adj*): connected with the rise and fall in the level of the sea

1 Read text A. Mark the statements true (T) or false (F) according to the text.

1 Governments should use water, solar and wind energy to keep the environment clean. __
2 Popular sources of energy cause a lot of pollution. __
3 There is nothing that people can do to help improve the environment. __
4 It is important to reuse and recycle products. __
5 Recycling has no negative effects on the environment. __

Usage note *resource* and *source*

Pay special attention to the difference in meaning when talking about something which can be used as a supply.

source **AWL** /sɔːs/ *noun* **1** a place, thing or person you get something from: *Their main source of heat was an open fire.*
resource **AWL** /rɪˈzɔːs/ *noun* **1** [C, usually pl.] a supply of something that a country, an organization or a person has and can use: *Japan has few natural resources and has to import raw materials.*

2 Choose the correct word to complete the sentences.

1 A small well is the village's only *source / resource* of clean drinking water.
2 As the population grows, it is using more of the Earth's *sources / resources*.
3 The university library is an important shared *source / resource* that benefits all students.
4 It is important to find an alternative energy *source / resource* as oil fields become less productive.

3 Complete the text using the correct form of the highlighted words in text A.

The government has recently announced a number of policies to protect the ¹_____ . They hope to cut ²_____ levels by reducing the amount of fossil fuels burned to make ³_____ . By moving towards using ⁴_____ energy such as wind and wave power, we will use fewer ⁵_____ and develop new industries. There are also plans to extend ⁶_____ programmes so that households can be involved in reducing ⁷_____ .

Why manage our world?

B Conservation is the term used to describe the **protection** and management of **natural** resources and the environment to ensure their long-term survival. Conservation recognizes that communities of plants and animals often change, but it involves managing the environment so that **habitats** and **species** are not affected by events that are not natural. An example of this is when conservation organizations move species to more suitable areas when a new road is built, etc.

There are many arguments in favour of conservation:
- moral – all species have a right to live
- aesthetic – **wild** habitats are attractive
- economic – plant and animal resources provide material for human life. If we **conserve** healthy species we can improve farm production and forestry, etc.
- environmental – most importantly, natural wildlife is essential to the **environmental** systems which all life on Earth depends on.

Source: Adapted from Park, C. (2007). 'conservation.' *A Dictionary of Environment and Conservation.* Oxford: Oxford University Press.

Glossary
aesthetic (*adj*): concerned with beauty and art
forestry (*n*): the science and practice of planting and taking care of trees
moral (*adj*): concerned with ideas of right and wrong behaviour

4 Read text B and answer the questions.

1 What does conservation help to do? _____
2 What kind of change does conservation try to stop? _____

5 Match the sentence halves to make common collocations.

1 A large number of animals can be found in **wild**
2 Attempts to **conserve**
3 The Amazonian rainforest is one of the most important **environmental**
4 Many **natural**
5 The national parks are protected by **conservation**

a **systems** on the planet.
b **species** like the African wild dog have been affected by overhunting and disease.
c **habitats** that are threatened by development.
d **organizations** who study any environmental change.
e **resources** are becoming harder to find and this is making them more expensive.

6 Choose the correct word to complete the sentences.

1 The Cairngorm mountains are considered an area of *nature / natural* beauty.
2 Attempts are being made to *conserve / conservation* a number of at-risk bird species.
3 Many companies are trying to increase their use of *renew / renewable* energy while reducing costs.
4 Increasing levels of *pollution / polluter* have affected the air quality.
5 A decline in natural habitats has meant that more animal species need *protect / protection*.

Words to learn

community (n) AWL
cultural (adj) AWL
culture (n) AWL

custom (n)
lifestyle (n)
security (n) AWL

social (adj)
society (n)
tradition (n) AWL

traditional (adj) AWL
welfare (n) AWL

What is culture?

A In **social** science, **culture** is a general term for aspects of the human experience that are learned, and the way that people behave together. These patterns of behaviour are shown by the shared knowledge, beliefs, art, morals, laws and **customs** of a group.

Many modern ideas of culture come from the work of researchers and anthropologists working with different groups and **communities**. These academics view culture as relative. This means that they describe, compare and contrast **lifestyles** and beliefs, rather than ranking them in terms of importance. This view of culture also looks at how **traditional** ideas and practices are shared by cultures as they meet and mix – a concept known as **cultural** transmission.

Source: Adapted from Scott, J. (2014). *A Dictionary of Sociology*. (4th ed.). Oxford: Oxford University Press.

Glossary
anthropologist (n): a person who studies the human race and its origins and customs
transmission (n): the act of passing something from one person to another

1 Do the paraphrases have a similar meaning (S) to the original text or a different meaning (D)?

1 'In social science, **culture** is a general term describing aspects of the human experience that are learned, and the way that people behave together.'
Social scientists define culture as a way of describing what people know and how they relate to each other. __

2 '... patterns of behaviour are shown by the shared knowledge, beliefs, art, morals, laws and **customs** of a group.'
The things that people know, believe and agree on form behaviour patterns. __

3 'These academics view culture as relative. This means that they describe, compare and contrast **lifestyles** and beliefs, rather than ranking them in terms of importance.'
Cultural relativism is when academics decide which culture is the most important in relation to another. __

4 'This view of culture also looks at how **traditional** ideas and practices are shared by cultures as they meet and mix – a concept known as **cultural** transmission.'
Cultural transmission describes the way that ideas and customs move between cultures. __

2 Choose the best word to complete the sentences.

1 In many *cultures / cultural*, the oldest son in a family is seen as the most important child.
2 A number of small *cultures / communities* living in the Amazon have little contact with the outside world.
3 As the use of technology grows, *traditional / cultural* approaches to teaching languages are changing.
4 Earning more money helped the family to change their *behaviour / lifestyle*.
5 Travellers should always try to learn some of the local *customs / traditions* so that they don't make mistakes when meeting people.
6 Social and *cultural / traditional* influences can affect the way students study.

Helping society?

B In times of financial difficulty, members of **society** often need more support from the state. This support may be through medical care, education, housing or other benefits. In addition, many people are given payments from the government to help them with living costs. In this essay, I will argue that such **welfare** has a negative impact on economic growth and makes people too dependent upon the help of others. I will show that the **tradition** of relying upon the government to provide **security** has led to an economic slowdown.

3 Read text B, the introduction to a student's essay. Does the writer think that 'welfare' is positive or negative?

4 Read text B again. Which is the most suitable conclusion, a or b?

a In conclusion, people need state support in times of financial difficulty to help them feel more secure. Although this tradition costs the government money, increased security means that people will still spend, helping the economy to grow. __

b In conclusion, when people rely too much on the government for welfare payments or social security, they are less likely to actively look for a job that will improve their lifestyle. This means that their earnings will not increase, and they will not pay taxes to help the economy grow. Therefore, the tradition of state support negatively affects progress. __

5 Complete the definitions using words from the box.

security   society   tradition   welfare

1 _____ (n): a belief or way of doing something which has existed for a long time
2 _____ (n): protection against something bad happening in the future
3 _____ (n): practical or financial help provided by a government
4 _____ (n): people in general, living together and sharing customs, laws, etc.

6 Choose the correct words to complete the pairs of sentences. Use the glossary on pp.127–141 to help you.

1 social – society
   a The government has increased funding to deal with the _____ problems facing inner-city areas.
   b One of the biggest challenges for _____ is the impact of climate change on how we live.

2 culture – cultural
   a Foreign students often find _____ differences as challenging as their academic work.
   b Many people think that increased internet use has changed our _____ for the worse.

3 traditional – tradition
   a There is a strong _____ of supporting new families in Scandinavian countries.
   b She wore a _____ dress to work today. They make them in her home village.

4 secure – security
   a In general, children need a stable and _____ family environment to achieve.
   b Lack of government funding has threatened the _____ of many public services.

7 Write a short paragraph (two or three sentences) about one of the following. Try to use some of the words from the unit.

- Compare two cultures you know about.
- How has your culture changed in recent years?
- Describe a social problem and discuss how to solve it.

43 Medicine

Words to learn

disease (n)	infection (n)	mental (adj) AWL	treatment (n)
health (n)	injury (n) AWL	physical (adj) AWL	virus (n)
health care (n)	medical (adj) AWL	symptom (n)	
healthy (adj)	medicine (n)	treat (v)	

Diet, exercise and health

A To stay in good **health**, people need to understand how their body works and how their behaviour affects it. A **healthy** diet and regular **physical** activity help the body to function properly. They improve the immune system, which protects the body against **diseases**. This means that people are able to fight off **viruses** or **infections**. There is also evidence that people who eat well and exercise regularly have better **mental** health. However, in some cases, too much exercise is bad for the body and can lead to long-term **injury**.

Glossary
immune system (n):
the organs and processes in the body that help it to fight against infection and disease

Usage note describing ill health

- An **infection** is an illness caused by bacteria or a virus that usually affects one part of the body.
- A **disease** is an illness often caused by an infection.
- A **virus** is a living organism that causes infectious diseases in people or animals.
- An **injury** describes harm done to a person's body, for example in an accident.

1 a Read text A. Mark the statements true (T) or false (F) according to the texts.

1 The immune system can be improved by eating the right kind of food and taking part in sports. __
2 A good diet and active lifestyle make people feel better in body and mind. __
3 Increasing physical activity does not make a difference to a person's health. __
4 Too much exercise can be physically harmful. __

2 Complete the sentences using words from the box.

disease   health   healthy   infection   injury   mental   physical   virus

1 By changing their diets and exercising more frequently, the patients improved their _____ .
2 He seems to be very stressed. We're worried about his _____ health.
3 Heart _____ is one of the most common causes of death in the UK.
4 After running a marathon she was suffering from _____ exhaustion.
5 If a patient appears _____ but still complains of pain, doctors might take further tests.
6 When people suffer a head _____ , for example after falling, they should be examined for signs of brain damage.
7 Breathing problems in the very old and very young can often be caused by a chest _____ .
8 Medical teams were sent to Western Africa to stop the spread of the Ebola _____ .

3 Match the sentence halves to make collocations.

1 He wore a monitor to measure his **physical**
2 Stress is a leading cause of **mental**
3 Exercise and a balanced diet are indicators of **good**
4 Taking vitamins can help **fight off**
5 Brushing teeth regularly **protects against**
6 A balanced, **healthy**
7 She suffered from a **long-term**

a **viruses** and **infections** during winter.
b **health** in patients.
c **injury** which affected her movement.
d **diet** is low in fat and avoids too much salt.
e **health** problems in young adults.
f gum **disease** or other dental problems.
g **activity** throughout the day.

Stopping the spread of diseases

B **Medical** research has shown that pathogens – microorganisms that can cause infectious disease – are often found on the surface of our skin. In the past, **health care** staff didn't understand this and didn't wash their hands regularly; as a result, hospital patients often acquired infection.

Modern hospitals have strict hygiene rules, so that people receiving **treatment** are not at risk of infection. However, advances in **medicine** have not completely stopped the spread of diseases. Some harmful bacteria, previously killed by antibiotics, have become resistant to the drugs. This means that the infections which people get in hospital are now more difficult to **treat** and that people's **symptoms** can be much more serious.

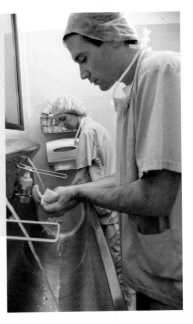

Glossary
antibiotics (*n, pl*): a substance that can destroy or prevent the growth of bacteria and cure infections
bacteria (*n*): the simplest and smallest forms of life, often a cause of disease
hygiene (*n*): the practice of keeping a place or person clean to prevent illness and disease
microorganism (*n*): a very small living thing
resistant (*adj*): not affected by a drug or medicine

4 Choose the correct words to complete the definitions.

1 *Health care / A symptom* is the service that provides medical care in a country.
2 *Medicine / Treatment* is the study of diseases and injuries.
3 *Health care / Treatment* is something that is done to try to cure an illness or injury.
4 *A symptom / treatment* is a change in your body or mind that shows you are not well.

5 a Complete the sentences with the correct words. Use the glossary on pp.127–141 to help you.

1 **treatment – treat – treating**
   a Doctors use a combination of drugs to _____ serious illnesses.
   b After six months of _____ , she left hospital.
2 **medically – medical – medicine**
   a He needed urgent _____ attention after he was hit by a car.
   b A lot of research in modern _____ is focused on creating new antibiotics.
3 **health care – healthy – health**
   a An indicator of good _____ is how quickly a person's pulse slows after exercise.
   b People who have a _____ lifestyle are statistically likely to live longer.
4 **symptom – symptoms – symptomatic**
   a Early _____ of disease are sometimes ignored by the public.
   b A headache is a common _____ of lack of water.

b Identify the part of speech (noun, verb or adjective) of the keyword in each sentence in 5a.

1 a __   2 a __   3 a __   4 a __
  b __   b __   b __   b __

44 Law

Words to learn

commit (v) AWL   guilty (adj)   jury (n)   punish (v)   witness (n)
court (n)   illegal (adj) AWL   law (n)   punishment (n)
crime (n)   innocent (adj)   lawyer (n)   sentence (n)
criminal (adj)   judge (n)   legal (adj) AWL   trial (n)

Types of law

A The British **legal** system is divided into two types of **law** to cover different situations – public and private law. Public law is defined as laws that affect the whole of society at any one time, for example **criminal** law. Private law (also known as civil law) affects individuals and businesses. Examples of this could be where people working in a company have a dispute, or when a married couple are considering divorce.

The main purpose of criminal law is to stop, and **punish**, certain types of behaviour that can cause physical danger or distress to others. Criminal law ensures that we have a civilized society, **illegal** activity is reduced, and the population as a whole feels safe. If a person **commits** a **crime**, then the legal system allows them to be punished.

Glossary
civil (adj): connected with people, involving personal matters
civilized (adj): well organized, with good laws that are fair
distress (adj): a feeling of great worry or unhappiness

B British legal system:

- Public law (including criminal law) – affects whole society. Should stop/punish dangerous + illegal behaviour; ensure civilized society.
- Private law (= civil law) – affects individuals/ business, e.g. disagreement re. work/divorce.

C British legal system:

- Public law (= criminal law) – affects whole society. Stops illegal behaviour. Makes people safe.
- Private law (= civil law) – focus on business, e.g. disagreements.

1 Read the extract from a law textbook, text A, and the student notes, texts B and C. Choose the most accurate student notes, B or C.

2 Read text A again. Which situations refer to criminal law (A) and which refer to civil law (B)?

1 Jane and Peter Hammond have been married for 20 years. Since their children left home they have had many disagreements about money, and now live apart. Jane wants to marry someone else. __
2 A young man has been recorded by speed cameras driving at 95 miles per hour on a road where the limit is 70 miles per hour. __
3 Clare Johnson has been caught taking money from the shop where she works. __
4 McPherson and Sons completed building work for a large company last year. They still have not been paid. The company is refusing to discuss the matter. __

3 Choose the correct words to complete the sentences.

1 When entering a business agreement, it is important to know your *law / legal* rights

2 There has been an increase in *crime / criminal* activity across European borders.

3 It is estimated that the sale of *criminal / illegal* drugs accounts for nearly 1% of global trade.

4 Psychologists think you can change a child's attitude by ignoring, rather than *committing / punishing*, bad behaviour.

5 The government passed a series of *laws / crimes* relating to working conditions in factories.

6 Violent *crime / law* rates have steadily been declining since 2008.

7 Research suggests that minority groups are less likely to *commit / punish* crimes than other members of society.

A criminal trial

D In English law, a **jury** comprises of twelve randomly selected people who decide the facts of a case and give a **verdict**. In a criminal **trial**, the jury are directed by a **judge** on points of law. The judge also summarizes the evidence presented by **lawyers** to the **court**. He or she can draw attention to statements made by key **witnesses** (people who have seen the criminal activity), but must leave the jury to decide all questions of fact for themselves. If the jury are sure that the defendant is '**guilty** beyond all reasonable doubt', then the judge will often give a **sentence** of time in prison. However, if the person is judged to be **innocent**, then they will be found 'not guilty' and allowed to go free.

Source: Adapted from Law, J. (2015). 'jury.' *A Dictionary of Law*. (8th ed.). Oxford: Oxford University Press.

Glossary
defendant (*n*): the person in a trial who is accused of committing a crime
randomly (*adv*): done or chosen without deciding in advance, or without a regular pattern
verdict (*n*): a decision made in court which says if somebody is guilty or not

4 Complete the definitions using words from the box.

| jury | guilty | court | lawyer | sentence | trial |

1 _____ (*adj*): having done something illegal

2 _____ (*n*): a person who is trained and qualified to advise people about the law, and to represent them

3 _____ (*n*): a formal explanation of evidence to decide if somebody who is accused of a crime is guilty or not

4 _____ (*n*): the place where legal cases are judged

5 _____ (*n*): a group of people who listen to the facts of a case and decide whether someone is guilty or not

6 _____ (*n*): the punishment given by a court

5 Choose the correct word to complete the sentences.

1 After she was found *guilty / not guilty*, she was allowed to return to her normal life.

2 Towards the end of the trial, the *judge / jury* reminded everyone that this was a serious crime.

3 The *court / trial* lasted for several months, and was often discussed in the press.

4 *Judges / Lawyers* representing Mr Barolo asked if they could have more time to prepare for the trial.

5 Several *juries / witnesses* were called to say what they had seen during the robbery.

6 The *judge / jury* could not come to an agreement on a final verdict.

7 Companies who ignore the tax laws are often taken to *court / trial*.

8 He was found *innocent / guilty* and went to prison for 15 years.

9 When the judge read out the *sentence / witness*, everyone was shocked.

10 People thought that he was *innocent / guilty* because there was no evidence that he had done wrong.

Words to learn

authority (*n*) AWL   election (*n*)   policy (*n*) AWL   politics (*n*)   vote (*n*)
campaign (*n*)   government (*n*)   political (*adj*)   power (*n*)   vote (*v*)
democracy (*n*)   ministry (*n*) AWL   politician (*n*)   scheme (*n*) AWL   voter (*n*)

What is politics?

A Within every society people have different ideas, goals and demands. The **political** process is one way of ensuring that arguments over these differences are resolved without harming society. **Politics** examines the way that **power** is divided between individuals and the state, and the different institutions that make up the state, for example the **ministries** which control health care, education and the armed services.

Democracy, which means 'people power', is one way of giving the population some control over the **government**. When the public **votes** for a particular party which goes on to form a government, they give them the **authority** to use their power to make decisions which should benefit society as a whole. Another form of control is exercised through a referendum, when the public are asked to cast **votes** on an issue to give direct input into the **policies** that shape their lives. By discussing these policies, the general public feels more engaged with the political process and more open to discussing political opinions. The greater the levels of interest, the more likely these people will be active **voters**.

Glossary
referendum (*n*): an occasion when all the people of a country can vote on important issues
state (*n*): the government of a country

1 Read text A. Mark the statements true (T) or false (F) according to the text.

1 The political process is a way of avoiding situations which could damage society. __
2 Politics just focuses on the power of the state. __
3 In a democracy, people can have some control over government. __
4 A democratic government should make decisions which benefit small parts of society. __
5 Sometimes voters are asked to give their opinions on important matters. __

2 Choose the correct words to complete the sentences. Use the glossary on pp.127–141 to help you.

1 His first job in the *Ministry* / *Minister* of Health was to review hospital spending.
2 Many political scientists agree that economic stability is the first step in creating a *democracy* / *democratic*.
3 *Governing* / *Government* spending is set to increase over the next five years.
4 Following a long debate, ministers *authority* / *authorized* changes to the current report.
5 The *votes* / *voters* were counted electronically to ensure there were no errors in the process.
6 Questions were asked about the *political* / *politics* influence of big business.
7 The votes were shared so no one party held all the *policies* / *power* in government.
8 A series of new *politics* / *policies* has been put forward to control climate change.

3 Complete the quotations with the correct words. Use the glossary on pp.127–141 to help you.

1 '*Democracy* / *Power* must be built through open societies that share information … When there is debate there are solutions. When there is no sharing of *democracy* / *power*, no rule of law, no accountability, there is corruption.' (Atifete Jahjaga, Kosovan politician)
2 'One of the penalties for refusing to participate in *governed* / *politics* is that you end up being *governed* / *politics* by your inferiors.' (Plato, Greek philosopher and mathematician)
3 'Here is my first principle of foreign *policy* / *government*: a good *policy* / *government* at home.' (William Gladstone, four times British prime minister)

Compulsory voting

B In some countries, people are required by law to vote during an **election**. This is known as 'compulsory voting'. The **scheme**, which is used in Australia and Belgium, has been studied by political scientists who are keen to determine its effect on voter choice and election results. In recent years, the main effect has been that liberal **politicians** tend to get greater support than they would if the choice to vote was free. These politicians are usually popular during **campaigns**, but their supporters are less motivated to vote when the election is held.

Another effect is that uninterested voters tend to vote for the first name on the list presented to them ...

Source: Adapted from McLean, I. & McMillan, A. (2009). 'compulsory voting.' *The Concise Oxford Dictionary of Politics*. (3rd ed.). Oxford: Oxford University Press.

Glossary
compulsory (*adj*): that must be done because of a rule or law
liberal (*adj*): wanting a lot of political and economic freedom and supporting gradual social change

4 Read text B. Choose the best sentence to complete the second paragraph.

a To address this, politicians agreed to place names on ballot papers in a random order, ensuring that the results of voting were more accurate. __
b To address this, voters were told which politician to vote for, ensuring that the results were shared between political parties. __

5 Complete the sentences using words from the box.

campaigns   election   politicians   scheme

1 Critics suggested that once the party were in government they would break the promises they made before the _____ .
2 In the US, large businesses contribute to political _____ .
3 The project has been supported by a number of influential _____ and members of the current government.
4 The government proposed a new _____ to deal with the issue of graduates leaving the country to work abroad.

6 Match the sentence halves to make collocations.

1 After winning the election, the party was **given**
2 Although we agree on a lot, our **political**
3 In the referendum, 16-year-olds were allowed to **cast**
4 Ministers met to **discuss**
5 There was a decision to **hold**
6 A fair government should use

a **policies** for the next term in power.
b **votes** for the first time.
c **authority** to form a government.
d the **election** the following year.
e **opinions** are quite different.
f its **power** to bring about greater equality.

7 Write a short paragraph (two or three sentences) about one of the following. Try to use some of the words from the unit.

- How the political system works in your country
- A well-known politician and their achievements
- Whether young people are interested in politics, and why/why not

Student writing: arguments and counter-arguments

When writing an argument, it is important to show that you have considered arguments on both sides of a question. This can make your argument stronger, because it allows you to deal with possible criticisms that people might make.

A Recycling policy in the UK is set partly at a national level and partly by local **government**. The EU has also introduced a number of **laws** and targets to encourage people to use more **renewable resources** and reduce **waste**. All local councils in the UK have **designed** their own recycling **schemes**, with most organizing the collection of paper, glass, cans and plastics from people's homes. As a result, according to DEFRA, there was a 235% increase in household recycling between 2000/01 and 2009/10. However, the **financial investment** needed for improving recycling facilities is considerable, and in some places, the number of collections has been reduced in order to meet some of these costs. The number of containers needed for recycling in some places has also been criticized. Some councils have introduced up to seven bins, which can be confusing to residents and difficult to store.

---

1 Read text A. What are the two possible problems with recycling?

Focus on collocation

2 Match the following verbs and nouns from the text.

1	introduce	a	waste
2	reduce	b	a scheme
3	designed	c	a law
4	use	d	resources

3 Complete the sentences using an appropriate form of the verb + noun combinations from exercise 2.

1 The government has _____ _____ which makes it illegal for businesses to pollute the environment.
2 This new _____ was _____ by a local charity to encourage people to conserve energy.
3 We cannot continue to _____ the world's _____ at the current rate or they will run out.
4 The company is trying to find ways of _____ _____ by using less packaging.

Student writing: summarizing and paraphrasing

In academic writing, you will often need to summarize ideas from your reading. If you summarize rather than quoting directly, you can show that you have understood the ideas clearly. You should make sure that you use your own words when summarizing.

B A recent report suggests that the government needs to focus on **mental health** problems in our **communities**. The causes of mental illness vary, and include both biological and **environmental** factors, but stressful modern **lifestyles** are also contributing to a rise in the number of patients showing **symptoms** of mental illness. The researchers claim that **politicians** and **health care** professionals need to give mental health the same attention that they give to **physical** health, so that effective **treatment** can be provided.

---

4 According to the text, which of the following can cause mental health problems? Tick any that apply.

a biological factors __

b modern lifestyles __

c financial factors __

d environmental factors __

Focus on word families

5 Complete the following word families.

Noun	Verb	Adjective	Adverb
health	-	1 _____	2 _____
3 _____	-	environmental	4 _____
-	-	physical	5 _____
treatment	6 _____	-	-
-	-	mental	7 _____

6 Complete the pairs of sentences using one of the words shown.

1 treating – treatment

   a Doctors are _____ people with the virus in special centres.

   b There is no known _____ for this disease.

2 environmentally – environment

   a The company is trying to develop more _____ friendly packaging.

   b Protection of the _____ is one of this government's main priorities.

3 physical – physically

   a The club provides facilities so that _____ disabled children can take part in sports.

   b This disease is difficult to identify as there are few _____ symptoms.

4 healthy – healthily

   a Modern society needs to find ways for people to live more _____ .

   b _____ meals are provided in the canteen every day.

5 mental – mentally

   a It is important for employers to protect their employees' _____ health.

   b The research questionnaire is too _____ challenging for children to complete.

Writing task

7 Write a few sentences describing possible arguments *against* one or more of the following statements.

- Children need to learn about new technology, so they should have free access to electronic devices such as mobile phones and computers.
- The most effective way to punish criminals is by sending them to prison.
- Conservation of endangered species is a waste of time.

Language reference

Nouns

Countable and uncountable nouns

Nouns can be countable, uncountable or both. Most nouns are countable, but some nouns refer to things that typically cannot be counted and so they do not usually have a plural form. These are known as **uncountable nouns**. Examples in this book include: *knowledge, pollution, research*. Uncountable nouns can't be used with *a* or *an*.

Academic English often includes many **abstract nouns.** These are words like *knowledge, happiness, security*, which refer to an idea, a quality or a state. Abstract nouns are usually uncountable.

Some nouns can be uncountable or countable, depending on the meaning or context.
For example:

Business was good last year. (= uncountable)
This refers to the activity of buying and selling in general.

Businesses in the city suffered during the economic crisis. (= countable)

This refers to individual companies.
Remember to use *much* and *less* with uncountable nouns, and *many* and *few* with countable nouns:

*How **much research** have you done for the project?*

*How **many words** have you written for the assignment?*

*There is **less employment** in this sector now.*

***Fewer people** are employed in this sector than in the past.*

Noun phrases

Noun phrases are very common in academic writing. A noun phrase can be a single noun, or it can be a noun combined with words which give more information about the main noun.

All of the following are noun phrases (main noun = **company**):

*The **companies** ...* (= article + **noun**)

*A computer **company** ...* (= article + noun + **noun**)

*A Californian computer **company** ...* (= article + adjective + noun + **noun**)

*A Californian computer **company** with offices in San Francisco ...* (= article + adjective + noun + **noun** + prepositional phrase)

*The Californian computer **company** that he works for ...* (= article + adjective + noun + **noun** + relative clause)

Notice that the information in a noun phrase can come before and after the main noun. Adjectives are most commonly used before a noun: *economic growth, a computer company, a high percentage*.

Formal written English uses more noun phrases than informal English. Compare the highlighted words below. The use of a noun phrase gives the first sentence a more academic style.

*The council is considering **less frequent refuse collection**.*

*The council is considering **collecting refuse less frequently**.*

We often use noun + noun combinations to talk about academic study and academic departments:

a(n) law / science / university / undergraduate student

the history / geography / engineering department (or the department of history / geography / engineering)

a(n) law / science / university / undergraduate degree

But, we use the adjective *medical*: *a medical student / degree* (NOT ~~a medicine student / degree~~)

When you are writing in academic English, try to think about changing verb clauses into noun phrases. Use the word families in the glossary on pp.127–141 to help you do this.

Irregular plurals

Some nouns in English have an irregular plural form. The following list includes some useful irregular plurals for academic English.

Singular -on, -um	Plural -a
datum*	data
phenomenon	phenomena
Singular -is	**Plural -es**
analysis	analyses
crisis	crises
emphasis	emphases
thesis	theses
Singular -ex	**Plural –ices, -es**
index	indices, indexes**
Singular -a	**Plural -ae**
formula	formulae
Singular -f, -fe	**Plural -ves**
half	halves
life	lives
wife	wives
Singular and plural forms are the same	
contents	contents
news	news
series	series
species	species
Others	
child	children
foot	feet
man	men
person	people
woman	women

* the singular form is rare – the plural form is usually used

** *indexes* is more commonly used

Verbs

Tenses in academic writing

In academic English, certain tenses are much more common than others. The most useful by far is the **present simple**. This is because academic writing often describes a situation or discusses opinions. You can use the present simple:

- to describe the situation in your introduction: *This paper **looks at** …*
- to make generalizations about findings, research, etc.: *The evidence **suggests** that …*
- when citing other writers' work: *Macdonald (2007) **argues** that …*

When you are describing the methods or results of a study, the **past simple** may be useful. This tense is also common when you refer back to these results (for example in a conclusion): *Respondents **were asked** a number of questions …*; *Our findings **suggested** that …*

You may also use the past simple to refer to the specific findings of a piece of research: *Smith (2014) **showed** that …*

The **present perfect simple** can be useful in literature reviews, when you want to show why previous work is relevant to what you are writing about now. This is because the tense links the past with the present. Often, the subjects of sentences in the present perfect are general in academic English: *Several studies **have found** that …*; *There **has been** a great deal of research on this subject …*

The future with *will* or *going to* is not common in academic writing. When writing about the future in academic English, modal verbs such as *may*, *might* and *could* are frequently used, in order to show caution. (See 'Hedging' on page 110.)

Transitive and intransitive verbs

The basic sentence in English usually takes the form **subject** + **verb** + **object**:

He studies engineering.
The research found a problem.

The verb *to be* uses a different pattern:

subject + *be* + noun: *She is a doctor.*
subject + *be* + adjective: *The course is interesting.*

Remember that some verbs (transitive verbs) are followed by an object:

The website provides some useful advice. (*provide* = transitive verb; *advice* = object)

But other verbs (intransitive verbs) are not followed by an object:

Wage costs are rising in certain areas. (*rise* = intransitive verb, so there is no object)

Some verbs can be both transitive and intransitive, depending on the context:

She manages an IT company in London. (= transitive)

The experiment wasn't difficult, so he was able to manage without any help. (= intransitive)

The passive voice

The passive is used more frequently in academic English than in general English. Compare these two sentences:

People reported the first case of the disease in Guinea.

The first case of the disease was reported in Guinea.

We don't know who the people in the first sentence are (doctors? local people? patients?). In academic English, it is better to avoid using general words like 'people' or 'they' as the subject of the sentence. The passive is used instead. So, the object in the first sentence ('the first case of the disease') becomes the subject of the passive verb in the second sentence. In this case, it doesn't matter who reported the first case; the focus is on the disease.

The passive is formed by a form of the verb *be* + past participle: e.g. *it was reported*; *it is known*.

Note that intransitive verbs do not have objects, so they cannot be used in the passive voice:

Costs have risen. (NOT ~~Costs have been risen.~~)

Verb patterns

Some verbs can be followed by an *-ing* form; others can be followed by an infinitive with *to*. Note that some verbs appear in more than one group.

Verb + *-ing* form

admit	delay	insist on	recommend
avoid	deny	involve	risk
consider	discuss	postpone	suggest

They **admitted copying** the data.

The project **involves studying** elephant behaviour.

He **risks losing** his place on the course if he fails the exam.

Verb + infinitive with *to*

agree	decide	learn	plan
appear	expect	manage	promise
arrange	fail	need	refuse
claim	hope	offer	seem

New research **claims to show** a link between the drug and cancer.

The university **expects to publish** the book next year.

The chimpanzees **learned to communicate** in sign language.

Verb + *that* + subject + verb

admit	claim	discover	say
agree	conclude	explain	show
argue	decide	find	suggest
believe	deny	prove	think

They **admitted that** their research was not original.

The author **argues that** more research needs to be done.

20% of patients **believed that** their health had improved.

Verb + noun/pronoun + infinitive with *to*

advise	encourage	persuade	tell
ask	expect	remind	want
enable	need	teach	warn

The money **enabled him to complete** his research.

Economists **expect the market to grow** this year.

Scientists have **warned politicians to consider** the impact of global warming.

Irregular verbs

The following list includes all of the irregular verbs in the Words to learn lists in this book, along with some other useful irregular verbs. Use a good dictionary or grammar book to give you a full list of irregular verbs.

Infinitive	Past tense	Past participle	▶ Unit
be	was	been	-
become	became	became	-
begin	began	begun	-
break	broke	broken	-
bring	brought	brought	-
buy	bought	bought	-
choose	chose	chosen	-
come	came	come	-
cost	cost	cost	-
deal	dealt	dealt	-
do	did	done	-
draw	drew	drawn	33
fall	fell	fallen	22
find	found	found	-
get	got	got	-
give	gave	given	-
go	went	gone	-
grow	grew	grown	22
have	had	had	-
input	input or inputted	input or inputted	40
know	knew	known	27
lead	led	led	24
leave	left	left	-
lend	lent	lent	39
let	let	let	-
lose	lost	lost	39
make	made	made	5
mean	meant	meant	24
mistake	mistook	mistaken	-
misunderstand	misunderstood	misunderstood	4
pay	paid	paid	-
prove	proved	proved or proven	30
put	put	put	30
read	read	read	-
rise	rose	risen	22
say	said	said	-
see	saw	seen	-
sell	sold	sold	-
set	set	set	30, 38

Infinitive	Past tense	Past participle	▶ Unit
show	showed	shown	28
spread	spread	spread	3
speak	spoke	spoken	-
spend	spent	spent	-
stand	stood	stood	-
take	took	taken	13, 26
teach	taught	taught	8
tell	told	told	-
think	thought	thought	-
understand	understood	understood	-
write	wrote	written	-

Hedging

In academic writing we use hedging language to show the difference between proven facts and ideas which *may* be true, based on the evidence we have. There are several ways of doing this, and you should try to use a variety of these structures in your own writing. Compare the pairs of sentences below to see how the hedging language changes them.

Adverbs: *perhaps, potentially, possibly*

This was the most important law passed by the government.

*This was **perhaps** the most important law passed by the government.*

Adjectives: *likely, possible, potential*

Students will achieve better exam grades by using these methods.

*Students **are likely to** achieve better exam grades by using these methods.*

Verbs: *appear to, seem to, tend to, indicate, suggest*

The results show that the drug causes heart problems.

*The results **seem to** show that the drug causes heart problems.*

Modal verbs: *may, might, could*

The findings are significant for future research.

*The findings **could be** significant for future research.*

Note: We can use *appear/seem/tend* + infinitive with *to*:

*At first, the new law **seemed to be** very successful.*

We can also use *appear/seem* + adjective: *A change in policy **appears** very **unlikely**.*

Hedging language is also used in academic writing for generalizations: statements that are true in most situations, but not all the time. For example, if we say *Shoppers buy the same goods each week*, this is clearly not accurate. Not everyone buys exactly the same things every week. So we use hedging language to show that we are talking in general: ***Many** shoppers buy **more or less** the same goods each week.* This makes your argument stronger because it shows that you understand that there may be exceptions. Compare the following pairs of sentences:

Cities suffer from serious air pollution.

***Many** cities suffer from serious air pollution.*

This book is used by undergraduates.

*This book is **often** used by undergraduates.*

Children watch too much television.

***Many** children **in western countries** watch too much television.*

Collocation

In English certain words are often found together. We call this **collocation**. Various combinations are possible: verb + noun (*to give a presentation*), adjective + noun (*chemical engineering*), adverb + adjective (*statistically significant*), and so on. The list below shows examples of some common types of collocations that are used in this book. You will come across many more in your reading. Learners' dictionaries usually include useful information on common collocations. For more on collocation ▶ Unit 5.

Verb + noun	▶ Unit
to answer a question	13
to collect/obtain evidence/information	27
to give sb feedback	11
to make/take notes	13

Adjective + noun	
a beneficial/harmful effect	32
accurate data/information/assessment	31
a high proportion of sth	21
cultural/religious/moral beliefs	29

Adverb + adjective	
increasingly rapid	22

Verb + adverb	
to develop gradually	23
to increase/decrease considerably/ significantly/dramatically	20, 22
to vary significantly	21

Noun + noun	
internet access	14
bullet point	12

Verb + adjective	
become inflamed	23

Noun + verb	
evidence suggests	20
statistics show	21
a survey finds	21, 28

Prepositions

Many nouns, verbs and adjectives in English are typically followed by a particular preposition. Others are often used in phrases with a preposition before them. The following list shows examples of the most common types.

You can find many other fixed phrases in the dictionary. They are often shown in **bold** followed by an example sentence, or sometimes in the idioms section, where they have a full definition.

+ against	▶ Unit
to protect against sth	43

by +	
by law	44
by the deadline	10

+ for	
a deadline for sth	11
a reason for sth	24
support for sb/sth	11

+ from	
be absent from sth	32
to suffer from sth	43

+ in	
a course in sth	8
to invest in sth	39
to participate in sth	6

+ in/of

Note: We use this group of words talk about changes; *in* tells you what sort of change it is (*an increase **in** wages/employment/population*); *of* tells you how much the change is (*an increase **of** £300/20%/9 million*).

a decrease in/of	22
investment in/of sth	39

+ of	
an advantage of sth	31
to approve of sth	29
be capable of sth	6

+ on	
to concentrate on sth	6
a presentation on sth	13
to focus on sth	6

+ to	
according to sb/sth	35
an introduction to sth	9

+ with	
be concerned with sth	6
to deal with sth	3
together with sth	5

in +	
in general	3
in particular	3
in fact	27

Other common uses	
on average	3
be different from sth	6
have an effect on sth	24

Affixes

Understanding prefixes (at the beginning of words) and suffixes (at the end of words) can help you to work out the meaning of the word or the part of speech. For more about affixes ▶ Unit 4

Prefixes

Negative prefixes

Many prefixes give a word a negative or opposite meaning. The two most common are *un-* and *in-*:

fortunately → unfortunately; like → unlike
effective → ineffective; correct → incorrect

Sometimes, the *in-* prefix change before words with particular first letters:

il-: legal → illegal
im-: possible → impossible
ir-: regular → irregular

Other prefixes with negative meanings

There are several other prefixes which form words with negative meanings.
The following list shows some of the most common examples.

Prefix	Meaning	Examples
anti-	against, preventing	*antisocial, antifreeze*
dis-	not, opposite	*disadvantage, disagree*
mis-	badly, wrongly	*misunderstand, misuse*

Prefixes connected with amount, number or size

For example, the prefix *bi-* means 'two', so someone who is *bilingual* speaks two languages, and a *biannual event* happens twice a year.

Prefix	Meaning	Examples
bi-	two	*bilingual, biannual*
micro-	small	*microscope, microelectronics*
mono-	one, single	*monolingual, monotone*

Prefixes connected with position, time or direction

For example, an *international agreement* is an agreement between different nations and an *intercity train* travels between one city and another.

Prefix	Meaning	Examples
inter-	between	*international, intercity*
post-	after	*post-war, postpone*
pre-	before	*pre-war, predict*
trans-	across, from one place or state to another	*transport, transfer, trans-atlantic*

Prefixes connected with a particular subject

The following list shows some of the most common examples.

Prefix	Meaning	Examples
bio-	connected with life or living things	*biology, biotechnology*
eco-	connected with the environment	*ecology, ecosystem*
geo-	connected with the earth	*geology, geopolitical*
socio-	connected with society	*sociology, sociolinguistics*

Suffixes

Suffixes often give you useful information about a word's part of speech. For example: *legal* (adj), *legally* (adv), *legalize* (v), *legalization* (n). Together, we call a group like this a **word family**. Knowing a word family can help you to paraphrase another writer's ideas, or to express yourself in a more formal academic style.

The lists below show some of the most common suffixes in English. However, be aware that many common words do not follow a predictable pattern. This often causes students to make mistakes, for example with the words *different* (adj) and *difference* (n), or the words *effect* (n) and *affect* (v). Remember to record words from the same word family together in your vocabulary notes with a note of the part of speech to help avoid mistakes like this. You can find word families in the glossary on page 127.

Nouns

Nouns can be formed by adding a suffix to a verb, an adjective or another noun:

Verb to noun

-ment *develop → development*
-ion/-sion/-tion *collect → collection; discuss → discussion*
-ation *inform → information; investigate → investigation*
-ing *compute → computing; write → writing*

Adjective to noun

-ity *legal → legality; active → activity*
-ness *aware → awareness; ill → illness*

Noun to noun

A suffix can make an abstract noun.

-hood *child → childhood; adult → adulthood*
-ship *friend → friendship* (the quality of being friends); *member → membership* (belonging to a group of members)

Nouns referring to people

A suffix can show us that a noun refers to a person who does a particular job or who has a particular quality.

-ant/-ent	*participate → participant; immigrate → immigrant*
-er/-or	*teach → teacher; foreign → foreigner*
-ist	*science → scientist; communism → communist*
-ian	*politics → politician; history → historian*

Verbs

A suffix can be added to a noun or an adjective to make a verb. Often these have a meaning of 'to make' or 'to become'.

-en	*wide → widen; length → lengthen*
-ify	*false → falsify; example → exemplify**
-ize/-ise	*equal → equalize; emphasis → emphasize*

*notice the spelling change

Adjectives

-ful	*success → successful; use → useful*
-ive	*progress → progressive; communicate → communicative*
-ous	*number → numerous; poison → poisonous*
-less	*use → useless* (= not useful)

Adverbs

-ly	*negative → negatively* (in a negative manner); *political → politically*

Be careful – not all words ending in *-ly* are adverbs; some are adjectives. For example, the words *daily* and *hourly* in *a daily newspaper* or *an hourly train* are adjectives.

Notice also that many common words that do not end in *-ly* are adverbs. For example, the word *fast* can be either an adjective (*a fast train*) or an adverb: *The train was travelling very fast.* (NOT ~~fastly~~)

Academic and language terms

adjective: a word that describes a person or a thing. For example, *serious, interesting* or *scientific* in *a serious illness, interesting research* and *scientific knowledge.* ▶ Unit 2

adverb: a word that adds more information about place, time, manner, cause or degree to a **verb** (*easily* in *easily understand*), an **adjective** (*severely* in *severely ill*), a phrase (*quickly* in *quickly draw attention to*) or another **adverb** (*extremely* in *extremely easily*). ▶ Unit 3

affix: a **prefix** or a **suffix**. ▶ Unit 4

citation: a **summary**, **paraphrase** or **quotation** from another piece of writing; when you cite something from a **source**, you always give a **reference** to identify the original writer. ▶ Unit 35

collocation: a combination of words that are typically used together. For example, *make a decision.* ▶ Unit 5

countable noun: a noun that can be used in the plural (*numbers, ideas, people*) or with *a* or *an* (*a number, an idea, a person*). ▶ Unit 2

dependent preposition: a **preposition** that is typically used together with another word, such as a **noun** (*assessment of, insight into*), a **verb** (*overlap with, discriminate against*) or an **adjective** (*capable of, responsible for*). The choice of **preposition** depends on the word it is used with. ▶ Unit 6

emphasis: the use of language to show that something has special importance (*a central argument*) or that you are very confident about something (*it is absolutely certain that…*). ▶ Unit 33

evaluation: in academic writing, **evaluation** is the writer's response to an idea based on evidence; whether it is accurate, effective, etc. ▶ Units 31 and 32

hedging: in academic writing, **hedging** is the language a writer uses to show how they feel about an idea. It is used to express ideas accurately (*most people, potentially harmful …*), and to show whether something is an established fact or an opinion based on evidence (*appear to be, it is likely that …*). ▶ Unit 34

noun: a word that refers to a person (*scientist*), a place (*city*) a thing (*book*), a quality (*accuracy*) or an activity (*development*). ▶ Unit 2

noun phrase: a group of words in a sentence that behaves in the same way as a **noun**. For example, *the difference in temperature, individual members of the team.* ▶ Unit 2

paraphrase: to express what someone has said or written using different words. ▶ Unit 35

part of speech: one of the classes which words are divided into according to their grammar, such as **noun**, **verb**, **adjective**, etc.

phrasal verb: a **verb** combined with an **adverb** or a **preposition** to give a new meaning. For example, *print out, set out* and *tend to.*

plural: a form of a **noun** or a **verb** that refers to more than one person or thing, for example *assignments, are.*

prefix: a letter or group of letters added to the beginning of a word to change its meaning, such as *un-* in *unnecessary* and *re-* in *review.* ▶ Unit 4

preposition: a word, such as *in, from, to* and *of*, used before a **noun** or pronoun to show place (*in the city, at university*), position (*on the table, under the microscope*) time (*before Wednesday, by now*) or method (*with a computer, by email*). ▶ Unit 6

quotation: a sentence or short paragraph taken directly from the source material, with no words changed. Quotations are placed inside quotation marks ('…') to show clearly that the writer is using someone else's words. ▶ Unit 35

reference: in academic writing, a **reference** is a mention of a source of information. A **reference** is always used with a quotation or a **citation** to give details about the **source**. ▶ Unit 12

singular: a form of a **noun** or **verb** that refers to one person or thing. For example, *assignment, is.*

source: a text or person that provides information, especially for a piece of written work. ▶ Unit 12

suffix: a letter or group of letters added to the end of a word to make another word, such as *-ly* in *greatly* or *-ness* in *awareness.* ▶ Unit 4

summary: a shorter version of the **source** text, written in your own words and including the main points. ▶ Unit 35

synonym: a word or expression that has the same or nearly the same meaning as another word. For example, *completely* and *entirely* are synonyms.

uncountable noun: a **noun** that cannot be made **plural** or used with *a* or *an*. For example, *water, information* and *importance.* ▶ Unit 2

verb: a word or group of words that expresses an action (*write*), an event (*happen*) or a state (*live*). ▶ Unit 3

word family: all the forms or **parts of speech** of a word, for example *differ, difference, different, differently.* ▶ Unit 4

word formation: the way in which words are made up of different parts, such as **prefixes** and **suffixes**. ▶ Unit 4

Answer key

Unit 1

1 1 the *Academic Word List*
2 uncountable
3 of, for
4 it is present and clearly seen
5 found
6 evidence, support

2 a, b, c, d, f, g

Unit 2

1 1 U 2 C 3 U 4 U 5 U 6 C 7 U 8 C

2 1 information
2 work
3 lives
4 media
5 uses

3 1 change
2 makes
3 helps
4 is

4 1 T
2 F ('They argue that increased use of fossil fuel is necessary for economic growth.')
3 F ('We are becoming increasingly aware that when we pollute a particular location, we are polluting the world.')

5 1 particular
2 low
3 aware
4 necessary

Unit 3

1 a 1 e 2 c 3 a 4 f 5 b 6 d

1 b 1 I 2 T 3 T 4 T 5 T 6 I

2 1 spread
2 lost
3 chose
4 found
5 cost

3 1 C
2 I (the largest proportion of international students *come* from Central Asia; the US and UK are the most popular destinations)
3 C
4 I (students prefer to stay in their own region, they study in a country that is near to their own)

4 1 abroad
2 overseas
3 easily
4 well
5 fast
6 In general

5 1 spread   2 abroad (*overseas* does not fit naturally here because these countries are close together and you do not have to go 'over the sea' to travel between them)   3 deal with   4 globally
5 largely

Unit 4

1 1 behaviour   2 behavioural   3 difference
4 differ   5 different   6 measurement

2 1 provision   2 provide   3 competitor
4 compete   5 competitive   6 attract
7 attractive

3 a 1 behaviour
2 competitors
3 attract
4 measurements
5 provide

3 b 1 noun
2 noun
3 verb
4 noun
5 verb

4 1 repeated
2 Fortunately
3 misunderstood
4 unaware
5 attractive
6 reuse

5 1 A 2 A 3 N 4 A 5 N 6 A

Unit 5

1 1 to give a presentation
2 It was quick to complete, giving more time for interviews.

2 a 1 skills
2 questionnaire
3 option
4 feedback
5 work
6 positive

2 b 1 choose
2 follow
3 regular
4 complete
5 communication (*language skills* usually refer to speaking different (foreign) languages; *communication skills* are about communicating well with people (in your own language))

3 1 in return for
2 together with
3 on behalf of
4 in terms of

4 1 on
   2 come
   3 makes
   4 in
   5 in
   6 on

5 **suggested answers**
   1 ask / answer
   2 country / economy
   3 mass
   4 play / have

Unit 6

1 1 on, of
   2 of, to
   3 with, of, on

2 1 a new approach to language learning.
   2 concerned with human rights issues
   3 the impact of the floods on the local people / the impact of floods on local people
   4 aspects of contemporary culture
   5 focuses on the role of technology in education
   6 aware of the health risks of smoking

3 1 to take, to write, noting
   2 to participate, picking up

4 1 of achieving
   2 on finding
   3 to leave
   4 patients not to drive

5 1 c 2 d 3 a 4 b

Unit 7

1 1 use
   2 get / get to
   3 try
   4 get
   5 right

2 1 receive
   2 attempt
   3 correct
   4 strategies
   5 employed

3 1 2 2 4

4 1 b 2 a 3 b

5 a 1 enjoy
   2 right
   3 cycle
   4 odd
   5 table

5 b 1 S
   2 D (in **5a** the meaning is 'the right side'; in extract G the meaning is 'a thing that you are allowed to do according to the law')
   3 S
   4 D (in **5a** the meaning is 'strange; unusual'; in extract H the meaning is 'that cannot be divided by two')
   5 S

Unit 8

1 1 student
   2 course
   3 studying
   4 university
   5 undergraduate, international student

2 1 at
   2 doing
   3 studying
   4 in
   5 students

3 1 F (higher education does not include high schools)
   2 T
   3 T
   4 T
   5 F (a university department usually teaches one general subject (e.g. history, engineering, law))

4 1 University
   2 Faculty
   3 Department
   4 courses

5 1 noun
   2 adjective
   3 noun
   4 verb
   5 noun

6 1 b 2 d 3 a 4 c 5 e

Unit 9

1 1 teaches
   2 History of Art
   3 philosophy department
   4 the philosophy of science

2 1 b 2 c 3 a 4 d

3 c

4 1 historian 2 philosophical 3 education
   4 sociological 5 economist 6 law
   7 political

5 1 social 2 perspective 3 topic
   4 field 5 sociologists

6 1 philosopher
   2 historical
   3 economics
   4 political
   5 literary

Unit 10

1 1 T
   2 F (he says that they have *dissimilar/very different* types of personality)
   3 F (different types of scientists generally/often work *in teams*)
   4 T

2 1 B 2 A 3 C

3 1 physicists
   2 experimented
   3 scientific
   4 observe
   5 laboratory
   6 team

4 **suggested answer**
   The objectives of basic science and applied science are different (basic science aims to understand the physical world, applied science aims to design something for a purpose).

5 1 An objective
   2 Engineering
   3 Applied science
   4 methodology

6 a 1 a. science
        b. scientists
    2 a. biologists
        b. biological
    3 a. physics
        b. physical
    4 a. chemical
        b. chemists
    5 a. experimental
        b. experiments

6 b 1 a. noun
        b. noun
    2 a. noun
        b. adjective
    3 a. noun
        b. adjective
    4 a. adjective
        b. noun
    5 a. adjective
        b. noun

Unit 11

1 1 d 2 e 3 b 4 a 5 c

2 1 submit
   2 write
   3 give
   4 edit

3 1 ✔
   2 ✗
   3 ✔
   4 ✔ / ✗ (the feedback on this section contains both positive and negative comments)
   5 ✗
   6 ✗

4 1 conclusion
   2 summary
   3 introduction
   4 support

5 1 concludes
   2 assessment
   3 summarizes
   4 introduction
   5 edit
   6 assigned

Unit 12

1 1 Business Economics
   2 Andrew Gillespie
   3 the contents page
   4 Thinking like an economist
   5 26 pages

2 1 textbook 2 title 3 author
   4 contents 5 chapters 6 page numbers

3 1 reading
   2 publication
   3 author
   4 title

4 1 heading
   2 paragraph
   3 bullet points
   4 illustration

5 **suggested answers**
   1 a science textbook
   2 Survival in hot, dry climates
   3 three
   4 an elephant

6 1 index 2 glossary 3 terms 4 references

7 1 author
   2 on the contents page
   3 author, date of publication, title of the book (or article)
   4 in the references
   5 in the glossary (of terms)
   6 in the index / using the contents page

Unit 13

1 a, b, c

2 1 give, take, ask
   2 discuss, present, answer, interrupt

3 1 ask and answer
   2 give presentations
   3 interrupt speakers
   4 take notes

4 1 lecturer / lecture
   2 lecture
   3 tutorial, tutor
   4 debate

5 1 lecture
2 take notes
3 ask questions
4 presentation
5 tutorial

6 1 lectures 2 arguments 3 lecturers / lectures
4 take notes 5 ask questions 6 discuss
7 a presentation 8 seminar

Unit 14

1 a, b, d

2 1 communicate
2 access
3 slides
4 administration
5 registered, log on
6 connection (you can also say *internet access*, but
access is an uncountable noun so it isn't used
with *an*)
7 links

3 1 Y
2 Y
3 N (they remember it better when they read it on
paper)
4 Y

4 1 f 2 h 3 a 4 g 5 b 6 c 7 d 8 e

5 1 a slide
2 a link
3 log on
4 keyword search
5 a document
6 print out

Review 1

1 email interviews and online questionnaires

2 1 2 2 1 3 - 4 3 5 -

3 1 access
2 submit
3 contribute
4 giving
5 meeting
6 take

4 1 T
2 F ('engineering students often work in teams on
practical projects')
3 F (in seminars students discuss their ideas and
listen to arguments from other students and
tutors)

5 1 d 2 b 3 a 4 e 5 c

6 1 at 2 of 3 to 4 with 5 about

Unit 15

1 1 F (Buildings are important culturally and
socially, as well as providing shelter.)
2 F (Architects and builders think about buildings
in different stages.)
3 T
4 T
5 F (Builders use computer-generated design to
check their work against plans.)

2 1 contain
2 item
3 section
4 structure
5 attached to
6 complex
7 elements
8 specific
9 version

3 1 specific
2 section
3 contain
4 structure
5 element

4 a

5 1 consist of
2 exist
3 category
4 pattern
5 type
6 include

6 1 patterns
2 exist
3 categories
4 includes
5 consists of / includes
6 types

Unit 16

1 1 As 2 Firstly 3 At this stage 4 Then
5 Finally

2 1 series
2 process
3 constant
4 removed
5 steps

3 1 C 2 B

4 1 previous
2 task
3 stage
4 procedure
5 regularly
6 transfer

5 1 regular
  2 stage
  3 last
  4 previously
  5 involves / involved / will involve
  6 transfers

Unit 17

1 1 Recent
  2 annual
  3 temporary
  4 current
  5 present

2 1 permanent
  2 period
  3 decade
  4 a century
  5 ongoing

3 suggested answers
At the present time, During the period from 1950 to 1990, By 2030, In the five decades from 1950 to 2000, by the middle of the 21st century

4 a

5 1 long-term
  2 short-term
  3 brief
  4 recently
  5 currently
  6 contemporary
  7 duration

6 1 current
  2 Presently
  3 permanently
  4 briefly

Unit 18

1 1 F ("people's life experiences worldwide have become increasingly similar")
  2 T
  3 T

2 1 c 2 a 3 b

3 1 locations
  2 an international football match
  3 global support
  4 national average
  5 urban areas
  6 site
  7 Rural

4 b

5 1 b 2 a 3 d 4 c

6 1 a. international
    b. national
  2 a. location
    b. Local
  3 a. national
    b. nation
  4 a. regions
    b. regional
  5 a. foreigner
    b. foreign

Unit 19

1 1 peer group
  2 family members
  3 gender
  4 adolescence
  5 ethnicity

2 1 gender
  2 relationships / their relationship
  3 role
  4 identity / identities
  5 adolescence

3 suggested answers
  1 as individuals / as adults
  2 a person's occupation
  3 their colleagues
  4 a community / a community of local residents

4 1 with
  2 in
  3 in
  4 to

5 a 1 a. adolescence
      b. adolescents
  2 a. ethnic
    b. ethnicity
  3 a. residents
    b. residential

5 b 1 a. noun
      b. noun
  2 a. adjective
    b. noun
  3 a. noun
    b. adjective

Unit 20

1 1 S
  2 D (*numerous* causes means that there are many of them; the *main* cause is the one that happens most often)
  3 S
  4 S (these are different word forms (verb and adverb) but both are about numbers that are not exact)
  5 S

2 1 amounts
2 quantities
3 figures
4 numerous
5 approximately
6 estimate
7 significantly
8 considerably

3 1 T
2 F (they say you should do a *minimum of* / *at least* 30 minutes five times a week)
3 T
4 F (it is the maximum number of animals that *can* live in an area)

4 1 f 2 e 3 a 4 d 5 c 6 b

5 **suggested answers**
1 The adult birds reach *approximately* 35 cm in length.
2 The male birds are *significantly* larger than the females.
3 People were asked to *estimate* the number of hours they spend online each day.
4 There have been *numerous* studies into the effects of computer games on behaviour.
5 Students were given *a 30-minute time limit* to complete the task. / Students were given *a time limit of 30 minutes* to complete the task.
6 The government published *the latest unemployment figures*.

Unit 21

1 1 the highest proportion of smokers
2 (only) a small minority of US workers

2 1 S 2 S 3 L 4 L 5 S

3 **suggested answers**
1 a fraction of / a small fraction of / a tiny fraction of
2 the majority of
3 Only a small proportion of / A small proportion of
4 per cent of
5 a minority of

4 1 average, value
2 mean
3 calculate, formula
4 total, divide

5 1 formula
2 divide by
3 total
4 majority
5 percentage
6 minority

6 1 calculate   2 average / mean   3 total
4 values   5 divide   6 mean / average
7 statistics / values   8 percentage / proportion
9 majority   10 percentage / proportion

Unit 22

1 a, c, e

2 1 b 2 g 3 f 4 a 5 e 6 d 7 c

3 a, b, d

4 a 1 fell   2 fallen   3 rose   4 risen   5 a reduction
6 declined

4 b 1 fell
2 risen
3 decline
4 growth
5 reduction

5 1 in
2 by
3 in
4 by

Unit 23

1 b

2 1 become
2 vary
3 trigger
4 occur
5 develop

3 1 occur
2 triggered
3 develop
4 vary

4 a 1 progress, innovations, invention
2 disrupted, create, reversed, reviewed, revised, improved

4 b 1 progress
2 creation
3 innovate
4 invent
5 reversal
6 review
7 revision
8 improvement

4 c 1 reversed
2 disruption
3 revision
4 improve
5 creation
6 invent
7 progress
8 innovations
9 reviewed

Review 2

1 1 B 2 C 3 A 4 D

2 a 1 increase   2 growth   3 change
4 variety   5 rise   6 decrease

2 b 1 rapidly
2 significant
3 considerable
4 dramatically

3 1 significant, increase
2 considerable, variations
3 change, dramatically / rapidly

4 1 2   2 3   3 4   4 1   5 5   6 6

5 1 I   2 T   3 T

6 1 contains
2 will be created
3 were transferred
4 involves
5 be calculated

Unit 24

1 1 F (they only kill bacteria, not viruses)
2 T
3 T (they mutate and become resistant)
4 F (they are caused by viruses)

2 1 f   2 c   3 a   4 d   5 e   6 b

3 1 C   2 -   3 B   4 -

4 1 effective
2 effects
3 affects
4 effect

5 1 consequences
2 reason
3 link
4 risk
5 associated with

6 1 on   4 to
2 for   5 to
3 as   6 of

Unit 25

1 1 b   2 a

2 1 c   2 d   3 e   4 a   5 b

3 a 1 various
2 separate
3 alternative

3 b 1 Various   2 Separate   3 Alternative

4 1 S   2 D   3 S

5 1 unique
2 equally
3 resembles
4 as well as
5 unlike
6 Similarly

6 1 3   2 1   3 2

7 1 various
2 similar to / very similar to

Unit 26

1 1 suffered
2 a lack
3 disposal, problem
4 regulations

2 a 1 disaster, disaster
2 emergency, emergency, emergency

2 b 1 emergency
2 disasters
3 accidents

3 1 address   2 issues   3 minimize
4 enforce   5 aimed   6 successfully
7 quality   8 account

4 1 solve
2 cause
3 addressing
4 find
5 experienced
6 face

5 a 1 a   2 c   3 b

Unit 27

1 1 T
2 F (you can assume an expert audience knows about the topic; you may need to explain more for a general audience)
3 T

2 1 explain   2 detail   3 experts
4 assume   5 knowledge   6 definitions
7 terminology

3 a 1 assumption   2 define   3 explanation
4 know

3 b 1 define / explain
2 explanation
3 assumptions
4 explains / explained
5 knowledge

4 a 1 QL
2 QL
3 QN
4 QL
5 QN

4 b **suggested answers**
1 education / TESOL
2 medicine / health science
3 economics
4 engineering / business studies
5 geography / environmental science

5 1 evidence
2 piece of information / item of information
3 facts
4 items of data / pieces of data
5 knowledge
6 details

6 1 collect 2 obtained 3 sources 4 available
    5 in the form of 6 explain 7 details
    8 for example

Unit 28

1 1 research 2 activities 3 conduct 4 projects
    5 organize 6 record 7 results 8 analysis

2 a 1 N 2 V 3 V 4 N

2 b 1 research
    2 organization
    3 record
    4 analyse

2 c 1 analysed
    2 researching
    3 record
    4 analysis
    5 organization

3 1 T
    2 F (they disagree with his data collection)
    3 F (a national survey was conducted)
    4 F (women's academic qualifications are no lower than men's)
    5 T

4 1 S
    2 S
    3 D (*method* is all the steps involved in a piece of research; *analysis* is only the stage where you examine the results/data)
    4 S
    5 D (if research *shows* something, it is clear; if research *suggests* something, it may be true)

5 1 conducted
    2 projects
    3 shown
    4 suggest
    5 recent
    6 on
    7 scientific
    8 further

Unit 29

1 b

2 1 point of view
    2 opinions
    3 view
    4 beliefs
    5 justify
    6 argue that
    7 approved of

3 1 point of view / view
    2 view / point of view
    3 approve
    4 beliefs
    5 argue
    6 justify
    7 opinions

4 a

5 1 f 2 c 3 a 4 e 5 g 6 b 7 d

6 1 Critics of
    2 consider
    3 definitely
    4 believe
    5 views on
    6 presume
    7 In turn

Unit 30

1 1 ✔
    2 ✘ (statistics don't tell us the reasons why people live longer)
    3 ✔
    4 ✘ (theories can suggest ways to improve our quality of life)

2 1 theory
    2 relationship
    3 proposed
    4 explain
    5 prove
    6 predictions
    7 concept
    8 set out

3 1 f 2 b 3 e 4 c 5 a 6 d

4 1 Model 2 physical 3 negative 4 perceptions
    5 Theory 6 choices 7 less decline

5 1 models
    2 predict
    3 persuade
    4 put forward
    5 principle
    6 based on

6 1 set out
    2 predict
    3 a principle
    4 prove
    5 persuade

Unit 31

1 1 convincing
    2 accurate
    3 precise
    4 successful
    5 positive
    6 effective
    7 benefits

2 1 f 2 d 3 e 4 a 5 c 6 b

3 1 T
    2 F (page popularity is a very basic measure of how popular a website is)
    3 F (page popularity is worked out by counting links from other websites)
    4 T
    5 T

4 1 popular
    2 advantage
    3 interesting
    4 efficient
    5 appropriate

5 1 efficient
    2 interesting
    3 most popular
    4 appropriate
    5 advantage of
    6 an accurate

Unit 32

1 1 ✔
    2 ✔
    3 ✘ (*direction* describes how people approach tasks and how they avoid harmful behaviour)
    4 ✘ (without pressure they may have less direction)

2 1 absent
    2 risks
    3 harmful
    4 disadvantage
    5 pressures
    6 challenging

3 1 d 2 a 3 f 4 b 5 c 6 e

4 1 blame 2 work theory 3 mistakes 4 discuss
    5 false sense 6 weakness

5 1 false
    2 blame
    3 negative
    4 threat
    5 weakness
    6 criticism
    7 mistake

6 1 absent
    2 harmful
    3 false
    4 weakness
    5 threats
    6 blame bankers

Review 3

1 1 a/e 2 d/f 3 b/c

2 1 d 2 b 3 a 4 e 5 c

3 1 suggested
    2 associated
    3 believe
    4 meant
    5 minimize
    6 predict

4 1 T
    2 F (students can be successful in both small and large classes)
    3 T

5 1 To some extent
    2 a great deal
    3 successful
    4 assume
    5 harmful

6 1 c 2 a 3 b 4 d

Unit 33

1 1 A 2 – 3 C 4 B

2 1 entirely
    2 essential
    3 importance
    4 central
    5 actually
    6 especially
    7 stress
    8 absolutely

3 1 E 2 D 3 F

4 1 c 2 b 3 d 4 a

5 1 emphasis
    2 highlighted
    3 obviously
    4 actual
    5 drew
    6 importantly
    7 central

6 **suggested answers**
    1 The paper explains a completely/an entirely new method for identifying the age of samples.
    2 There are obvious/major differences between print books and online information.
    3 The authors stress/emphasize that the findings only apply to this specific environment.
    4 Working as a team is a central/essential/important part of nursing.

Unit 34

1 1 T
    2 F (the texts use words like *perhaps*, *likely* and *possible* to show that these are not proven facts)

2 1 seem to
    2 perhaps
    3 indicate
    4 possible

3 1 to have
    2 perhaps
    3 to occur
    4 likely
    5 potentially
    6 seems
    7 indicates

4 1 quite equally
    2 there is generally more industry
    3 are mostly not very interested in
    4 often buy many of the same things

5 1 overall
2 relatively, typically
3 more or less
4 somewhat
5 normally

Unit 35

1 1 F (Good academic writing requires references to other academic work.)
2 F (Using references shows that the writer can understand and evaluate others' academic work.)
3 F (There are three main ways to refer to other academic writing in your essays.)
4 T
5 T
6 T

2 b

3 1 quotes
2 quotation
3 discussed
4 sources
5 explain
6 citations

4 1 According to 2 references 3 stated
4 plagiarizing

Unit 36

1 a, b

2 1 to 2 of 3 to 4 of 5 of 6 to

3 1 a 2 a 3 a

4 1 despite
2 Although / Even though
3 However
4 Despite
5 whereas

Unit 37

1 1 in recent years
2 At first
3 As soon as
4 subsequently
5 By the time
6 eventually
7 initial
8 After that

2 a

3 1 whenever
2 initially
3 at last
4 In the meantime

4 1 a. At first
b. firstly
2 a. eventual
b. eventually

3 a. initial
b. initially
4 a. At last
b. Lastly
5 a. subsequent
b. subsequently

Review 4

1 1 language problems
2 adjusting to a new culture
3 financial concerns

2 1 appears
2 although
3 tended to
4 likely

3 1 Air travel tends to be less expensive than ten years ago.
2 Women typically earn less than men. / Typically, women earn less than men.
3 This vaccine will potentially change people's lives in the developing world.
4 It appears that there is a mistake in that data. / There appears to be a mistake in that data.
5 The research indicates that inflation contributes to poverty.
6 Violent crime is likely to increase if guns are more available.

4 1 5 2 4 3 1 4 7 5 6 6 2 7 3

5 1 The researchers wanted to continue with the research project. However, there was not enough money.
2 As soon as the earthquake struck the city, the electricity supply was cut.
3 By the time the company launched the new vaccine, ten thousand people had already died.
4 Despite the risk of failure, the team decided to go ahead with the operation.

Unit 38

1 1 F (location can have a big effect on a company's success)
2 F (employees have higher salaries in some places than others)
3 T
4 T

2 1 a. employee
b. employers
c. professional
2 a. career
b. job
3 a. industry
b. organizations

3 1 D (people can buy more different things than before and have more choice of where to buy them)
2 S

4 1 product
    2 consumer
    3 service
    4 customer
    5 purchase
    6 guarantee

5 1 c 2 d 3 b 4 a 5 e

Unit 39

1 1 n 2 adj 3 n 4 adj

2 1 economy
    2 currency
    3 income
    4 finance
    5 investment
    6 Financial

3 a 1 investment 2 financial 3 economic 4 profit

3 b 1 invest
    2 financial
    3 economic
    4 profitable

4 1 lend
    2 borrow
    3 owes
    4 borrow
    5 lend

5 1 earn 2 profits 3 income 4 invest

6 1 P 2 L 3 L 4 P

Unit 40

1 b

2 1 data
    2 devices
    3 software
    4 technical
    5 design
    6 digital
    7 technology
    8 equipment
    9 system

3 1 designed
    2 Technology is
    3 technical knowledge
    4 devices
    5 software
    6 data

4 a, b, d

5 1 automatic
    2 applications
    3 store
    4 coding
    5 input

6 1 a 2 b 3 a 4 b

7 1 design 2 device 3 electronic
    4 applications 5 store 6 data 7 security

Unit 41

1 1 T
    2 T
    3 F ('Individuals can also protect the environment by
    trying to reuse and recycle as much as possible.')
    4 T
    5 F ('the process still causes some levels of pollution')

2 1 source
    2 resources
    3 resource
    4 source

3 1 environment 2 pollution 3 energy
    4 renewable 5 resources 6 recycling
    7 waste

4 1 protect natural resources and the environment
    2 change which is not natural

5 1 c 2 b 3 a 4 e 5 d

6 1 natural
    2 conserve
    3 renewable
    4 pollution
    5 protection

Unit 42

1 1 S 2 S 3 D 4 S

2 1 cultures
    2 communities
    3 traditional
    4 lifestyle
    5 customs
    6 cultural

3 negative

4 b

5 1 tradition
    2 security
    3 welfare
    4 society

6 1 a. social
      b. society
    2 a. cultural
      b. culture
    3 a. tradition
      b. traditional
    4 a. secure
      b. security

Unit 43

1 1 T
    2 T
    3 F (regular physical activity improves the immune
    system and also leads to better mental health)
    4 T

2
1 health
2 mental
3 disease
4 physical
5 healthy
6 injury
7 infection
8 virus

3 1 g 2 e 3 b 4 a 5 f 6 d 7 c

4
1 Health care
2 Medicine
3 Treatment
4 symptom

5 a
1 a. treat
   b. treatment
2 a. medical
   b. medicine
3 a. health
   b. healthy
4 a. symptoms
   b. symptom

5 b
1 a. verb
   b. noun
2 a. adjective
   b. noun
3 a. noun
   b. adjective
4 a. noun
   b. noun

Unit 44

1 B

2 1 B 2 A 3 A 4 B

3
1 legal
2 criminal
3 illegal
4 punishing
5 laws
6 crime
7 commit

4
1 guilty
2 lawyer
3 trial
4 court
5 jury
6 sentence

5
1 not guilty
2 judge
3 trial
4 Lawyers
5 witnesses
6 jury
7 court
8 guilty
9 sentence
10 innocent

Unit 45

1
1 T
2 F ('Politics examines the way that power is divided between individuals and the state')
3 T
4 F (their decisions should benefit society as a whole)
5 T

2
1 Ministry
2 democracy
3 Government
4 authorized
5 votes
6 political
7 power
8 policies

3
1 Democracy, power
2 politics, governed
3 policy, government

4 a

5
1 election
2 campaigns
3 politicians
4 scheme

6 1 c 2 e 3 b 4 a 5 d 6 f

Review 5

1
1 the cost means that the number of collections has been reduced in some areas
2 the number of bins can be confusing and uses lots of space

2 1 c 2 a 3 b 4 d

3
1 introduced, a law
2 scheme, designed
3 use, resources
4 reducing, waste

4 a, b, d

5
1 healthy 2 healthily 3 environment
4 environmentally 5 physically 6 treat
7 mentally

6
1 a. treating
   b. treatment
2 a. environmentally
   b. environment
3 a. physically
   b. physical
4 a. healthily
   b. Healthy
5 a. mental
   b. mentally

Glossary

abroad /əˈbrɔːd/ *adv* in or to a foreign country U3

absent /ˈæbsənt/ *adj* not present as part of sth U32 WF **absence** *n*

absolutely /ˈæbsəluːtli/ *adv* totally; without any limitation U33 WF **absolute** *adj*

academic AWL /ˌækəˈdemɪk/ *adj* connected with education, especially studying in schools and universities U8 WF **academia** *n*, **academic** *n*, **academically** *adv*, **academy** *n*

access[1] AWL /ˈækses/ *n* the process of connecting to the internet or of opening a computer file to get or add information U14

access[2] AWL /ˈækses/ *v* to connect to the internet or open a computer file in order to get or add information U14 WF **accessible** *adj*, **accessibility** *n*, **inaccessible** *adj*

accident /ˈæksɪdənt/ *n* an unpleasant event, especially in a vehicle, that happens unexpectedly and causes injury or damage U26

according to /əˈkɔːdɪŋ tu/ *prep* as stated or reported by sb/sth U35

accurate AWL /ˈækjərət/ *adj* representing sb/sth in a way that is true and exact U31 WF **accuracy** *n*, **accurately** *adv*, **inaccuracy** *n*, **inaccurate** *adj*

achieve AWL /əˈtʃiːv/ *v* to succeed in reaching a particular goal or result, especially by effort or skill U7 WF **achievable** *adj*, **achievement** *n*

activity /ækˈtɪvəti/ *n* (pl. -ies) a thing that a person or group does or has done, usually in order to achieve a particular aim U28 WF **active** *adj*, **actively** *adv*

actually /ˈæktʃuəli/ *adv* used to emphasize a fact or the truth about a situation U33 WF **actual** *adj*

address /əˈdres/ *v* to think about a problem or a situation and decide how you are going to deal with it U26

administration AWL /ədˌmɪnɪˈstreɪʃn/ *n* the activity of running a business, school or other organization U14 WF **administer** *v*

adolescence /ˌædəˈlesns/ *n* the time in a person's life when they develop from a child into an adult U19

adolescent /ˌædəˈlesnt/ *n* a young person who is developing from a child into an adult U19

adult AWL /ˈædʌlt/ *n* a fully grown person who is legally responsible for their actions U19 WF **adult** *adj*, **adulthood** *n*

advantage /ədˈvɑːntɪdʒ/ *n* a quality of sth that makes it better or more useful U31 WF **advantageous** *adj*

advise /ədˈvaɪz/ *v* to tell sb what you think they should do in a particular situation U6 WF **advice** *n*, **advisor** *n*

affect AWL /əˈfekt/ *v* **1** to make a difference to sb/sth or to what sb thinks or does U24 **2** (of a disease) to attack a part of the body; to make sb become ill U24 WF **unaffected** *adj*

after that /ˌɑːftə ˈðæt/ *prep* later than sth; following sth in time U37

afterwards /ˈɑːftəwədz/ *adv* at a later time; after an event that has already been mentioned U37

aim to /ˈeɪm tu/ *v* to try or plan to achieve sth U26 WF **aim** *n*

alternative AWL /ɔːlˈtɜːnətɪv/ *adj* that can be used instead of sth else U25 WF **alternative** *n*, **alternatively** *adv*

although /ɔːlˈðəʊ/ *conj* used for introducing a statement that makes the main statement in a sentence seem surprising U36

amount /əˈmaʊnt/ *n* (used especially with uncountable ns) a quantity of sth U20

analysis AWL /əˈnæləsɪs/ *n* (pl. analyses /əˈnæləsiːz/) the detailed study or examination of sth in order to understand more about it; the result of the study U28 WF **analyst** *n*, **analytic** *adj*, **analytical** *adj*, **analytically** *adv*

analyse AWL /ˈænəlaɪz/ *v* to examine the nature or structure of sth, especially by separating it into its parts, in order to understand or explain it U28

ancient /ˈeɪnʃənt/ *adj* belonging to a period of history that is thousands of years in the past U9

annual AWL /ˈænjuəl/ *adj* covering a period of one year U17 WF **annually** *adv*

appear /əˈpɪə(r)/ *v* (not used in the progressive tenses) to give the impression of being or doing sth U34 WF **appearance** *n*

application /ˌæplɪˈkeɪʃn/ *n* a program or piece of software designed to do a particular job U40

applied science /əˌplaɪd ˈsaɪəns/ *n* the area of science concerned with studying the use of scientific knowledge to solve practical problems, for example engineering and computer science U10

approach AWL /əˈprəʊtʃ/ *n* a way of doing or thinking about sth such as a problem or task U6 WF **approach** *v*

appropriate AWL /əˈprəʊpriət/ *adj* suitable, acceptable or correct for the particular circumstances U31 WF **appropriacy** *n*, **appropriateness** *n*, **appropriately** *adv*, **inappropriate** *adj*, **inappropriately** *adv*

approve of /əˈpruːv ɒv/ *phrasal v* to think that sb/sth is good, acceptable or suitable U29 WF **approval** *n*

approximately AWL /əˈprɒksɪmətli/ *adv* (abbr. approx.) in a way that is almost accurate or exact, but not completely so U20 WF **approximate** *adj v*, **approximation** *n*

area AWL /ˈeəriə/ *n* part of a town, a country or the world U18

argue /ˈɑːgjuː/ *v* to give reasons why you think that sth is right/wrong, true/not true, etc., especially to persuade people that you are right U29 WF **arguably** *adv*

argument /ˈɑːgjumənt/ *n* a reason or set of reasons that sb uses to show that sth is true or correct U13

art /ɑːt/ *n* **1** the use of the imagination to express ideas or feelings, especially in painting, drawing or sculpture, but also in dance, music, film, etc. U9 **2** examples of objects such as paintings, drawings or sculptures U9

artist /ˈɑːtɪst/ *n* a person who creates works of art, especially paintings or drawings U9 WF **artistic** *adj*

as a result /ˌæz ə rɪˈzʌlt/ *phr* because of the thing that has just been mentioned U24

as a result of /ˌæz ə rɪˈzʌlt əv/ *prep* caused or produced because of sth else U36

aspect AWL /ˈæspekt/ *n* a particular feature of a situation, an idea or a process; a way in which sth may be considered U6

assess AWL /əˈses/ *v* to make a judgement about the nature or quality of sb/sth U11

assessment AWL /əˈsesmənt/ *n* the act of judging or forming an opinion about sb/sth; an occasion when this is done U11

assign AWL /əˈsaɪn/ *v* to give sb sth that they can use, or some work or a duty U11

assignment AWL /əˈsaɪnmənt/ *n* a task or piece of work that sb is given to do, usually as part of their job or studies; the act of giving a task to sb U11

associated with /əˈsəʊʃieɪtɪd wɪð/ *adj* if one thing is associated with another, the two things are connected because they happen together or one thing causes the other U24 WF associate *v*, association *n*

as soon as /əz ˈsuːn æz/ *phr* immediately after U37

assume AWL /əˈsjuːm/ *v* to think or accept that sth is true but without having proof of it U27 WF assumption *n*

as well as /əz ˈwel æz/ *phr* in addition to U25

at first /ˌæt ˈfɜːst/ *phr* at or in the beginning U37

at last /ˌæt ˈlɑːst/ *phr* after much delay or effort; in the end U37

attached to AWL /əˈtætʃt tu/ *adj* joined or connected to sth U15 WF attachment *n*, unattached *adj*

attempt /əˈtempt/ *v* to try to do or provide sth, especially sth difficult U7 WF attempt *n*

at the same time /ˌæt ðə seɪm ˈtaɪm/ *phr* at one time; together U37

attitude AWL /ˈætɪtjuːd/ *n* a way of thinking or feeling about sb/sth; the way of behaving towards sb/sth that shows how sb thinks or feels U29

attract /əˈtrækt/ *v* to make sb/sth come somewhere or take part in sth U4 WF attraction *n*, attractive *adj*

attraction /əˈtrækʃn/ *n* a feature, quality or person that makes sth seem interesting and enjoyable, and worth having or doing U4

attractive /əˈtræktɪv/ *adj* having features or qualities that make sth seem interesting and worth having U4 WF attractively *adv*, unattractive *adj*

author AWL /ˈɔːθə(r)/ *n* the person who wrote a particular article, book or document U12 WF author *v*, authorship *n*

authority AWL /ɔːˈθɒrəti/ *n* (pl. -ies) the power to give orders to people or to say how things should be done U45 WF authoritative *adj*, authorize *v*

automatically AWL /ˌɔːtəˈmætɪkli/ *adv* by machine or computer U40 WF automate *v*, automatic *adj*, automation *n*

available AWL /əˈveɪləbl/ *adj* (of things) that you can use or obtain U27 WF availability *n*, unavailable *adj*

average[1] /ˈævərɪdʒ/ *adj* calculated by adding several amounts together, finding a total, and dividing the total by the number of amounts U21

average[2] /ˈævərɪdʒ/ *n* a number that expresses the central or typical value of a set of data U21

avoid /əˈvɔɪd/ *v* to choose not to do sth, especially to prevent sth bad from happening U32 WF avoidable *adj*, unavoidable *adj*

aware AWL /əˈweə(r)/ *adj* knowing or realizing that sth is true or exists U2 WF awareness *n*, unaware *adj*

based on /ˈbeɪst ɒn/ *adj* using or developing from sth U30

because of /bɪˈkɒz əv/ *prep* used when giving a reason U36

become /bɪˈkʌm/ *v* (became, become) to start to be sth U23

be concerned with /ˌbiː kənˈsɜːnd wɪð/ *v* **1** to be about sth U6 **2** to take an interest in sth; to cause sb to take an interest in sth U6 WF concern *n v*, concerned *adj*, concerning *adj*

behave /bɪˈheɪv/ *v* to function or react in a particular way U4 WF behaviour *n*, behavioural *adj*

behaviour /bɪˈheɪvjə(r)/ *n* the way that sb/sth functions or reacts in a particular situation U4

behavioural /bɪˈheɪvjərəl/ *adj* involving or connected with behaviour U4

belief /bɪˈliːf/ *n* something that you believe, often as part of your religion U29

believe /bɪˈliːv/ *v* (not used in the progressive tenses) to think that sth is true or possible, although you are not completely certain U29

benefit AWL /ˈbenɪfɪt/ *n* a helpful and useful effect that sth has; an advantage that sth provides U31 WF benefit *v*, beneficial *adj*, beneficiary *n*

biological /ˌbaɪəˈlɒdʒɪkl/ *adj* connected with the processes that take place within living things U10

biologist /baɪˈɒlədʒɪst/ *n* a scientist who studies biology U10

biology /baɪˈɒlədʒi/ *n* the scientific study of the life and structure of plants and animals U10

blame[1] /bleɪm/ *v* to think or say that sb/sth is responsible for sth bad U32

blame[2] /bleɪm/ *n* responsibility for doing sth badly or wrongly; saying that sb/sth is responsible for sth U32

borrow /ˈbɒrəʊ/ *v* to take money from a person or bank and agree to pay it back to them/it at a later time U39 WF borrower *n*, borrowing *n*

brief AWL /briːf/ *adj* (briefer, briefest) **1** using few words U17 **2** lasting only a short time U17 WF briefly *adv*, brevity *n*, in brief *phr*

bullet point /ˈbʊlɪt pɔɪnt/ *n* an item in a list in a document, that is printed with a square, diamond or circle in front of it in order to show that it is important. The square, etc. is also called a bullet point. U12

business /ˈbɪznəs/ *n* a commercial organization such as a company, shop or factory U38

by far /ˌbaɪ ˈfɑː(r)/ *phr* (used with comparative or superlative adjs or advs) by a great amount U25

by the time /ˌbaɪ ðə ˈtaɪm/ *phr* when the time that sth happens is reached U37

calculate /ˈkælkjuleɪt/ *v* to use numbers or mathematics to find out a total number, amount, distance, etc. U21 WF calculation *n*, calculator *n*

campaign /kæmˈpeɪn/ *n* a series of planned activities that are intended to achieve a particular social, commercial or political aim U45 WF campaign *v*, campaigner *n*

capable AWL /ˈkeɪpəbl/ *adj* having the ability or qualities necessary for doing sth U6 WF capability *n*, incapable *adj*

capacity AWL /kəˈpæsəti/ *n* (pl. -ies) the number of things or people that a container or space can hold U20

career /kəˈrɪə(r)/ n the series of jobs that a person has in a particular area of work, usually involving more responsibility as time passes U38

catalogue /ˈkætəlɒg/ n a complete list of items, for example of all the books or resources in a library, or of items for sale U14

category AWL /ˈkætəgəri/ n (pl. -ies) a group of people or things with particular features in common U15 WF **categorize** v, **categorization** n

cause[1] /kɔːz/ v to make sth happen, especially sth bad or unpleasant U24

cause[2] /kɔːz/ n a person or thing that makes sth happen U24

central /ˈsentrəl/ adj very important or essential U33 WF **centrally** adv, **centre** n

century /ˈsentʃəri/ n (pl. -ies) **1** (abbr. **cent.**) any of the periods of 100 years before or after the birth of Christ U17 **2** a period of 100 years U17

challenging AWL /ˈtʃælɪndʒɪŋ/ adj difficult in an interesting way that tests your ability U32 WF **challenge** v

change /tʃeɪndʒ/ n the act or process of sth becoming different; the result of this U23 WF **change** v

chapter AWL /ˈtʃæptə(r)/ n (abbr. **chap.**) a separate section of a book, usually with a number or title U12

chemical AWL /ˈkemɪkl/ adj involving atoms and molecules and how they cause substances to have different structures, properties and reactions U10 WF **chemical** n

chemist /ˈkemɪst/ n a scientist who studies chemistry U10

chemistry /ˈkemɪstri/ n the scientific study of substances, including the study of their chemical structures, properties and reactions U10

citation AWL /saɪˈteɪʃn/ n **1** words taken from a piece of writing or a speech; a reference, usually consisting of a name and a date, that identifies the original writer or speaker of these words U35 **2** an act of citing or being cited U35 WF **cite** v

code AWL /kəʊd/ n (computing) a system of computer programming instructions U40 WF **code** v

colleague AWL /ˈkɒliːg/ n a person that you work with, especially in a profession or business U19

collect /kəˈlekt/ v **1** to bring things together from different people or places U27 **2** to obtain sth, especially for use in tests U27 WF **collection** n

come into contact with AWL /ˌkʌm ɪntə ˈkɒntækt wɪð/ phr to meet sb or experience sth U5 WF **contact** v n

commercial /kəˈmɜːʃl/ adj making or intended to make a profit U38 WF **commerce** n, **commercialization** n, **commercialize** v, **commercially** adv

commit AWL /kəˈmɪt/ v (-tt-) to do sth wrong or illegal U44

communicate AWL /kəˈmjuːnɪkeɪt/ v to exchange information, news, ideas, etc. with sb U14 WF **communicative** adj, **communicatively** adv

communication AWL /kə,mjuːnɪˈkeɪʃn/ n the activity or process of expressing ideas and feelings or of giving people information U14

community AWL /kəˈmjuːnəti/ n (pl. -ies) (used in compounds) a group of people who share the same religion, race, job, etc. U42

company /ˈkʌmpəni/ n (pl. -ies) (abbr. **Co.**) (often in names) a business organization that makes money by producing or selling goods or services U38

compare /kəmˈpeə(r)/ v to examine people or things to see how they are similar and how they are different U25 WF **comparison** n, **comparable** adj

compete /kəmˈpiːt/ v to try to get sth or do sth, rather than letting sb/sth else get it or do it U4 WF **competition** n, **competitive** adj, **competitor** n

competition /ˌkɒmpəˈtɪʃn/ n (used especially about the world of business) a situation in which sb/sth tries to be more successful than sb/sth else, or tries to get sth rather than let sb/sth else get it U4

competitive /kəmˈpetətɪv/ adj connected with competition, especially in the world of business U4 WF **competitively** adv, **competitiveness** n

complete /kəmˈpliːt/ v to write all the information you are asked for on a form U5 WF **complete** adj, **incomplete** adj

completely /kəmˈpliːtli/ adv (used to emphasize the following word or phr) in every way possible U33

complex AWL /ˈkɒmpleks/ adj **1** made of many different things or parts that are connected U15 **2** difficult to understand or deal with U15 WF **complexity** n

concentrate AWL /ˈkɒnsntreɪt/ v to give all your attention to sth and not think about anything else U6 WF **concentration** n

concept AWL /ˈkɒnsept/ n an idea; a basic principle U30 WF **conceptual** adj, **conceptually** adv

conclude AWL /kənˈkluːd/ v to come to an end; to bring sth to an end U11

conclusion AWL /kənˈkluːʒn/ n the end of sth such as a piece of writing or a process U11

conduct AWL /kənˈdʌkt/ v to organize and/or do a particular activity U28

connection /kəˈnekʃn/ n the action of connecting sth to a supply of water, electricity, etc. or to a computer or telephone network; the fact of being connected in this way U14 WF **connect** v, **connectivity** n

consequence AWL /ˈkɒnsɪkwəns/ n (often pl.) a result of sth that has happened U24 WF **consequent** adj, **consequently** adv

conservation /ˌkɒnsəˈveɪʃn/ n the protection of the natural environment U41 WF **conservationist** n

conserve /kənˈsɜːv/ v to protect the natural environment and prevent it from being changed or destroyed U41

consider /kənˈsɪdə(r)/ v to think about sth, especially the needs and feelings of other people, and be influenced by this when making a decision or taking action U29 WF **consideration** n, **reconsider** v

considerably AWL /kənˈsɪdərəbli/ adv much; a lot U20 WF **considerable** adj

consist of AWL /kənˈsɪst ɒv/ phrasal v (not used in the progressive tenses) to be formed from the people or things mentioned U15

constant AWL /ˈkɒnstənt/ adj that does not change U16 WF **constancy** n, **constantly** adv, **inconstancy** n

consumer AWL /kənˈsjuːmə(r)/ n a person who buys goods or uses services U38 WF **consume** v, **consumption** n

contain /kənˈteɪn/ v (not used in the progressive tenses) if sth contains sth else, it has that thing inside it or as part of it U15 WF **container** n

contemporary AWL /kənˈtemprəri/ adj belonging to the present time U17

contents /'kɒntents/ *n* the different sections that are contained in a book, magazine, or website; a list of these sections U12

continue /kən'tɪnjuː/ *v* **1** to keep existing or happening without stopping U3 **2** to keep doing sth without stopping U3 WF continuous *adj*, continuously *adv*, continuation *n*

contrast AWL /kən'trɑːst/ *v* to show a clear difference when close together or when compared U36 WF contrast /'kɒntrɑːst/ *n*, contrastive *adj*

convincing AWL /kən'vɪnsɪŋ/ *adj* that makes sb believe that sth is true U31 WF convince *v*, convincingly *adv*, unconvincing *adj*

correct /kə'rekt/ *adj* accurate or true, without any mistakes U7 WF correction *n*, correctly *adv*

country /'kʌntri/ *n* (pl. -ies) an area of land that has or used to have its own government and laws U18

course /kɔːs/ *n* **1** a series of classes or lectures on a particular subject U8 **2** a period of study at a college or university that leads to an exam or a qualification U8 WF coursework *n*

court /kɔːt/ *n* **1** the place where legal trials take place and where crimes and legal cases are judged; the process of taking legal action against sb U44 **2** the court the people in a court, especially those who make the decisions, such as the judge and jury U44

create AWL /kri'eɪt/ *v* to make sth happen or exist U23 WF creation *n*, creator *n*, recreate *v*

crime /kraɪm/ *n* **1** activities that involve breaking the law U44 **2** an illegal act or activity that can be punished by law U44

criminal /'krɪmɪnl/ *adj* **1** connected with or involving crime U44 **2** connected with the laws that deal with crime U44 WF criminal *n*

critic /'krɪtɪk/ *n* a person who expresses disapproval of sb/sth and talks about their/its bad qualities, especially publicly U29 WF critical *adj*, critically *adv*

critical thinking /ˌkrɪtɪkl 'θɪŋkɪŋ/ *n* the process of analysing information in order to reach a logical decision about the extent to which you believe sth to be true or false U4

criticism /'krɪtɪsɪzəm/ *n* the act of expressing disapproval of sb/sth and opinions about their faults or bad qualities; a statement showing disapproval U32 WF criticize *v*

cultural AWL /'kʌltʃərəl/ *adj* connected with the customs, beliefs, art, way of life or social organization of a particular country or group U42 WF culturally *adv*

culture AWL /'kʌltʃə(r)/ *n* **1** the customs, beliefs, art, way of life or social organization of a particular country or group U42 **2** a country or group with its own customs and beliefs, art, way of life and social organization U42

currency AWL /'kʌrənsi/ *n* (pl. -ies) the system of money that a country uses U39

current /'kʌrənt/ *adj* **1** existing, happening or being used now; of the present time U17 **2** being used by or accepted by many people at the present time U17

currently /'kʌrəntli/ *adv* at the present time U17

custom /'kʌstəm/ *n* an accepted way of behaving or of doing things in a society or a community U42 WF customary *adj*

customer /'kʌstəmə(r)/ *n* a person or an organization that buys goods and services U38

cycle AWL /'saɪkl/ *n* the fact of a series of events being repeated many times, always in the same order U7

damage /'dæmɪdʒ/ *v* to cause physical harm to sth U3 WF damage *n*

data AWL /'deɪtə/ *n* facts that are stored by a computer or transferred between computers U40

date of publication /ˌdeɪt əv ˌpʌblɪ'keɪʃn/ *n* the year in which a book, a report, an article, etc. was printed and made available to the public U12

deadline /'dedlaɪn/ *n* a point in time by which sth must be done U11

deal with /'diːl wɪð/ *phrasal v* (dealt) to take action in order to solve a problem or complete a task U3

debate AWL /dɪ'beɪt/ *n* a formal discussion of an issue at a public meeting or in a parliament U13 WF debatable *adj*

decade AWL /'dekeɪd/ *n* a period of ten years, especially one beginning with a year ending in zero U17

decline AWL /dɪ'klaɪn/ *n* a continuous decrease in the number, strength, value, etc. of sth U22 WF decline *v*

decrease /dɪ'kriːs/ *v* to become smaller in size, number, etc.; to make sth smaller in size, number, etc. U22 WF decrease /'diːkriːs/ *n*

definitely AWL /'defɪnətli/ *adv* without doubt U29 WF definite *adj*

definition AWL /ˌdefɪ'nɪʃn/ *n* a statement of the exact meaning of a word or phr, especially in a dictionary U27 WF define *v*

degree /dɪ'griː/ *n* a qualification obtained by a student who successfully completes a university or college course U8

delete /dɪ'liːt/ *v* to remove sth that has been written or printed U14 WF deletion *n*

democracy /dɪ'mɒkrəsi/ *n* (pl. -ies) **1** a system of government in which all the people of a country can vote to elect their representatives U45 **2** a country which has this system of government U45 WF democratic *adj*, democratically *adv*

department /dɪ'pɑːtmənt/ *n* (abbr. Dept) a section of a large organization such as a government, business or university U8

describe /dɪ'skraɪb/ *v* **1** to give an account of sth in words **2** to say what sb/sth is like; to say what sb/sth is U15 WF description *n*, descriptive *adj*

design¹ AWL /dɪ'zaɪn/ *n* the way that sth works, looks or is used; the process of planning how sth will work, look or be used U40

design² AWL /dɪ'zaɪn/ *v* to plan how sth will work, look or be used U40 WF designer *n*

despite AWL /dɪ'spaɪt/ *prep* without being affected by sth U36

detail AWL /'diːteɪl/ *n* exact information about sth U27 WF detailed *adj*

develop /dɪ'veləp/ *v* to begin to have sth such as a disease or a problem; (of a disease or problem) to start to affect sb/sth U23 WF development *n*

developed /dɪ'veləpt/ *adj* a developed country, region or society has many industries and a complicated economic system U2

developing /dɪ'veləpɪŋ/ *adj* a developing country, region or society is poor, and trying to make its industry and economic system more advanced U2

device AWL /dɪ'vaɪs/ *n* an object or a piece of equipment that has been designed for a particular purpose U40

differ /ˈdɪfə(r)/ v to be different from sb/sth U4 WF difference n, different adj, differently adv

difference /ˈdɪfrəns/ n the way in which two people or things are not like each other; the state of being different U4

different /ˈdɪfrənt/ adj (of things of the same kind) separate and individual U4

differently /ˈdɪfrəntli/ adv in a way that is not the same as sb/sth U4

digital /ˈdɪdʒɪtl/ adj using a system of receiving and sending information as a series of the numbers one and zero, showing that an electronic signal is there or is not there; connected with computer technology U40 WF digitally adv

disadvantage /ˌdɪsədˈvɑːntɪdʒ/ n a factor that makes sb/sth less effective or less likely to succeed; a circumstance that makes a situation difficult U32

disaster /dɪˈzɑːstə(r)/ n an unexpected event that kills a lot of people or causes a lot of damage U26

discipline /ˈdɪsəplɪn/ n a subject of study, especially in a university U8

discuss /dɪˈskʌs/ v 1 to write or talk about sth in detail, showing the different ideas and opinions about it U35 2 to talk about sth with sb, especially in order to decide sth or in order to increase knowledge or understanding U13

discussion /dɪˈskʌʃn/ n a conversation about sb/sth; the process of discussing sb/sth U13

disease /dɪˈziːz/ n an illness of the body in humans, animals or plants U43

disposal AWL /dɪˈspəʊzl/ n the act of getting rid of sth U26 WF disposable adj, dispose v

disrupt /dɪsˈrʌpt/ v to make it difficult for sth to act or continue in the normal way U23 WF disruption n, disruptive adj

divide by /dɪˈvaɪd baɪ/ phrasal v to calculate sth by finding out how many times one number or amount is contained in another U21 WF division n

document AWL /ˈdɒkjumənt/ n a computer file that contains text and that has a name that identifies it U14

draft AWL /drɑːft/ n a rough written version of sth that is not yet in its final form U11 WF draft v adj, redraft v

dramatic AWL /drəˈmætɪk/ adj (of a change or an event) sudden, very great and often surprising U22 WF drama n, dramatically adv

draw attention to /ˌdrɔː əˈtenʃn tu/ phr to make people listen to, look at or think about sth/sb carefully U33

due to /ˈdjuː tu/ prep because of sth/sb U36

duration AWL /djuˈreɪʃn/ n the length of time that sth lasts or continues U17

earn /ɜːn/ v to get money for work that you do U39 WF earnings n

easily /ˈiːzəli/ adv without problems or difficulty U3 WF easy adj

economic AWL /ˌiːkəˈnɒmɪk/ adj connected with the trade, industry and development of wealth of a country, an area or a society U39 WF economical adj, economically adv, economize v, uneconomical adj

economics AWL /ˌiːkəˈnɒmɪks/ n the study of how a society organizes its money, trade and industry U39 WF economist n

economy AWL /ɪˈkɒnəmi/ n (pl. -ies) (often the economy) the relationship between production, trade and the supply of money in a particular country or region U39

edit AWL /ˈedɪt/ v to prepare a piece of writing to be published, or read by sb else, by correcting the mistakes and making improvements to it U11 WF edition n, editorial adj n

editor AWL /ˈedɪtə(r)/ n a person who prepares a book to be published, for example by checking and correcting the text and making improvements U11

education /ˌedʒuˈkeɪʃn/ n (usually Education) the subject of study that deals with how to teach U9 WF educate v, educational adj, educator n

effect /ɪˈfekt/ n a change that sb/sth causes in sb/sth else U24

effective /ɪˈfektɪv/ adj producing the result that is wanted or intended; producing a successful result U31 WF effectively adv, effectiveness n

efficient /ɪˈfɪʃnt/ adj doing sth well and with no waste of time, money or energy U31 WF efficiency n, efficiently adv

effort /ˈefət/ n the physical or mental energy that you need to do sth; sth that takes a lot of energy U32

election /ɪˈlekʃn/ n the process of choosing a person or a group of people for a position, especially a political position, by voting U45 WF elect v

electrical /ɪˈlektrɪkl/ adj connected with electricity; using or producing electricity U40 WF electric adj, electrically adv, electricity n

electronic /ɪˌlekˈtrɒnɪk/ adj done by means of a computer or other electronic device, especially over a network U40 WF electronics n

element AWL /ˈelɪmənt/ n a necessary or typical part of sth U15

emergency /iˈmɜːdʒənsi/ n (pl. -ies) a sudden serious and dangerous event or situation which needs immediate action to deal with it U26

emphasize, -ise AWL /ˈemfəsaɪz/ v to give special importance to sth U33 WF emphasis n, emphatic adj, emphatically adv

employ /ɪmˈplɔɪ/ v 1 to use sth such as a skill, method, device or word for a particular purpose U7 2 to give sb a job to do for payment U38

employee /ɪmˈplɔɪiː/ n a person who is paid to work for sb U38

employer /ɪmˈplɔɪə(r)/ n a person or company that pays people to work for them U38

enable AWL /ɪˈneɪbl/ v to make it possible for sb to do sth U6

energy AWL /ˈenədʒi/ n a source of power that can be used by sb/sth, for example to provide light and heat, or to work machines U41

enforce AWL /ɪnˈfɔːs/ v to make sure that people obey a particular law or rule U26 WF enforcement n

engineering /ˌendʒɪˈnɪərɪŋ/ n the activity of using scientific knowledge to design and build things U10 WF engineer n

enjoy /ɪnˈdʒɔɪ/ v to have sth good that is an advantage to you U7

ensure AWL /ɪnˈʃɔː(r)/ v to make sure that sth happens or is definite U6

entirely /ɪnˈtaɪəli/ adv in every way possible U33 WF entire adj

environment AWL /ɪnˈvaɪrənmənt/ n the environment the natural world (used in discussing ways in which the natural world is damaged or protected, especially by humans) U41

environmental AWL /ɪnˌvaɪrənˈmentl/ *adj* connected with the natural world; connected with the ways in which the natural world is damaged or protected, especially by humans U41 WF **environmentalist** *n*, **environmentally** *adv*

equally /ˈiːkwəli/ *adv* to the same degree; in the same way U25 WF **equal** *adj*, **equality** *n*, **equalize** *v*, **inequality** *n*, **unequal** *adj*

equipment AWL /ɪˈkwɪpmənt/ *n* the necessary items for a particular purpose or activity U40 WF **equip** *v*, **equipped** *adj*

especially /ɪˈspeʃəli/ *adv* (abbr. **esp.**) very much; to a particular degree U33

essay /ˈeseɪ/ *n* a short piece of writing by a student as part of a course of study U11

essential /ɪˈsenʃl/ *adj* completely necessary; extremely important in a particular situation or for a particular activity U33 WF **essentially** *adv*

estimate AWL /ˈestɪmeɪt/ *v* to approximately calculate or judge the value, number, quantity or extent of sth U20 WF **estimate** /ˈestɪmət/ *n*, **estimation** *n*, **overestimate** *v n*, **underestimate** *v n*

ethnic AWL /ˈeθnɪk/ *adj* connected with or belonging to a race or people that shares a cultural tradition U19

ethnicity AWL /eθˈnɪsəti/ *n* (pl. -ies) the fact or state of belonging to a social group that has a shared national or cultural tradition U19

even though /ˌiːvn ˈðəʊ/ *conj* despite the fact that U36

eventually AWL /ɪˈventʃuəli/ *adv* at the end of a period of time or a series of events U37 WF **eventual** *adj*

evidence AWL /ˈevɪdəns/ *n* the facts, signs or objects that make you believe that sth is true U27

exist /ɪɡˈzɪst/ *v* (not used in the progressive tenses) to happen or be found in a particular place, time or situation; to be U15 WF **existence** *n*

experiment /ɪkˈsperɪmənt/ *v* to do a scientific experiment or experiments U10 WF **experiment** *n*

experimental /ɪkˌsperɪˈmentl/ *adj* connected with scientific experiments U10 WF **experimentally** *adv*

expert AWL /ˈekspɜːt/ *n* a person with special knowledge, skill or training in sth U27 WF **expert** *adj*, **expertise** *n*, **expertly** *adv*

explain /ɪkˈspleɪn/ *v* **1** to tell sb about sth in a way that makes it easy to understand U27 **2** to give a reason for sth; to be a reason for sth U30 U35 WF **explanation** *n*

face /feɪs/ *v* if you face a particular situation, or it faces you, you have to deal with it U26

fact /fækt/ *n* a thing that is known to be true, especially when it can be proved U27 WF **factual** *adj*, **factually** *adv*

factor AWL /ˈfæktə(r)/ *n* one of several things that cause or affect sth U24

faculty /ˈfæklti/ *n* (pl. -ies) a department or group of related departments in a college or university U8

fall /fɔːl/ *v* (fell, fallen) to decrease in amount, number or strength U22 WF **fall** *n*

false /fɔːls/ *adj* **1** wrong; not correct or true U32 **2** wrong, because it is based on sth that is not true or correct U32 WF **falsely** *adv*, **falsification** *n*, **falsify** *v*

family member /ˈfæməli membə(r)/ *n* a person who is related to you, for example a parent, child, brother, sister, etc. U19

fee AWL /fiː/ *n* an amount of money that you pay for professional advice or services U39

feedback /ˈfiːdbæk/ *n* advice, criticism or information about how good or useful sth or sb's work is U11

field /fiːld/ *n* a particular subject or activity that sb works in or is interested in U9

figure /ˈfɪɡə(r)/ *n* a number representing a particular amount, especially one given in official information U20

finally AWL /ˈfaɪnəli/ *adv* used to introduce the last in a list of things or the final point that you want to make U16 WF **final** *adj*, **finalize** *v*

finance AWL /ˈfaɪnæns/ *n* the activity of managing money, especially by a government or commercial organization U39 WF **finance** *v*, **financier** *n*

financial AWL /faɪˈnænʃl/ *adj* connected with money and finance U39 WF **financially** *adv*

finding /ˈfaɪndɪŋ/ *n* information that is discovered as the result of research into sth U28

firm /fɜːm/ *n* a business or company, especially one involving a partnership of two or more people U38

firstly /ˈfɜːstli/ *adv* used to introduce the first of a list of points you want to make in a piece of writing or a speech U37 WF **first of all** *phr*

focus AWL /ˈfəʊkəs/ *v* (-s- or -ss-) to give attention or effort to a particular thing (or to just a few things), rather than to many things U6 WF **focus** *n*, **refocus** *v*

foreign /ˈfɒrən/ *adj* **1** in or from a country that is not your own U18 **2** dealing with or involving other countries U18 WF **foreigner** *n*

for example /fɔːr ɪɡˈzɑːmpl/ *phr* (abbr. **e.g.**) used to emphasize sth that explains or supports what you are saying; used to give an example of what you are saying U27 WF **exemplify** *v*

formula AWL /ˈfɔːmjələ/ *n* (pl. formulae or formulas) (mathematics) a series of letters, numbers or symbols that represent a rule or law U21

fraction /ˈfrækʃn/ *n* a small part or amount of sth U21

fund AWL /fʌnd/ *v* to provide money for sth, usually sth official U38 WF **fund** *n*, **funder** *n*

gender AWL /ˈdʒendə(r)/ *n* the fact of being male or female, especially when considered with reference to social and cultural differences, not differences in biology U19

generally /ˈdʒenrəli/ *adv* in most cases U3

global AWL /ˈɡləʊbl/ *adj* covering or affecting the whole world U18 WF **globalization** *n*

globally AWL /ˈɡləʊbəli/ *adv* in a way that involves the whole world U3

glossary /ˈɡlɒsəri/ *n* (pl. -ies) a list of technical or special words, especially those in a particular text, explaining their meanings U12

goal /ɡəʊl/ *n* something that you hope to achieve U31

government /ˈɡʌvənmənt/ *n* (often **the Government**) (abbr. **govt**) the group of people and the institutions connected with them that are responsible for controlling a country or state U45 WF **govern** *v*

a great deal /ə ˌɡreɪt ˈdiːl/ *phr* much; a lot U25

grow /ɡrəʊ/ *v* (grew, grown) to increase in size, number, strength or quality U22

growth /grəʊθ/ n an increase in the size, amount or degree of sth U22

guarantee AWL /ˌgærənˈtiː/ v to promise to do or keep sth; to promise sth will happen or exist U38 WF **guarantee** n

guideline /ˈgaɪdlaɪn/ n (usually pl.) a rule or intruction that is given by an official organization telling you how to do sth U5

guilty /ˈgɪlti/ adj (guiltier, guiltiest) (**more guilty** and **most guilty** are more frequent) having done sth illegal U44 WF **guilt** n

habitat /ˈhæbɪtæt/ n the natural environment of a particular type of animal or plant U41

happen /ˈhæpən/ v to take place, especially without being planned; to take place as the result of sth U3

harmful /ˈhɑːmfl/ adj causing damage or injury to sb/sth, especially to a person's health or to the environment U32 WF **harm** n v

heading /ˈhedɪŋ/ n a title printed at the top of a page or at the beginning of a section of a book U12

health /helθ/ n the condition of a person's body or mind U43

health care /ˈhelθ keə(r)/ n the service of providing medical care U43

healthy /ˈhelθi/ adj (healthier, healthiest) **1** having good health; in good physical or mental condition U43 **2** good for your health U43

higher education /ˌhaɪər edʒuˈkeɪʃn/ n (abbr. HE) education and training at college and university, especially to degree level U8

highlight AWL /ˈhaɪlaɪt/ v to emphasize sth, especially so that people give it more attention U33 WF **highlight** n

history /ˈhɪstri/ n (pl. -ies) the study of past events as a subject at school or university U9 WF **historical** adj, **historically** adv, **historian** n

however /haʊˈevə(r)/ adv used to introduce a statement that contrasts with sth that has just been said U36

identity AWL /aɪˈdentəti/ n (pl. -ies) the characteristics that make a person or thing who or what they are and make them different from others U19

illegal AWL /ɪˈliːgl/ adj not allowed by the law U44 WF **illegally** adv

illustration AWL /ˌɪləˈstreɪʃn/ n a picture or drawing in a book, etc. especially one that explains sth U12 WF **illustrate** v, **illustrative** adj

impact AWL /ˈɪmpækt/ n the powerful effect that sth has on sb/sth U6 WF **impact** v

importance /ɪmˈpɔːtns/ n the quality of being important U33

important /ɪmˈpɔːtnt/ adj having a great effect on people or things; of great value U33 WF **importantly** adv, **unimportant** adj

improve /ɪmˈpruːv/ v to become better than before; to make sth/sb better than before U23 WF **improvement** n

include /ɪnˈkluːd/ v (not used in the progressive tenses) if one thing includes another, it has the second thing as one of its parts U15 WF **including** prep, **inclusion** n

income AWL /ˈɪnkʌm/ n the money that a person, region, country, etc. earns from work, from investing money or from business U39

increase /ɪnˈkriːs/ v to become or make sth greater in size, amount or degree U22 WF **increase** n

increasingly /ɪnˈkriːsɪŋli/ adv more and more all the time U22

in detail /ˌɪn ˈdiːteɪl/ phr including exact information U27

index AWL /ˈɪndeks/ n (pl. indexes) (in a book or set of books) an alphabetical list of names, subjects, etc. with the numbers of the pages on which they are mentioned U12 WF **index** v

indicate AWL /ˈɪndɪkeɪt/ v **1** to show that sth is true or exists U34 **2** to be a sign of sth; to show that sth is possible or likely U34 WF **indication** n, **indicator** n, **indicative** adj

individual AWL /ˌɪndɪˈvɪdʒuəl/ n a person considered separately rather than as part of a group U19 WF **individuality** n, **individually** adv

industry /ˈɪndəstri/ n (pl. -ies) the people and activities involved in producing a particular thing, or in providing a particular service U38 WF **industrial** adj

ineffective /ˌɪnɪˈfektɪv/ adj not achieving what you want to achieve; not having any effect U24 WF **ineffectively** adv, **ineffectiveness** n

in fact /ˌɪn ˈfækt/ phr used to emphasize a statement, especially one that is the opposite of what has just been mentioned U27

infection /ɪnˈfekʃn/ n a disease that is caused by sth such as bacteria or a virus U43 WF **infect** v, **infectious** adj

information /ˌɪnfəˈmeɪʃn/ n facts or details about sb/ sth that are provided or learned U2 WF **inform** v, **informative** adj

information technology /ˌɪnfəˌmeɪʃn tekˈnɒlədʒi/ n (abbr. IT) the study or use of electronic equipment, especially computers, for storing, analysing and sending information U5

in general /ˌɪn ˈdʒenrəl/ phr usually; mainly U3 WF **generalization** n, **generalize** v

initial AWL /ɪˈnɪʃl/ adj happening at the beginning; first U37

initially AWL /ɪˈnɪʃəli/ adv at the beginning U37

injury AWL /ˈɪndʒəri/ n (pl. -ies) harm done to a person's or an animal's body, for example in an accident; harm done to a person's mind U43 WF **injure** v

innocent /ˈɪnəsnt/ adj not guilty of a crime, etc.; not having done sth wrong U44 WF **innocence** n

innovation AWL /ˌɪnəˈveɪʃn/ n a new thing, idea or way of doing sth that has been introduced U23 WF **innovate** v, **innovative** adj, **innovatively** adv

in order that … /ˌɪn ˈɔːdə ðæt/ phr so that sth can happen U5

input AWL /ˈɪnpʊt/ v (inputting, input or inputting, inputted) to put data into a computer U40 WF **input** n

in recent years /ˌɪn ˈriːsnt jɪəz/ phr during the period of time that was not long ago U37

in relation to /ˌɪn rɪˈleɪʃn tu/ phr in comparison with sth U19

in return for /ˌɪn rɪˈtɜːn fɔː(r)/ phr as an exchange or a reward for sth; as a response to sth U5

insert AWL /ɪnˈsɜːt/ v to add sth to a piece of writing U14 WF **insertion** n

institution AWL /ˌɪnstɪˈtjuːʃn/ n an important, often large, organization that has a particular purpose, for example a university or bank U8 WF **institute** n, **institutional** adj, **institutionally** adv

interesting /ˈɪntrəstɪŋ/ adj attracting your attention because it is special, exciting or unusual U31 WF interest n v, interested adj

in terms of /ˌɪn ˈtɜːmz ɒv/ phr used to show what aspect of a subject you are talking about or how you are thinking about it U5 U29

international /ˌɪntəˈnæʃnəl/ adj connected with or involving two or more countries U18 WF internationally adv

international student /ˌɪntəˈnæʃnəl stjuːdnt/ n a person who is studying in a country that is not their own U8

interrupt /ˌɪntəˈrʌpt/ v to say or do sth that makes sb stop what they are saying or doing U13 WF interruption n

in the form of /ˌɪn ðə ˈfɔːm ɒv/ phr a particular way in which a thing exists or appears U27 WF formation n

in the meantime /ˌɪn ðə ˈmiːntaɪm/ phr in the period of time between two times or two events; between now and a future event U37

in the past /ˌɪn ðə ˈpɑːst/ phr in a time that has gone by U37

introduce /ˌɪntrəˈdjuːs/ v (especially in a piece of writing) to bring sth into discussion U11

introduction /ˌɪntrəˈdʌkʃn/ n the first part of a book, report or speech that gives a general idea of what is to follow U11 WF introductory adj

in turn /ˌɪn ˈtɜːn/ phr as a result of sth in a series of events U29

invention /ɪnˈvenʃn/ n the act of creating or designing sth that has not existed before U23 WF invent v, inventive adj, inventively adv

invest AWL /ɪnˈvest/ v (of an organization or government, etc.) to spend money on sth in order to make it better or more successful U39 WF investor n, reinvest v

investment AWL /ɪnˈvestmənt/ n the action or process of investing money for profit U39 WF reinvestment n

involve AWL /ɪnˈvɒlv/ v if a situation, an event or an activity involves sth, that thing is an important or necessary part or result of it U16 WF involvement n

issue AWL /ˈɪʃuː/ n (often issues) a problem, concern or difficulty U26

item AWL /ˈaɪtəm/ n a single object or thing, especially one that is part of a list, collection or set U15 U27

job AWL /dʒɒb/ n work for which you receive regular payment U38

judge /dʒʌdʒ/ n a person in a court who has the authority to decide how criminals should be punished or to make legal decisions U44 WF judge v, judgement n

jury /ˈdʒʊəri/ n (pl. -ies) a group of members of the public who listen to the facts of a case in a court and decide whether or not sb is guilty of a crime U44 WF juror n

justify AWL /ˈdʒʌstɪfaɪ/ v (justifies, justifying, justified) to give an explanation or excuse for sth or for doing sth; to show that sb/sth is right or reasonable U29 WF justification n, unjustified adj

keyword search /ˈkiːwɜːd sɜːtʃ/ n an act of looking for something on the internet, in a computer database, etc. by typing a particular word or phr that you are interested in U14

knowledge /ˈnɒlɪdʒ/ n the understanding of a subject that is gained through study, research or experience U27 WF know v, knowledgeable adj

laboratory /ləˈbɒrətri/ n (pl. -ies) a room or building containing equipment for scientific experiments, research or teaching, or for making drugs or chemicals U10

lack of /ˈlæk ɒv/ n the state of not having sth or not having enough of sth U26 WF lack v

largely /ˈlɑːdʒli/ adv to a great extent; mostly or mainly U3

last /lɑːst/ det, adj 1 happening or coming after all other similar things or people U16 2 most recent U16

lastly /ˈlɑːstli/ adv used to introduce the final point that you want to make U37

law /lɔː/ n 1 (also the law) the whole system of rules that everyone in a country or society must obey U44 2 a particular branch of the law U44 3 a rule that deals with a particular crime, relationship or agreement U44

lawyer /ˈlɔːjə(r)/ n a person who is trained and qualified to advise people about the law, to represent them in court and to write legal documents U44

lead to /ˈliːd tu/ phrasal v (led) to have sth as a result U24

lecture AWL /ˈlektʃə(r)/ n a talk that is given to a group of people to teach them about a particular subject, often as part of a university or college course U13

lecturer AWL /ˈlektʃərə(r)/ n a person who gives lectures, especially as a teacher at a university or college in Britain U13 WF lecture v

legal AWL /ˈliːgl/ adj 1 connected with the law U44 2 allowed or required by law U44 WF legality n, legally adv

lend /lend/ v (lent) (of a bank or financial institution) to give money to sb on condition that they pay it back over a period of time and pay interest on it U39 WF lender n

level /ˈlevl/ n the amount of sth that exists in a particular situation at a particular time U20

life /laɪf/ n (pl. lives) the activities, events or situations that are experienced as part of being alive or as part of being in a particular situation U2

lifestyle /ˈlaɪfstaɪl/ n the way in which a person or a group of people lives and works U42

likely /ˈlaɪkli/ adj (likelier, likeliest) (more likely and most likely are the usual forms.) if sb is likely to do sth, or sth is likely to happen, they will probably do it or it will probably happen U34 WF likelihood n, likely adv, unlikely adj

limit /ˈlɪmɪt/ n the greatest or smallest amount or level of sth that is possible or allowed U20 WF limit v, limitation n, limited adj

link AWL /lɪŋk/ n 1 a connection between two or more people or things, especially where one affects the other U24 2 (computing) a place in an electronic document that is connected to another electronic document or to another part of the same document U14 WF link v

literature /ˈlɪtrətʃə(r)/ n pieces of writing that are considered to be works of art, especially novels, plays and poems (in contrast to technical books and newspapers, magazines, etc.) U9 WF literary adj

loan /ləʊn/ n money that an organization such as a bank loans and sb borrows U39 WF loan v

local /ˈləʊkl/ *adj* belonging to or connected with the particular place or area that you are talking about or with the place where you live U18 WF **locally** *adv*

location AWL /ləʊˈkeɪʃn/ *n* a place where sth happens or exists; the position of sth U18 WF **locate** *v*, **relocate** *v*

log on /ˌlɒg ˈɒn/ *phrasal v* (-gg-) (computing) to perform the actions that allow you to begin using a computer system U14

long-term /ˌlɒŋ ˈtɜːm/ *adj* that will last or have an effect over a long period of time into the future U17

loss /lɒs/ *n* money that has been lost by a business or an organization U39 WF **lose** *v*

low /ləʊ/ *adj* (lower, lowest) less or worse than normal in quantity, quality, size or level U2

major AWL /ˈmeɪdʒə(r)/ *adj* large, important or serious U33

majority AWL /məˈdʒɒrəti/ *n* (pl. -ies) the greater number or part U21

make sense /ˌmeɪk ˈsens/ *phr* to be a sensible thing to do U5

maximum AWL /ˈmæksɪməm/ *adj* (abbr. max.) as large, fast, etc. as is possible; the most that is possible or allowed U20 WF **maximum** *n*, **maximize** *v*, **maximization** *n*

mean[1] /miːn/ *v* (meant) (not used in the progressive tenses) to have sth as a result or a likely result U24

mean[2] /miːn/ *n* the value found by adding together all the numbers in a group, and dividing the total by the number of numbers U21 WF **mean** *adj*

measure /ˈmeʒə(r)/ *v* to find the size, quantity, etc. of sth in standard units U4 WF **measurement** *n*

measurement /ˈmeʒəmənt/ *n* the size, length or amount of sth, as established by measuring U4

media AWL /ˈmiːdiə/ *n* the media the main ways, such as television, newspapers and the internet, that are used to communicate information and provide entertainment to large numbers of people U2

medical AWL /ˈmedɪkl/ *adj* connected with the science or practice of medicine U43 WF **medically** *adv*

medicine /ˈmedsn/ *n* the study and treatment of diseases and injuries U43

medium AWL /ˈmiːdiəm/ *n* a way of communicating information to people U2

mental AWL /ˈmentl/ *adj* connected with the state of health of the mind or with the treatment of illnesses of the mind U43 WF **mentally** *adv*

method AWL /ˈmeθəd/ *n* a particular way of doing sth U28 WF **methodical** *adj*

methodology AWL /ˌmeθəˈdɒlədʒi/ *n* (pl. -ies) a set of methods and principles used to perform a particular activity U10 WF **methodological** *adj*

minimize, -ise AWL /ˈmɪnɪmaɪz/ *v* to reduce sth, especially sth bad, to the lowest possible level U26

minimum AWL /ˈmɪnɪməm/ *adj* (abbr. min.) the smallest or lowest that is possible, required or recorded U20 WF **minimum** *n*

ministry AWL /ˈmɪnɪstri/ *n* (pl. -ies) (in the UK and some other countries) a government department that has a particular area of responsibility U45 WF **minister** *n*, **ministerial** *adj*

minority AWL /maɪˈnɒrəti/ *n* (pl. -ies) the smaller part of a group; less than half of the people or things in a large group U21

mistake /mɪˈsteɪk/ *n* an action or opinion that is not correct, or that produces a result that is not wanted U32

misunderstand /ˌmɪsʌndəˈstænd/ *v* (misunderstood) to fail to understand sb/sth correctly U4 WF **understand** *v*

model /ˈmɒdl/ *n* a simple description, especially a mathematical one, of a group of complex systems or processes, used for understanding or explaining how sth works U30 WF **model** *v*

moderate /ˈmɒdərət/ *adj* average rather than large or small in amount or level U20 WF **moderately** *adv*, **moderation** *n*

modern /ˈmɒdn/ *adj* of the present time or recent times U9

more or less /ˌmɔːr ɔː ˈles/ *phr* almost U34

nation /ˈneɪʃn/ *n* a country considered as a group of people with the same language, culture and history, who live in a particular area under one government U18 WF **nationality** *n*

national /ˈnæʃnəl/ *adj* **1** connected with a particular nation; shared by a whole nation U18 **2** owned, controlled or paid for by the government U18 WF **nationally** *adv*

natural /ˈnætʃrəl/ *adj* existing in nature; not made or caused by humans U41 WF **nature** *n*, **naturally** *adv*

necessary /ˈnesəsəri/ *adj* that is needed for a purpose or a reason U2 WF **necessarily** *adv*, **necessity** *n*, **unnecessary** *adj*

need /niːd/ *n* a situation when sth is necessary or must be done U6

negative AWL /ˈnegətɪv/ *adj* **1** bad or harmful U32 **2** considering only the bad side of sth/sb; lacking enthusiasm or hope U32 WF **negatively** *adv*

news /njuːz/ *n* reports of recent events that appear in newspapers or on television or radio U2

normally AWL /ˈnɔːməli/ *adv* usually; in normal circumstances U34 WF **normal** *adj*, **normality** *n*, **abnormal** *adj*, **abnormally** *adv*

numerous /ˈnjuːmərəs/ *adj* existing in large numbers U20

objective AWL /əbˈdʒektɪv/ *n* something that you are trying to achieve U10

observe /əbˈzɜːv/ *v* to watch sb/sth carefully, especially in order to learn more about them U10 WF **observation** *n*, **observer** *n*

obtain AWL /əbˈteɪn/ *v* to get sth, especially by making an effort U27 WF **obtainable** *adj*, **unobtainable** *adj*

obvious AWL /ˈɒbviəs/ *adj* easy to see or understand U33 WF **obviously** *adv*

occupation AWL /ˌɒkjuˈpeɪʃn/ *n* a job or profession U19 WF **occupational** *adj*

occur AWL /əˈkɜː(r)/ *v* (-rr-) to happen U23 WF **occurrence** *n*

odd AWL /ɒd/ *adj* **1** (no comparative or superlative) (of numbers) that cannot be divided exactly by the number two U7 **2** (odder, oddest) strange or unusual U7

on a ... basis /ˌɒn ə ... ˈbeɪsɪs/ *phr* the way sth is organized or arranged U5

on behalf of AWL /ˌɒn bɪˈhɑːf ɒv/ *phr* as the representative of sb U5

ongoing AWL /ˈɒngəʊɪŋ/ *adj* continuing to exist or develop U17

on screen /ˌɒn ˈskriːn/ adv on a computer or other electronic device U14

on the whole /ˌɒn ðə ˈhəʊl/ phr considering everything; in general U34

opinion /əˈpɪnjən/ n someone's feelings or thoughts about sb/sth, rather than a fact U29

option AWL /ˈɒpʃn/ n something that sb can choose to do or have U5 WF **optional** adj

organization, -isation /ˌɔːɡənaɪˈzeɪʃn/ n **1** an organized group of people with a particular purpose, such as a business or government department U38 **2** the act of making arrangements or preparations for sth U28

organize, -ise /ˈɔːɡənaɪz/ v to arrange sth or the parts of sth into a particular order or structure U28

overall AWL /ˌəʊvərˈɔːl/ adv generally; when everything is considered U34 WF **overall** adj

overseas AWL /ˌəʊvəˈsiːz/ adv to or in a foreign country, especially those separated from your country by the sea or ocean U3 WF **overseas** adj

owe /əʊ/ v (not used in the progressive tenses) to have to pay sb for sth that you have already received or return money that you have borrowed U39

owing to /ˈəʊɪŋ tu/ prep because of U36

page number /ˈpeɪdʒ nʌmbə(r)/ n a number printed on a page to show its position in a book, etc. U12

paragraph AWL /ˈpærəɡrɑːf/ n (abbr. **par.**/ **para.**) a section of a piece of writing, usually consisting of several sentences dealing with a single subject. The first sentence of a paragraph starts on a new line. U12

participate AWL /pɑːˈtɪsɪpeɪt/ v to take part in or become involved in an activity U6 WF **participation** n, **participant** n, **participatory** adj

particular /pəˈtɪkjələ(r)/ adj used to emphasize that you are referring to one individual person, thing or type of thing and not others U2 WF **in particular** phr, **particularly** adv

pattern /ˈpætn/ n **1** the regular way in which sth happens or is done U15 **2** a regular arrangement of lines, shapes, colours, etc. found in similar objects or as a design on material, etc. U15

peak /piːk/ v to reach the highest point or value U22 WF **peak** n adj

peer group /ˈpɪə ɡruːp/ n a group of people of the same age or social position U19

per cent AWL /pə ˈsent/ n (symb. **%**) one part in every hundred U21

percentage AWL /pəˈsentɪdʒ/ n the number, amount, rate of sth, expressed as if it is part of a total which is 100; a part or share of a whole U21

perhaps /pəˈhæps/ adv used when saying that sth may be true U34

period AWL /ˈpɪəriəd/ n **1** a particular length of time U17 **2** a length of time in the life of a particular person, the history of a particular country, etc. U17 WF **periodic** adj, **periodically** adv

permanent /ˈpɜːmənənt/ adj lasting for a long time or for all time in the future; existing all the time U17 WF **permanence** n, **permanently** adv

perspective AWL /pəˈspektɪv/ n a particular attitude towards sth; a way of thinking about sth U9

persuade /pəˈsweɪd/ v to make sb do sth by giving them good reasons for doing it U30 WF **persuasion** n, **persuasive** adj

philosophy AWL /fəˈlɒsəfi/ n (pl. -ies) the study of the nature and meaning of the universe and of human life U9 WF **philosopher** n, **philosophical** adj

physical AWL /ˈfɪzɪkl/ adj **1** connected with a person's body rather than their mind U43 **2** connected with things that actually exist or are present and can be seen, felt, etc. rather than things that only exist in a person's mind U10 WF **physically** adv

physicist /ˈfɪzɪsɪst/ n a scientist who studies physics U10

physics /ˈfɪzɪks/ n the scientific study of matter and energy and the relationships between them, including the study of forces, heat, light, sound, electricity and the structure of atoms U10

plagiarize, -ise /ˈpleɪdʒəraɪz/ v (disapproving) to copy another person's ideas, words or work and pretend that they are your own U35 WF **plagiarism** n

point of view /ˌpɔɪnt əv ˈvjuː/ n (pl. points of view) the particular attitude or opinion that sb has about sth U29

policy AWL /ˈpɒləsi/ n (pl. -ies) a plan of action agreed or chosen by a political party, a business, etc. U45

political /pəˈlɪtɪkl/ adj **1** connected with the state, government or public affairs U45 **2** connected with the different groups working in politics, especially their policies and the competition between them U45 WF **politically** adv

politician /ˌpɒləˈtɪʃn/ n a person whose job is concerned with politics, especially as an elected member of parliament, etc. U45

politics /ˈpɒlətɪks/ n **1** the activities involved in getting and using power in public life, and being able to influence decisions that affect a country or society U45 **2** the study of government and power U45

pollution /pəˈluːʃn/ n harmful or poisonous substances that make land, air, water, etc. no longer pleasant or safe to use; the process of adding these substances to the environment U41 WF **pollute** v, **polluted** adj, **polluter** n

popular /ˈpɒpjələ(r)/ adj liked or admired by many people or by a particular person or group U31 WF **popularity** n, **popularly** adv

position /pəˈzɪʃn/ n the level of importance of a person, organization or thing when compared with others U19

positive AWL /ˈpɒzətɪv/ adj **1** good or useful U31 **2** noticing or emphasizing what is good in sb/sth; showing confidence or hope U31 **3** expressing agreement, support or permission U31 **4** aimed at dealing with sth; taking action to produce a particular result U31 WF **positive** n, **positively** adv

possible /ˈpɒsəbl/ adj **1** that might exist, happen or be true but is not certain U34 **2** reasonable or acceptable in a particular situation U34 WF **possibility** n

possibly /ˈpɒsəbli/ adv used to say that sth might exist, happen or be true, but it is not certain U34

potential AWL /pəˈtenʃl/ adj that can develop into sth or be developed in the future U34 WF **potential** n

potentially AWL /pəˈtenʃəli/ adv possibly going to develop or be developed into sth, especially sth bad U34

power /ˈpaʊə(r)/ n political control of a country or an area U45 WF **powerful** adj, **powerfully** adv

precise AWL /prɪˈsaɪs/ adj clear and accurate U31 WF **precisely** adv, **precision** n, **imprecise** adj

predict AWL /prɪˈdɪkt/ v to say, expect or suggest that a particular thing will happen in the future or will be the result of sth U30 WF predictability n, predictable adj, predictably adv, unpredictable adj

prediction AWL /prɪˈdɪkʃn/ n a statement that says what you think will happen; the act of making such a statement U30

present /ˈpreznt/ adj 1 existing or happening now U17 2 (of a piece of work, etc.) being considered now U17 WF present n, presently adv

presentation /ˌpreznˈteɪʃn/ n the act of showing or offering information or ideas for other people to consider; an occasion when this happens U13 WF present v

pressure /ˈpreʃə(r)/ n the feeling that it is necessary to do sth; the action of making sb feel this; the problems caused by this U32

presume AWL /prɪˈzjuːm/ v to suppose that sth is true or exists, although it is not definitely proved or known U29 WF presumably adv, presumption n, presumptuous adj

previous AWL /ˈpriːviəs/ adj happening or existing before the event or object that you are talking about U16 WF previously adv

principle AWL /ˈprɪnsəpl/ n a law, rule or theory that sth is based on U30 WF principled adj, unprincipled adj

print out /ˌprɪnt ˈaʊt/ phrasal v to produce a document or information from a computer in printed form U14 WF printer n, printout n

problem /ˈprɒbləm/ n a thing that is difficult to deal with or to understand U26 WF problematic adj

procedure AWL /prəˈsiːdʒə(r)/ n a series of actions done in a particular order and way, especially the usual or correct way U16 WF procedural adj

process AWL /ˈprəʊses/ n 1 a series of actions that are taken in order to achieve a particular result U16 2 a series of things that happen, especially ones that result in natural changes U16 WF process v

product /ˈprɒdʌkt/ n a thing that is grown or produced, usually for sale U38 WF produce v, production n, productive adj, productively adv, productivity n, unproductive adj

professional AWL /prəˈfeʃnl/ n a person who does a job that needs special training and a high level of education U38 WF professional adj, professionally adv, professionalism n

professor /prəˈfesə(r)/ n (abbr. Prof.) a university teacher of the highest rank U9

profit /ˈprɒfɪt/ n the money that you make in business or by selling things, after paying the costs involved U39 WF profit v, profitable adj

programme /ˈprəʊɡræm/ n a course of study U9

progress /ˈprəʊɡres/ n the process of improving or developing, or of getting nearer to achieving or completing sth U23 WF progress /prəˈɡres/ v

project AWL /ˈprɒdʒekt/ n a planned piece of work that is designed to find information about sth, to produce sth new or to improve sth U28

proportion AWL /prəˈpɔːʃn/ n a part or share of a whole U21 WF proportional adj, proportionally adv, proportionate adj, proportionately adv, disproportionate adj

propose /prəˈpəʊz/ v to suggest a plan or an idea for people to consider and decide on U30 WF proposal n, proposition n

protect /prəˈtekt/ v to keep sb/sth safe from harm or injury U41

protection /prəˈtekʃn/ n the act of protecting sb/sth; the state of being protected U41

prove /pruːv/ v (proved or proven) to use evidence or argument to show that sth is true U30 WF disprove v, proof n

provide /prəˈvaɪd/ v to give sth to sb or make it available for them to use U4 WF provider n, provision n

provider /prəˈvaɪdə(r)/ n a person or an organization that supplies sb with sth they need or want U4

provision /prəˈvɪʒn/ n the act of supplying sb with sth that they need or want; sth that is supplied U4

public opinion /ˌpʌblɪk əˈpɪnjən/ n the opinions that people in society have about an issue U29

punish /ˈpʌnɪʃ/ v to make sb suffer because they have broken the law or done sth wrong U44

punishment /ˈpʌnɪʃmənt/ n an act or way of punishing sb U44

purchase AWL /ˈpɜːtʃəs/ v to buy sth U38 WF purchase n, purchaser n

purpose /ˈpɜːpəs/ n the aim, intention or function of sth; the thing that sth is supposed to achieve U6

put forward /ˌpʊt ˈfɔːwəd/ phrasal v (putting, put) to suggest sth for discussion U30

quality /ˈkwɒləti/ n (pl. -ies) the standard of sth when it is compared with other things like it; how good or bad sth is U26

quantity /ˈkwɒntəti/ n (pl. -ies) the amount of sth; a particular amount or number of sth U20

question /ˈkwestʃən/ n a sentence, phr or word that asks for information U13 WF question v

questionnaire /ˌkwestʃəˈneə(r)/ n a written list of questions that are answered by a number of people so that information can be collected from the answers U5

quotation AWL /kwəʊˈteɪʃn/ n words from another speaker or writer that sb uses in his/her own writing or speech, showing clearly that the words are from this source; the act of quoting the words of another speaker or writer U35 WF quote v n

quote AWL /kwəʊt/ v to use words from another speaker or writer in your writing or speech, showing clearly that the words are from this source U35 WF quote n

rapid /ˈræpɪd/ adj happening in a short period of time or at a fast rate U22 WF rapidly adv

rate /reɪt/ n a measurement of the speed at which sth happens U22

reading list /ˈriːdɪŋ lɪst/ n a list of books that students are told to read as part of their course of study U12

reason /ˈriːzn/ n a cause or an explanation for sth that has happened or that sb has done U24 WF reason v

receive /rɪˈsiːv/ v to get or accept sth that is sent or given to you U7 WF receipt n

recent /ˈriːsnt/ adj that happened or began only a short time ago U17

recently /ˈriːsntli/ adv not long ago U17

record¹ /ˈrekɔːd/ n something that gives you information about the past, especially an account kept in writing or some other permanent form so that it can be looked at and used in the future U28

record² /rɪˈkɔːd/ v to keep a permanent account of facts or events by writing them down, filming them, storing them in a computer, etc. U28

recycle /ˌriːˈsaɪkl/ v to treat things that have already been used so that they can be used again U41 WF **recycled** *adj*

recycling /ˌriːˈsaɪklɪŋ/ n the process of treating things that have already been used so that they can be used again U41

reduce /rɪˈdjuːs/ v to make sth less or smaller in size, amount or degree U22 WF **reduction** *n*

reference¹ /ˈrefrəns/ n a mention of a source of information in a book, an article, etc; a source of information that is mentioned in this way U12 WF **refer to** *phrasal v*, **with reference to** *phr*

reference² /ˈrefrəns/ v to provide a book, an article, etc. with references U35

region AWL /ˈriːdʒən/ n a large area of land, usually without exact limits or borders U18 WF **regional** *adj*

register AWL /ˈredʒɪstə(r)/ v to record the name of sb/sth on an official list U14 WF **deregister** v, **deregistration** n, **register** n, **registration** n

regularly /ˈregjələli/ adv often U16 WF **regular** *adj*

regulation AWL /ˌregjuˈleɪʃn/ n an official rule made by a government or some other authority U26 WF **regulate** v, **regulator** n, **regulatory** adj, **deregulate** v, **unregulated** adj

relationship /rɪˈleɪʃnʃɪp/ n **1** the way in which two people, groups or countries behave towards each other or deal with each other U19 **2** the way in which two or more people or things are connected U30 WF **related to** adj, **relation** n, **unrelated** adj

relatively /ˈrelətɪvli/ adv to a fairly large degree, especially in comparison with sth else U34 WF **relative** *adj*

reliable AWL /rɪˈlaɪəbl/ adj likely to be correct or true U4 WF **reliably** adv, **rely on** phrasal v, **unreliable** adj

religious /rɪˈlɪdʒəs/ adj connected with religion or with a particular religion U9 WF **religion** *n*

remove AWL /rɪˈmuːv/ v to get rid of sth; to make sth disappear U16 WF **removal** *n*

renewable /rɪˈnjuːəbl/ adj (of energy and natural resources) replaced naturally or controlled carefully and therefore able to be used without the risk of none being left U41

renewables /rɪˈnjuːəblz/ n types of energy that can be replaced naturally, such as energy produced from wind or water U41

repeat /rɪˈpiːt/ v to do or produce sth again or more than once U4

report¹ /rɪˈpɔːt/ v to tell people that sth has happened or exists, or to provide other information about sth U35

report² /rɪˈpɔːt/ n a written document in which a particular situation or subject is examined or discussed U11

research¹ AWL /ˈriːsɜːtʃ/ n careful study of a subject, especially in order to discover new facts or information about it U28

research² AWL /rɪˈsɜːtʃ/ v to study sth carefully and try to discover new facts about it U28

researcher AWL /rɪˈsɜːtʃə(r)/ n a person who does research U28

resemble /rɪˈzembl/ v (not used in the progressive tenses) to look like or be similar to another person or thing U25 WF **resemblance** *n*

resident AWL /ˈrezɪdənt/ n a person who lives in a particular place U19 WF **reside** v, **residence** n

residential AWL /ˌrezɪˈdenʃl/ adj (of an area of a town) suitable for living in; consisting of houses rather than factories or offices U19

resource AWL /rɪˈzɔːs/ n a supply of sth that a country, an organization or a person has and can use U41

respond AWL /rɪˈspɒnd/ v to give a spoken or written answer to sb/sth U28 WF **respondent** n, **response** n, **responsive** adj, **responsiveness** n, **unresponsive** adj

result /rɪˈzʌlt/ n the information that you get from a piece of research or from a scientific or medical test U28

reverse AWL /rɪˈvɜːs/ v to change a previous decision, law, etc. to the opposite one U23 WF **reversal** n, **reversible** adj, **irreversible** adj

review /rɪˈvjuː/ v to carefully examine and consider sth again, especially so that you can decide if it is necessary to make changes U23 WF **review** *n*

revise AWL /rɪˈvaɪz/ v to change sth, such as a book, process or rule, in order to improve it or make it more suitable U23 WF **revision** *n*

right /raɪt/ n **1** a legal or moral claim to have or get sth or to behave in a particular way U7 **2** the/sb's right side or direction U7

rise /raɪz/ v (rose, risen) to increase in amount or number U22 WF **rise** *n*

risk /rɪsk/ n the possibility of sth bad happening at some time in the future; a situation that could be dangerous or have a bad result U24 U32 WF **risky** *adj*

role AWL /rəʊl/ n the function that sb/sth has or the part sb/sth plays in a particular situation U19

rural /ˈrʊərəl/ adj connected with or like the countryside U18

scheme AWL /skiːm/ n a plan or system for doing or organizing sth U45

science /ˈsaɪəns/ n knowledge about the structure and behaviour of the natural and physical world, based on facts that you can prove, for example by experiments U10

scientific /ˌsaɪənˈtɪfɪk/ adj involving science; connected with science U10 WF **scientifically** *adv*

scientist /ˈsaɪəntɪst/ n a person who studies one or more of the natural sciences U10

section AWL /ˈsekʃn/ n **1** a separate part of a book, document, website, etc. U15 **2** any of the parts into which sth is divided U15

security AWL /sɪˈkjʊərəti/ n (pl. -ies) protection against sth bad that might happen in the future; the degree to which sth is safe and protected U40 U42 WF **insecure** adj, **secure** v adj, **securely** adv

seem /siːm/ v (not used in the progressive tenses) to give the impression of being or doing sth U34 WF **seeming** adj, **seemingly** adv

seminar /ˈsemɪnɑː(r)/ n a class at a university or college when a small group of students and a teacher discuss or study a particular topic U13

sentence /ˈsentəns/ n the punishment given by a court U44 WF **sentence** *v*

separate /ˈseprət/ *adj* different; not connected U25 WF **separate** *v*, **separately** *adv*, **separation** *n*

series AWL /ˈsɪəriːz/ *n* (pl. series) several events or things of a similar kind that come or happen one after the other U16

service /ˈsɜːvɪs/ *n* a business whose work involves doing sth for customers but not producing goods; the work that they do U38

set out /ˌset ˈaʊt/ *phrasal v* (setting, set) to present ideas, facts, etc. in an organized way, in speech or writing U30

set up /ˌset ˈʌp/ *phrasal v* (setting, set) to create sth or start it U38

short-term /ˌʃɔːt ˈtɜːm/ *adj* lasting a short time; designed only for a short period of time in the future U17

show /ʃəʊ/ *v* (showed, shown) to make sth clear; to prove sth U28

significantly AWL /sɪɡˈnɪfɪkəntli/ *adv* in a way that is large or important enough to have an effect on sth or to be noticed U20 WF **significant** *adj*, **insignificant** *adj*

similarly AWL /ˈsɪmələli/ *adv* used to say that two facts, actions or statements are like each other U25

similar to AWL /ˈsɪmələ tu/ *adj* like sb/sth but not exactly the same U25 WF **similarity** *n*, **dissimilar** *adj*

since /sɪns/ *conj* because; as U36

site AWL /saɪt/ *n* a place where sth has happened or that is used for sth U18

skill /skɪl/ *n* a particular ability or type of ability U5 WF **skilled** *adj*

slide /slaɪd/ *n* one page of an electronic presentation, that may contain text and images U14

so as to /ˈsəʊ əz tu/ *phr* with the intention of U24

social /ˈsəʊʃl/ *adj* connected with society and the way it is organized U42 WF **socially** *adv*, **socialize** *v*, **socialization** *n*

society /səˈsaɪəti/ *n* (pl. -ies) people in general, living together in communities; a particular community of people who share the same customs, laws, etc. U42

sociology /ˌsəʊsiˈɒlədʒi/ *n* the scientific study of the nature and development of society and social behaviour U9 WF **sociological** *adj*, **sociologically** *adv*, **sociologist** *n*

software /ˈsɒftweə(r)/ *n* the programs used by a computer for doing particular jobs U40

solution /səˈluːʃn/ *n* a way of solving a problem or dealing with a difficult situation U26

solve /sɒlv/ *v* to find a way of dealing with a problem or difficult situation U26

somewhat AWL /ˈsʌmwɒt/ *adv* to some degree U34

source AWL /sɔːs/ *n* a place, thing or person that you get sth from U27 U35

species /ˈspiːʃiːz/ *n* (pl. species) a group into which animals, plants, etc. that are able to breed with each other and produce healthy young are divided, smaller than a genus and identified by a Latin name U41

specific AWL /spəˈsɪfɪk/ *adj* **1** connected with one particular person, thing or group only U15 **2** detailed and exact U15 WF **specifically** *adv*

spread /spred/ *v* (spread) **1** to affect or be known or used by more and more people; to make sth do this U3 **2** to cover a larger and larger area; to make sth cover a larger and larger area U3 WF **spread** *n*

stage /steɪdʒ/ *n* a point, period or step in a process or in the development of sth U16

state /steɪt/ *v* to formally write or say sth, especially in a careful and clear way U35 WF **statement** *n*

statistics /stəˈtɪstɪks/ *n* a collection of information shown in numbers U21 WF **statistical** *adj*, **statistically** *adv*, **statistician** *n*

step /step/ *n* one of a series of things that sb does or that happen, which forms part of a process U16

storage /ˈstɔːrɪdʒ/ *n* (computing) the process of keeping data on a computer; the way it is kept U40

store /stɔː(r)/ *v* to keep information or facts in sth, for example in a computer or a brain U40 WF **store** *n*

strategy AWL /ˈstrætədʒi/ *n* (pl. -ies) a plan that is intended to achieve a particular purpose U7 WF **strategic** *adj*, **strategically** *adv*, **strategist** *n*

stress AWL /stres/ *v* to give particular emphasis or importance to a fact, an idea or a statement U33 WF **stress** *n*

structure AWL /ˈstrʌktʃə(r)/ *n* **1** the way in which the parts of sth are connected together, arranged or organized; a particular arrangement of parts U15 **2** a thing that is made of several parts arranged in a particular way, for example a building U15 WF **structural** *adj*, **structurally** *adv*, **structure** *v*

student /ˈstjuːdnt/ *n* a person who is studying at a university or college U8

study¹ /ˈstʌdi/ *n* (pl. -ies) a piece of research that examines a subject or question in detail U28

study² /ˈstʌdi/ *v* (studies, studying, studied) to spend time learning about a subject by reading, going to college, etc. U8

style AWL /staɪl/ *n* the correct use of language U11

subject /ˈsʌbdʒɪkt/ *n* an area of knowledge studied in a school, college, etc. U8

submit AWL /səbˈmɪt/ *v* (-tt-) to give a proposal, application or other document to sb in authority so that they can consider or judge it U11 WF **submission** *n*

subsequently AWL /ˈsʌbsɪkwəntli/ *adv* afterwards; after sth else has happened U37 WF **subsequent** *adj*

successful /səkˈsesfl/ *adj* achieving your aims or what was intended U31 WF **succeed** *v*, **success** *n*, **unsuccessful** *adj*

successfully /səkˈsesfəli/ *adv* in a way that achieves your aims or intentions U26

suffer /ˈsʌfə(r)/ *v* to experience sth unpleasant, such as injury, defeat or loss U26 WF **suffering** *n*

suggest /səˈdʒest/ *v* to put an idea into sb's mind; to make sb think that sth is true U28

summarize, -ise AWL /ˈsʌməraɪz/ *v* to give a summary of sth U11

summary AWL /ˈsʌməri/ *n* (pl. -ies) a short statement that gives only the main points of sth, not the details U11

support /səˈpɔːt/ *n* evidence that helps to show that sth is true or correct U11

survey AWL /ˈsɜːveɪ/ *n* an investigation of the opinions, behaviour, etc. of a particular group of people, which is usually done by asking them questions U28 WF **survey** /səˈveɪ/ *v*

survive AWL /səˈvaɪv/ *v* to continue to live or exist U3 WF **survival** *n*, **survivor** *n*

symptom /'sɪmptəm/ n a change in your body or mind that shows that you are not healthy U43 WF **symptomatic** adj

system /'sɪstəm/ n a group of things that work together in a particular way or for a particular purpose U40 WF **systematic** adj, **systematically** adv

table /'teɪbl/ n a list of facts or numbers arranged in a special order, usually in rows and columns U7

take into account /ˌteɪk ɪntu əˈkaʊnt/ phr to consider particular facts, circumstances, etc. when making a decision about sth U26

take notes /ˌteɪk ˈnəʊts/ phr to write down information while you are doing sth such as working on sth, reading sth or listening to sb speaking U13 WF **note** v n

task AWL /tɑːsk/ n a piece of work that has to be done U16

teach /tiːtʃ/ v (taught) to give lessons to students, for example in a school, college or university U8 WF **teacher** n

team AWL /tiːm/ n a group of people who work together at a particular job U10

technical AWL /'teknɪkl/ adj connected with the use of science or technology; involving the use of machines U40 WF **technically** adv

technology AWL /tekˈnɒlədʒi/ n (pl. -ies) equipment, machines and processes that are developed using knowledge of engineering and science; the knowledge used in developing them U40

temporary AWL /'temprəri/ adj lasting or intended to last or be used for a limited period of time U17 WF **temporarily** adv

tend to /'tend tu/ v to regularly or frequently behave in a particular way or have a particular characteristic U34 WF **tendency** n

term /tɜːm/ n a word or phr used to describe a thing or to express an idea, especially in a particular kind of language or area of study U12

terminology /ˌtɜːmɪˈnɒlədʒi/ n (pl. -ies) the set of technical words or expressions used in a particular subject U27

textbook /'tekstbʊk/ n a book that teaches a particular subject and that is used especially in schools and colleges U12 WF **text** n, **textual** adj

theory AWL /'θɪəri/ n (pl. -ies) a formal set of ideas that is intended to explain why sth happens or exists U30

therefore /'ðeəfɔː(r)/ adv used to introduce the logical result of sth that has just been mentioned U36

threat /θret/ n **1** a statement in which you tell sb that you will punish or harm them, especially if they do not do what you want U32 **2** the possibility of trouble, danger or disaster U32 WF **threaten** v, **under threat** phr

title /'taɪtl/ n the name of a book, poem, film, piece of music, etc. U12

together with /təˈgeðə wɪð/ phr in addition to; as well as U5

topic AWL /'tɒpɪk/ n a particular subject that is studied, written about or discussed U9 WF **topical** adj

to some extent /tə ˈsʌm ɪkstent/ phr partly; in a limited way U25

total /'təʊtl/ n the amount you get when you add several numbers or amounts together; the final number of people or things when they have all been counted U21 WF **total** adj, **totally** adv

tradition AWL /trəˈdɪʃn/ n a belief, custom, story or way of doing sth that has existed for a long time among a particular group of people; a set of these beliefs, etc. U42

traditional AWL /trəˈdɪʃənl/ adj **1** following older methods and ideas rather than modern or different ones U42 **2** being part of the beliefs, customs or way of life that have existed for a long time among a particular group of people U42 WF **traditionalist** n, **traditionally** adv

transfer AWL /trænsˈfɜː(r)/ v (-rr-) to move from one place to another; to move sth/sb from one place to another U16 WF **transferable** adj

treat /triːt/ v to give medical care or attention to a person, an illness or an injury U43

treatment /'triːtmənt/ n something that is done to cure an illness or injury, or to help sb with a physical or mental problem U43

trend AWL /trend/ n a general direction in which a situation is changing or developing U22

trial /'traɪəl/ n a formal examination of evidence in court by a judge and often a jury, to decide if sb accused of a crime is guilty or not U44 WF **try** v

trigger AWL /'trɪgə(r)/ v to make sth start to happen U23 WF **trigger** n

tutor /'tjuːtə(r)/ n a teacher in a college or university, especially one who is responsible for teaching or advising a student or a group of students U13

tutorial /tjuːˈtɔːriəl/ n a period of teaching in a university that involves discussion between an individual student or a small group of students and a U13

type /taɪp/ n a class or group of things or people that share particular qualities or features U15

typically /'tɪpɪkli/ adv in a way that shows the usual qualities or features of a particular type of person, thing or group U34 WF **atypical** adj, **typical** adj

undergraduate /ˌʌndəˈgrædʒuət/ n a university or college student who is studying for their first degree U8 WF **undergraduate** adj

unfortunately /ʌnˈfɔːtʃənətli/ adv used to say that a particular situation or fact makes you sad or disappointed U4 WF **unfortunate** adj

unique AWL /juˈniːk/ adj being the only one of their/its kind; different from everyone or everything else U25 WF **uniquely** adv, **uniqueness** n

university /ˌjuːnɪˈvɜːsəti/ n (pl. -ies) (abbr. Univ.) an institution at the highest level of education where you can study for a degree or do research U8

unlike /ˌʌnˈlaɪk/ prep in contrast to sb/sth U25

urban /'ɜːbən/ adj connected with a town or city U18 WF **urbanization** n

use /juːs/ n **1** the act of using sth; the state of being used U2 **2** a purpose for which sth is used; a way in which sth is or can be used U2 WF **use** /juːz/ v

useful /'juːsfl/ adj helping sb/sth to do or achieve sth U4

value /'væljuː/ n the amount represented by a letter or symbol; a size, number or quantity U21

variable AWL /'veəriəbl/ adj often changing; likely to change U22 WF **variable** n, **variability** n, **invariable** adj

various /'veəriəs/ adj several different U25

vary AWL /'veəri/ v (varying, varied) to change or be different according to the situation U23 WF **variation** n, **variety** n

version AWL /ˈvɜːʒn/ n a form of sth that is slightly different from an earlier form or from other forms of the same thing U15

view /vjuː/ n a personal opinion about sth; an attitude towards sth U29

virus /ˈvaɪrəs/ n **1** a living thing, too small to be seen without a microscope, that causes infectious disease in people, animals and plants **2** an infection or disease caused by a virus U43 WF viral adj

vote[1] /vəʊt/ n a formal choice that you make in an election or at a meeting in order to choose sb or decide sth U45

vote[2] /vəʊt/ v to show formally by marking a paper or raising your hand which person you want to win an election, or which plan or idea you support U45

voter /ˈvəʊtə(r)/ n a person who votes or has the right to vote, especially in a political election U45

waste[1] /weɪst/ n materials that are no longer needed and are thrown away U41 WF waste v

waste[2] /weɪst/ adj no longer needed for a particular process or remaining after a process has finished, and therefore thrown away U41

weakness /ˈwiːknəs/ n a weak point in an object, a system, sb's character, etc. U32 WF weak adj

welfare AWL /ˈwelfeə(r)/ n money that the government pays regularly to people who are poor, unemployed, sick, etc. U42

whenever /wenˈevə(r)/ conj at any time that; on any occasion that U37

whereas AWL /ˌweərˈæz/ conj used to compare or contrast two facts U36

while /waɪl/ conj used to contrast two things U16

wild /waɪld/ adj (wilder, wildest) (of land) in its natural state; not changed by people U41

witness /ˈwɪtnəs/ n a person who gives evidence in court U44 WF witness v

word count /ˈwɜːd kaʊnt/ n the number of words that a piece of writing contains, or should contain U11

work /wɜːk/ n **1** the job that a person does, especially in order to earn money U2 **2** tasks that need to be done U2 **3** the process of academic research; an academic article, book, etc. U2 WF work v

worldwide /ˈwɜːldwaɪd/ adj affecting all parts of the world U18 WF worldwide adv

KEY

abbr.	abbreviation	phrasal v	phrasal verb
adj	adjective	pl.	plural
adv	adverb	prep	prep
AWL	*Academic Word List*	sb	somebody
conj	conjunction	sth	something
det	determiner	v	verb
n	noun	WF	word family
phr	phrase		